Mike Perham was born on 16 March 1992 and started sailing as a six-year-old. At the age of fourteen, he became the youngest person to sail solo across the Atlantic, a record that stands to this day. In November 2008, he set off on a voyage around the world, and after celebrating his seventeenth birthday en route, broke the Guinness World Record for single-handed circumnavigation. His next challenge as a fully fledged adventurer is to become the youngest person to fly solo round the world.

When not off on one of his adventures, Mike lives in Hertfordshire with his father Peter, his mother Heather and sister Fiona. He is completing a National Diploma in Sport at the Oaklands Athletics Academy in St Albans.

Visit his website at www.challengemike.com

D1407218

SAILING THE DREAM

The amazing true story of the schoolboy who
sailed single-handed around the world

Mike Perham

BANTAM BOOKS

LONDON • TORONTO • SYDNEY • AUCKLAND • JOHANNESBURG

TRANSWORLD PUBLISHERS
61-63 Uxbridge Road, London W5 5SA
A Random House Group Company
www.transworldbooks.co.uk

SAILING THE DREAM
A BANTAM BOOK: 9780553825657

First published in Great Britain
in 2010 by Bantam Press
an imprint of Transworld Publishers
Bantam edition published 2011

Addresses for Random House Group Ltd companies outside the UK
can be found at: www.randomhouse.co.uk
The Random House Group Ltd Reg. No. 954009

The Random House Group Limited supports The Forest Stewardship
Council® (FSC®), the leading international forest certification organisation.
All our titles that are printed on Greenpeace approved FSC® certified
paper carry the FSC® logo. Our paper procurement policy can be found at
www.randomhouse.co.uk/environment

Typeset in Times New Roman by Falcon Oast Graphic Art Ltd.
Printed in the UK by CPI Cox & Wyman, Reading, RG1 8EX.

2 4 6 8 10 9 7 5 3 1

For Dad,
Not just a Dad; my best mate

For Mum,
Without your love and support,
none of this would have been possible

For Fiona,
I'm very lucky to have a sister like you

Contents

You're only as big as the dreams you dare to live

Portsmouth

Cascais

Cape Hatteras

Canary
Islands

Miami   *Bahamas*

Gibral

Cuba

Antigua

Panama City   *Galapagos
Islands*

*Cape Verde
Islands*

Equator

PACIFIC
OCEAN

ATLANTIC
OCEAN

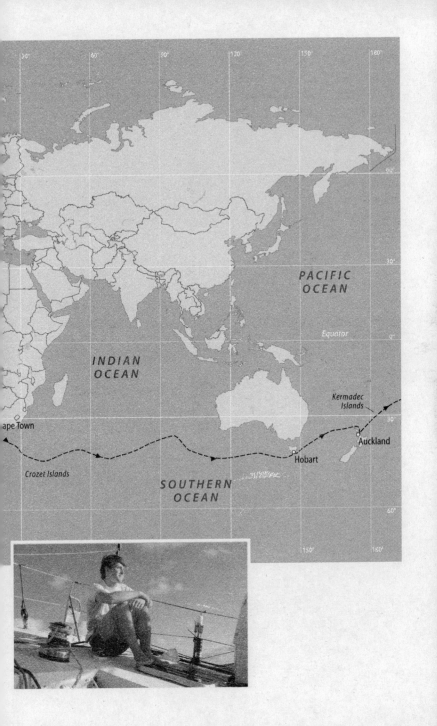

Prologue

Midnight. The boat flew over the raging Southern Ocean in the darkness. Everything inside rattled and shook as she surfed the monstrous waves.

I was in furious seas in the middle of the world's wildest ocean, somewhere between Australia and Africa, hundreds of miles from any shipping lane, about as far as it's possible to be from any other person.

I checked the wind speed. Still averaging 45 knots. I worried about my mast but I had three reefs in the main and this, along with my tiny bulletproof staysail, was the best possible set-up. I reminded myself my boat would outrun almost any wave and she was built to sail in the wildest seas imaginable.

'Well,' I thought, 'we are in those wild seas now.'

I looked outside. I could make out streaks of foam stretching across the sea, turning it white; I could see breakers collapsing under their own weight with a tremendous *whump*.

We shot over a huge wave and the boat surged forward as she passed the crest, picking up speed as she surfed downwards. I held my breath as we accelerated. Looking ahead, the boat was angled down at 20 degrees, flying towards the trough like an arrow.

I looked left and right, admiring the face of the huge roaring wave, its pure, unimaginable power; the speed rose to 18, 19, 20 knots as we surfed down its front. I continued to check the speed: 'Whoa! 22 . . . 24 . . . 26 knots! A new record!'

I braced myself for the drastic deceleration that was certain to come as we ploughed into the wall of water in front of us. The bow dug in and sent plumes of spray flying 20 feet into the air, turning my boat, essentially a 50-foot surf board, into a submarine for a few moments. Seconds later we were already on the crest of the next wave.

The speed! It was just amazing. I was setting new records by the minute. Twenty-six knots on my surfboard in these wild seas was just insane, like hurtling down a wet country lane in a Ferrari at 90mph.

Not for one moment did I wish I were on dry land. I was scared, for sure, but not panicked. Panic is not something I normally associate with the ocean. It's where I feel most at home. Its uncontrollable dangers are an unavoidable part of the ocean sailor's life.

I'd wedged myself inside the cabin at the chart table, which was the safest place to be in these conditions. Attempting to go anywhere on deck was just asking for a good test of my safety harness. I tried to work on the chart; it gave me something to do instead of just worry about the conditions, which were forecast to continue for at least another twenty-four hours. Everything was wet, except me. I had my fabulous dry-suit, and it was working a treat.

The sea became really lumpy; there were waves within waves. It seemed to boil. I was bounced every which way as the boat flew forward.

The freak wave that came thundering through the darkness from the port side must have been an enormous breaker. I was in the cabin so didn't see it coming but I had a one-second warning – its deafening roar. It scooped the boat up and slammed it flat on its starboard side in an instant.

All I could do was hold my breath and somersault with the boat as my world was flipped upside down. The fear that hit me was instant. The noise was ridiculous; the boat creaked, groaned, rattled and screamed.

Time seemed to slow as we went further and further over. Objects flew across the cabin. A 20-litre jerry can of diesel shot past me and hit the other side of the cabin with an almighty crack, spilling its contents.

This was about as bad as it could get. Speed had dropped to a few knots. A wave could sweep in from behind at any moment, turning or flipping the boat fully, ripping the carbon-fibre mast from the deck as if it were matchwood.

The water ballast was now above my head, on what was now the port side, turning the boat further and further over in the wrong direction, way past 90 degrees. The 4-metre keel was out of the water, the 70-foot mast was pointing down the front of the enormous wave. I was on the verge of turning all the way over.

I skidded as I fought to keep my balance; suddenly I was steadying myself with my feet against the roof.

Was this it? Was this the end of my dream?

Was this how I was going to die?

PART ONE

MAKING WAVES

1

Meet the Perhams

I screamed in delight; this was the most fantastic thing I'd ever done. Soaked in spray and shivering with pleasure, I scrambled to keep hold of the tiller. Mum looked nervously on from the bow as the wild steering of her insane six-year-old son threatened to tip both her and my sister into the water.

'Dad!' I yelled, feeling slightly panicked as the wind picked up, 'I need your help!'

'Hold on, Mike,' Dad answered, grinning as he joined me.

As far as I was concerned, *Blue Jay*, the Perham family's first boat, was a 14-foot piece of heaven. Dad had spotted it while we were caravanning in Suffolk. It was in tip-top condition. A family had bought it on a *Swallows and Amazons*-inspired whim and had used it just once. It had sat in their barn for the next fifteen years.

Dad snapped it up and we drove it round and round the caravan site in celebration. Deeply impressed by our spontaneous purchase – it was the finest and most wonderful thing I'd ever seen – I gave myself a stiff neck watching *Blue Jay* through the back window for the entire drive home.

Sailing and adventure is in my blood. I come from a long line of sailors, starting with my great-great-great-great-grandfather who served in the Marines as a gunner in the 1850s. Both of my grandfathers served in the Royal Navy, and my dad, Peter, joined the Merchant Navy at sixteen.

A glider pilot, sailor, climber and clown, Dad is one seriously tough and wiry ball of irrepressible energy. He cycled from Land's End to John O'Groats when he was seventeen and met and fell in love with Mum, Heather, a gentle, patient and adventurous woman, on their very first date. By the end of the evening they'd decided they were going to travel the globe.

Shortly after they'd backpacked through Southeast Asia, Dad managed to wangle his way aboard a custom-built 40-footer to take part in New Zealand's biggest sailing race. It was hit by one of the worst storms in living memory – just eight out of five hundred yachts finished.

Marriage brought my older sister Fiona and me, so Dad gave up the high seas for an oil-rig where he worked as a roustabout, guiding the drill, but after he nearly disappeared with the drill into the earth's core he chucked it in and went to the other extreme. He became a chartered surveyor, bought a house in landlocked Potters Bar and settled down.

My love for all things water-related meant that as I got older our garage became rammed with water sports equipment: windsurf, body and surfboards, canoes, dinghies and water-skis. I took up canoe polo and dabbled in athletics, rugby and biking. When I was six I also taught myself to ski on toy skis on a randomly discovered snowy hill in the Lake District.

Nothing compared to sailing, however. Nothing came close. We sailed in all weathers. In 1997, when we took *Blue Jay* to the Lake District, we woke up one morning on our inflatable mattresses drifting in floodwater. But the greater the adversity, the more determined I became, and we sailed our way across Lake Coniston in a big blow. Dad and I also terrified Mum and Fiona by sailing in Langston Harbour in Portsmouth in choppy waters.

I hated using the engine; it was always sail for me. When we went up the Thames on a windless day we had to use the outboard, which sounded like a scooter with a hole in the exhaust. I spent most of that trip cringing as people in their peaceful gardens and pubs looked up to see what the unholy racket was.

Just after I turned ten in 2002, Dad spotted a 27-foot yacht for sale in Germany. *Blue Jay* was laid up soon after we drove *The Odin* home, drawing stares as the car groaned its way through the streets, tugging *The Odin* into our little cul-de-sac.

We were inseparable from the start. I spent most of the naming party on board polishing and cleaning, dreaming of the high seas. If I wasn't in the house then everyone knew where to find me – on the boat.

The only problem was, I couldn't sail it. Even standing on tiptoe I couldn't see over the cockpit when I was at the wheel. Besides this, the way it held water ballast meant it wasn't all that seaworthy.

After a few frustrating sails, Dad had one of his brainwaves.

'Why don't we just design our own boat?' he said.

My heart jumped. 'Yes!'

2

The Idea

I stared at the paper. The cabin windows were wrong. I knew there was a better way of making them lighter, more watertight, and the right height and size for me. I sketched what I saw in my mind as best I could and showed Dad.

'That'll work,' he said, his eyes sparkling.

He had found a company, Harley Racing Yachts, that could build us a seaworthy 28-footer which we could tow on a trailer. Our boat was to be named *Arcturus* (after a very bright star; the model was called *Tide 28*), and we built her from scratch with Nigel Harley, a tireless boat enthusiast, an outgoing man with a massive shed filled to the rafters with every spare part under the sun. I learned how every piece of the boat was designed and made. It took us a year of long weekends and school holidays at Cowes, but Dad and I loved every minute.

We're like best mates. My dad's completely bonkers, and I think I must have a bit of his craziness too. We regularly hold 'loudest sneeze' competitions and score each other. You need to achieve sufficient volume so that everybody in the room stops what they're doing to see whether you've just sneezed your brains all over the carpet. Neither of us has scored a ten yet but I've got a nine a couple of times.

We're always mucking about; we just can't help it. Even a simple visit to a supermarket can involve a spontaneous game of badminton, football or trolley surfing. If we ever found any alarm clocks for sale, we'd set them so they'd go off hours later.

The day *Arcturus* was ready for a test sail I could hardly keep still. Her hull slid through the sea like an eel; I could feel the wind lifting her, and she tugged away, begging us to open her sails and let her go. *Arcturus* was truly beautiful. It felt as if she could sail for the horizon for ever.

It was then that I had my crazy idea.

Seb Clover, a few days shy of his sixteenth birthday, had just become the youngest person to sail the Atlantic. We'd seen him give a talk at the local cruising association. Mum and Dad have never lost their passion for trying all things new, and this is something I inevitably inherited from them.

I stared Dad in the eye. 'I want to sail across the Atlantic – in our boat – solo.'

We'd talked about sailing across the Atlantic every now and again, usually when we were in the car, driving home after a good sail, but now I was really serious. I wanted to do it as soon as possible.

I didn't know it then, but in August 1971, when he was a boy, Dad had written in his diary that he wanted to sail round the world on his own. 'Forget it,' his father told him, 'you'll never do that!' Now here was his fourteen-year-old son, saying almost exactly the same thing.

He was hardly going to say no, was he?

3

Ocean's 14

Nigel Harley suggested we take *Arcturus* to the Southampton Boat Show. People loved her. A 28-foot ocean-going trailer-sailer was unique and practical, really filling a gap in the market. Just pop it on the back of a 4×4 and off you go. No mooring fees. Five people wanted to buy one so we went into production. Nigel built them while Dad handled sales.

Fate took a hand when the very first guy we'd sold a boat to ran out of money and left us with a half-built boat. Dad said, 'Maybe we could both go across the Atlantic, one boat each,' and winked at me. Easier said than done as we had yet to get our scheme past Mum.

Dad took a deep breath one evening as we finished dinner and put forward his idea.

'What?' Mum said. 'I always knew *you* were crazy enough to fulfil your ambition, but I didn't think for a moment you were going to take Michael with you!'

Poor Mum! Most mothers only had to worry about their teenage kids staying out late, not about their only son spending months at sea facing deadly challenges and sleep deprivation.

Despite my best efforts to look serious, I was grinning from ear to ear.

There was a big issue here, though, a moral dilemma: should Mum and Dad let me take such a risk? I argued that getting out of bed and crossing the road is dangerous, and parents are always making life-or-death decisions on behalf of their kids. We agreed that the most important thing was to eliminate as much danger as possible, to make sure I was properly trained, and equipped with both the best gear and the best attitude. We knew that the Atlantic would throw up challenges guys twice my age and with twice my experience had not been able to overcome, so we did not take the decision lightly.

Then there was the financial side of things. We thought we'd have to re-mortgage the house. But by the end of the evening we were totally optimistic.

In this spirit I named my boat *Cheeky Monkey* and wondered whether she would become a sailing legend.

It was the spring of 2006, so we were going to have to get a move on as we needed to set off in November, the perfect time to go, when conditions would be at their best. Preparation needed to begin right away!

Researching the history of solo Atlantic crossing and solo sailing in general was a sobering experience. The Atlantic is, at 41 million square miles, massive, and many have died trying to cross it. It's not a place for the foolhardy or reckless. Death, serious injury and madness plague the solo adventurer.

One such tragic case was twenty-two-year-old Andrew Wilson who toiled away in his university's workshop every evening for five months working on his dream, the *Nautica*, a boat that would allow him to cross the Atlantic single-handed. He set off from Newfoundland in August 1980 bound for Ireland. Five months later, the empty *Nautica* was washed up on a remote Scottish isle.

Falling overboard was the biggest danger. If this happened then I'd have to watch *Cheeky Monkey* sail on without me, like Andrew Wilson probably watched the *Nautica*, and I wouldn't survive in open water for very long. Some single-handers tow a rope astern to give them a last desperate grasp for survival.

To deal with this I planned to wear a safety harness at all times, no excuses. Some sailors don't wear them, arguing that they restrict movement and can become entangled. Some even go so far as to believe that if you did fall overboard, the drag of the boat would make it impossible to pull yourself back on board so you'd drown anyway.

The harness is a belt that is fastened round the chest. It has short shoulder straps to hold the belt high up on the body. The boat has a wire lifeline stretched on each side next to the deck stanchions to give a free run from stem to stern, to which the harness is clipped. You get used to wearing one pretty quickly and use it automatically, like a seatbelt.

Then there was the danger of being hit by another boat or ship, or colliding with a whale or ocean debris. You might think there isn't much to hit in millions of square miles of sea, but there's all sorts of stuff to dodge. With no one to share watch, I'd only be able to sleep for minutes at a time. It would only take one small, simple mistake that at best would be dangerous and at worst, fatal. Even an entangled rudder can be disastrous when you're on your own.

Then there was accidental injury. Mum insisted we take two boxes of medical supplies – a huge amount for our little boats. 'You can never have too much,' she argued, so in they went. We had everything from splints to saline, antibiotics to painkillers (although our local doc would only let us take normal paracetamol). Dad and I also signed up for a sea-medical course which the instructors adapted especially for us. They'd ask us things like, 'OK, you've broken your arm, you're on your own, what are you going to do?' and then we'd work through various solutions together. We discovered we needed a mirror so we'd be able to see where we were hurt. We also took a pack of Pampers: with no time for stitches and bandages, a serious gash could be temporarily taken care of with a dollop of antiseptic, a nappy and a roll of miracle fix-all gaffer tape. There were hazards all over the boat and we could expect to suffer burns, sprains, breaks, gashes and concussion; and then there was always the possibility of hypothermia, even madness, which seemed to affect some long-distance solo sailors.

I visited a psychologist who asked me loads of very serious and very personal questions. 'What if you don't come back? What do you think will happen to your parents?' This was to make sure I understood the seriousness of our undertaking and to check my mental readiness. I'm happy to say it was a test I passed with flying colours.

Besides all this, in order to take the record for the youngest person to sail solo across the Atlantic I would have to follow all the stringent rules that apply to single-handed records. The 3,500-mile voyage had to be completed under sail operated and powered by wind and muscle power alone (so no electric/hydraulic winches to help with the sails).

The challenges brought the family closer than ever. Dad was my best mate and I could just as easily end up trying to save him if he got into trouble. When people asked us why we were doing it I felt like saying, 'For each other.' We shared the same dream and we were going to make it happen together.

Which meant we had a lot to do – and fast.

4

Money Troubles

The weeks became a whirlwind of courses, outings, schoolwork, training, sponsorship hunting, last-minute rebuilding of various parts of the boats, applying to Guinness World Records and appearing at the Southampton Boat Show. At weekends we trained night and day, sailing back and forth from Cowes to the Channel Islands.

In Southampton we met some people who had sailed the Atlantic who were amazed to hear of our plans and offered us some very useful practical advice, as well as enthusiastically telling us to go for it, something that reassured Mum no end.

I couldn't get a radio licence because I was under eighteen but that obviously wasn't going to stop me from mastering this vital bit of equipment. No one would insure me or the boat either, and the Royal Yachting Association said I was too young to take on such a challenge.

'Children can't even climb trees in this bloomin' country,' Dad moaned.

You don't need a 'sailing licence' to pilot a boat, but Dad was a Yacht Master and he took me through the syllabus until I knew it backwards. We studied the Atlantic crossing guide – the weather, ports to head for in a storm – and put together plans for a variety of scenarios at various stages of the crossing.

We also had to tell my school that I'd be away for six weeks.

Luckily, the headmaster agreed to the time off as long as I took my schoolwork with me. There was no escape.

Our finances soon became stretched to snapping point. Dad wouldn't earn a salary all the time we were away and we had already invested everything we could borrow in the boats. Any spare cash immediately went into our little pot. We had so many things to buy: two tracking devices, life rafts, satellite phones, sea anchors, assorted spares, supplies, clothing, self-steering equipment, solar panels for electricity, radar, GPS systems (two each, just in case one failed) and navigation charts. It seemed as if the trip wouldn't go ahead at all, not because we weren't prepared, simply because we'd run out of cash. We needed £30,000 and we had, with the help of some local businesses, scraped together £10,000. We desperately needed more sponsorship.

One day, Dad was late back from work and we were wondering where he'd got to, thinking that perhaps the trains were screwed up again, when he burst through the front door, panting. 'Ama-hurrr-zing news!' he said.

Every day, on his way home from Potters Bar train station, he passed by the European HQ of the US shoe giants Skechers. On a whim he had stepped through the sliding glass door, marched straight up to reception and outlined our scheme to the receptionist. The next day he had an interview with the marketing manager who became very interested as soon as she realized we lived locally. Dad walked calmly out of the building and waited until he was round the corner before sprinting down the road, desperate to give us the good news – although it was by no means a done deal.

Meetings with top brass and teleconferences with the US head office followed, as did a very anxious, nail-biting few weeks while we waited for an answer. Many businesses had eagerly said they'd sponsor us only to perform an about-turn once the decision reached the person who signed the cheques.

We were gloomily discussing our finances round the dinner table when the phone rang. Skechers had agreed to sponsor us. What's more, they'd stumped up the full £20,000! We danced round the table. My heart raced. That meant the trip would definitely go ahead.

The money came through a few days later and a PR company arranged for me to appear on BBC's *Newsround* sailing *Cheeky Monkey* with the Skechers logo on the sail and side. I grinned like a madman the whole time. Atlantic, here we come!

5

The Race to the Start Line

I awoke bursting with energy every single day, and boy, did I need it. We worked on *Cheeky Monkey* and *Arcturus* whenever we had time, there was so much equipment to fit. Once we were happy we then had to pack them up and find a transport company to drive them to Gibraltar. Although this made for a longer journey of 3,500 nautical miles – most Atlantic sailors leave from Gran Canaria in the Canary Islands, 600 nautical miles closer to Antigua – we liked the idea that we were starting from a British colony and were arriving in one. There'd be no language barriers.

Next we went shopping for supplies. We looked for the largest Tesco we could find, and each of us grabbed a trolley and filled it up with two months' worth of canned food. Soon we would realize that this was a very chaotic way to shop. Food is not merely fuel. There are times when all you have to look forward to is the next meal, and I would come to regret not being more careful.

In between all the preparations we managed to escape for a brief family weekend camping by the sea. This last trip together was especially poignant. As was our tradition, Dad and I gathered drift-wood for a fire on which we boiled a can of hotdogs. After eating our supper, watching the sunset and studying the ocean, we sat chatting, laughing and joking in the darkness as the fire shot sparks at us. It was the same as always, but our feelings ran deeper than normal; memories and thoughts for the future took on a greater significance. That frantic summer had brought us closer together than ever, and we were about to embark on a tremendous adventure.

Mum and Fiona were just as much a part of the mission as Dad and I. Apart from all their help with the preparations, they would run Mission Control – essentially our home computer with an internet connection in our front room, along with some charts, a telephone and a list of emergency numbers for everything from broadband repair to the satellite tracking company. Mum was more than happy to take all this on: it was the best way of keeping an eye on her two sailing madmen. Ours was a very economical operation (the satellite phones cost a dollar a minute to call the UK so I was under strict instructions not to abuse them), but we knew we had covered all the bases.

When the time came for Dad and me to head off, Mum gave me a hug and told me she loved me, and not to do anything stupid.

'What,' I replied, 'like sail across the Atlantic single-handed?'

6

Dry Land Disaster

We left Potters Bar before dawn to get to Southampton so we could supervise the loading of *Arcturus* on to the lorry that would take the boats to Gibraltar; *Cheeky Monkey* would be towed behind on its own trailer. It was close to midnight by the time they were ready. Seeing them both on the low-loader inspired feelings of pride in us both. Then, having given the lorry driver a good head start, we flew to Gibraltar.

We'd had a fairly sleepless night. We were tremendously excited. It was truly amazing to have arrived at this point. It taught me so much about what was possible when you really throw yourself into making a dream reality. Suddenly here we were, butterflies in our stomachs, about to embark on the adventure of a lifetime. I was so excited. This was going to be an amazing adventure, pure and simple!

The first thing I noticed about Gibraltar airport was that it was tiny. You step on to the tarmac, pick up your bags and turn right for Spain and left for Gibraltar. As we jiggled our trolleys round the corner we suddenly found ourselves in the town centre. We looked at each other in surprise. Because it seemed like the logical thing to do, we used the trolleys to wheel our bags all the way to the marina. We found out that everybody did this, and people wheeled them back up to the airport again when leaving.

When we arrived at the marina there was another surprise: my boat was on the lorry. Our hearts stopped as the driver approached us and began his explanation with the words, 'Mr Perham, there's been a terrible accident.'

He'd been racing along one of Spain's busiest motorways when one of the wheels on *Cheeky Monkey*'s trailer seized. The trailer gave an unexpected shudder and suddenly jack-knifed, tearing itself free of the lorry and catapulting itself towards the central reservation. The driver could only watch in his mirror as *Cheeky Monkey* smashed into the barrier with a sickening crunch. The trailer slithered along the barrier in a nails-down-the-blackboard screeching skid before finally coming to a standstill, pinned to the barrier in the middle of the motorway.

As cars veered round the unexpected obstacle, our brave driver had risked his neck working frantically to get the trailer lined up and hitched back on to the low-loader using his winch. He crawled into the next service station, where he chained *Cheeky Monkey* to a lamppost, raced to Gibraltar to deliver *Arcturus*, dashed back to collect *Cheeky Monkey* and drove back to Gibraltar again, desperately hoping he would arrive before we did. In the end, he beat us by just a few minutes.

We dropped our bags and sprinted over to my boat. A nasty black scuff mark showed us where it had hit the central reservation. But after we'd meticulously gone over every inch we concluded that she was still ship-shape – a testament to her toughness.

The next thing we thought was, 'What's Mum going to say?' We were worried she'd want to call the whole thing off. But once we'd argued that as far as we were concerned the boat was 100 per cent fit, she seemed reassured.

Apart from the scuff mark, various adjustments needed to be made to the boat, and the windows needed to be refitted. They'd been shaken loose during all the transporting and lifting. We decided to make them extra secure by bolting them in. The boat-yard was a mile away from where we were staying (appropriately enough, our B&B was on a boat, and while breakfast was great, the beds were awful and we slept terribly) and we were always forgetting stuff and having to march back and forth – in the pouring rain.

The weather was a major problem. It was blowing a gale, and it was three torturous days before we could put the boats in the water. In the meantime we bought hundreds of litres of fresh water and stocked up on some fresh food.

Finally, it was the night before the sail. Dad and I sat eating fish and chips, looking at our boats. 'It's amazing we've come this far,' he said, and I agreed wholeheartedly. It just showed what was possible when you really put your mind to it. We then talked about how we were going to look out for each other once we were out at sea – a reassuring exercise. Which reminded me that this was a first for Dad as well. He was also about to embark on his first solo sail!

One of my heroes, round-the-world sailor Pete Goss, once said, 'There are two challenges to any sailing project. The first is getting to the start line. The second is getting to the finish line.' Well, we had made it to the start line. It had proved extremely difficult, but here we were, only months after we'd decided to try the impossible. The only problem was, after three days of gales the wind had dropped to nothing, and barely a ripple creased the water. We had wanted to head off at ten a.m.

I hopped around with impatience, checking and rechecking *Cheeky Monkey*. She looked great. With our water bottles either side of the keel we had loads of space and the entire aft was given over to the stores department. The forward section, the driest part of the boat, was for our personal gear. Fully loaded, the boats weighed nearly 3 tonnes each.

I was fit to burst as we waited and waited in the still air.

7

An Emotional Departure

We had to get away soon. If we waited too long the weather reports predicted we'd hit the Strait of Gibraltar with the wind against us. We needed it behind us so we'd beat the strong tide and safely dodge our way through some of the most congested waters in the world.

We finally set off at midday on 18 November 2006. After all our hard work, leaving that day was so emotional. I called Mum at 12.47 and my voice croaked, 'It's just . . . just amazing.' I was so proud of what we were doing. Mum, trying to stay calm but streaming tears, told me she was thrilled. My body tingled with exhilaration; our dream had come true. Next, Mum called Dad. They had a conversation filled with raw emotion – love, jubilation and pride mixed with worry, fear and heartache. Fiona told me later that she'd never heard Dad get so emotional.

We sailed on, Europe on one side, Africa on the other. Once in the Strait the wind picked up and we scudded forward. We wanted to get out of the Strait as soon as possible, which meant no sleep for forty-eight hours, but I was far too fired up to worry about that. I could feel the power of the rolling sea below, although there were only ripples on the surface. Waves half a mile deep powered their way in from the Atlantic beneath me, discharging the grey ocean water into the deep blue Med. In the darkness I saw the lights of many supertankers.

Now the fun could really begin.

I gawped as we drew nearer to one of the supertankers. It was truly enormous, 500,000 tonnes and a quarter of a mile long. The distance from the keel to the top of the funnel rivalled the height of St Paul's. This was dangerous stuff. The Strait was chocka. Ships were funnelled in groups of three or four in ten-minute gaps so total concentration was required to pick your spot. One mistake and you'd be mown down. It wasn't as if they could put the brakes on: a supertanker's stopping distance is measured in kilometres.

We zigzagged our way round a constant line of shapes as darkness fell while the flow from the Atlantic – a million cubic metres of water through the 13km wide Strait every second – tried to push us back into the Med. It was just like being on a motorway jammed with juggernauts, incoming ships travelling on an eastbound lane while outgoing vessels travelled west.

I surged with confidence when we sailed out of the Strait and into the open Atlantic. Once we were clear, I made my way below to get some grub and was horrified to see there was water in my boat – lots of it.

Back in Potters Bar, Mum and Fiona were plotting our progress as a red line on a nautical map using info beamed from our satellite trackers. At eight a.m. Mum checked the charts again and again as the red lines had suddenly veered off course. She looked at Fiona and exclaimed, 'They're going the wrong way!'

Then Dad called home using the satellite phone and explained the problem. 'We're out of the Strait but we're heading north for Cadiz for housekeeping.' Mum said the reception was perfect. She could even hear the whoosh of the boat as it caught a wave and surged forward.

A few hours later, Dad and I were parked a couple of miles outside the ancient Spanish port city of Cadiz. The wind dropped to almost nothing and the sea lapped gently at our boats. We shouted our theories to each other as to what might be wrong in an effort to try and prevent us having to put in so early to fix the problem.

Then it hit me. It was rainwater! The rain had got in when we repaired the windows, which had come free of their mouldings during the journey. It had rained so much in Gibraltar that the bilges had filled to the top, so when I'd changed tack, water had slopped over the sides. No wonder *Cheeky Monkey* had felt so heavy!

I bailed and cleaned the bilges. I was soon ready but it was night-fall before the wind picked up again, so I passed the time marvelling at the lights of the remarkable cathedral city of Cadiz that juts out into the ocean in a star shape on the end of a short, narrow peninsula. I also tidied up. Like most teenagers, mess just seems to happen when I'm around, but in this situation you simply can't afford to leave things strewn about your boat.

Shortly after we set off again I saw my first wild dolphin. Just a silver strip breaking the waves at first, then it flew out of the water. I spotted another, then another, and soon twenty were playing around me. Overjoyed, I thought this would be a good time to call Mum.

She had some bad news. She emailed our position every morning as early as possible to the weather routing service and they'd email back the best course to avoid bad weather. The latest reports indicated a nasty blow was on the way, and there was no way round it.

But at that moment I was over the moon. I'd seen my first dolphin and was sailing along at 5 knots in 3-metre swells.

Then Mum asked me if I could see Dad.

'Yes,' I replied, 'he's a white dot on the horizon.'

And then the phone went dead.

8

Storm Horizons

On day seven I spied a mixture of silver and black-grey clouds rolling in fast from the southwest. Dad was out of range of the VHF and my sat phone was out of order.

The approaching storm was a gusting Force 9. Under such conditions dense streaks of foam in the direction of the wind would stretch for 30 feet; some waves would be so high they would become breakers, collapsing under their own weight, and the spray would make it difficult to see; the wind would blow at almost 40mph, strong enough to tear sails.

Sure enough, the wind rose rapidly. The barometer plummeted. The dolphins that had been playing alongside *Cheeky Monkey* vanished. Thunder rumbled in the distance as the air became thicker and colder, and spray started to hit my face.

The most important thing was to slow the boat down. If I ran before a gale at too great a speed and plummeted too fast down the face of a wave there would be a serious danger of pitchpoling – somersaulting stern over bow. The most likely hazard, however, was broaching, which is when the boat is pushed broadside to the face of the waves where it's smashed amidships and capsized by tonnes of water.

Working until my arms were aching, I wound the sails down,

fastened them securely and adjusted the self-steering. I then fed out the sea anchor, a parachute that holds water instead of air. This was the vital bit of kit that would keep *Cheeky Monkey*'s nose pointing at the waves during the blow. That way she wouldn't turn side on to the waves and end up being broached. Knowing how important they were, we'd bought sea anchors that were for bigger boats than ours, just to be safe.

As soon as that was done, I made sure everything was strapped down, then watched as the sea transformed into a dark, freezing maelstrom of violent waves. Spray blasted through the air, slapping me hard in the face. Night was falling; my adrenalin increased as the air pressure fell. A night-time storm was an exciting but frightening prospect, a bigger sailing challenge than anything I had ever faced before.

Not for one moment did I wish that I was on dry land. Ocean sailing is an on-the-edge sport and can be extremely hazardous, but dangers like this are part and parcel of the sailor's life.

At that moment, all I could think about was the impending storm. I was dead tired though, so, still fully togged up, I climbed into my bunk, raised the lee cloth and tried to doze – something that soon proved impossible as *Cheeky Monkey* see-sawed back and forth, her speed checked by the sea anchor.

Being so small and light, *Cheeky Monkey* bobbed up and down like a cork. It was like being inside a washing machine. The noise was intense, like car-crash after car-crash as the waves whacked the bow, everything inside the boat rattling and shaking like loose spanners in a metal toolbox.

It was hellish. For most of the time just standing up was a real mission. At one point I was thrown headfirst towards the stove, and on another occasion a wave put me to bed by throwing me back into my bunk. Wedged into my bunk was in fact the safest place for me to be, so I stayed put.

I held on as we shot down another huge swell. I loved every moment. This was even better than I'd been expecting!

9

Survival

I was so relieved that *Cheeky Monkey* was handling the storm so brilliantly, but a few waves later she suddenly jerked and turned, almost throwing me out of the bunk. I was side on to the waves, which could mean a capsize! The boat tilted until I was at 45 degrees to the water; the keel prevented the wave from taking me any further. I leapt from my bunk and saw on the anemometer that the wind had gusted to 46 knots. This really was a Force 9!

I palmed the sides of the cabin as I fought to get on deck. I quickly clipped on my safety harness. Spray hit me like bullets; the wind sounded like an express train; streams of water poured over the deck. *Cheeky Monkey* reared like a bucking horse. I quickly slammed the deck hatch shut behind me as the last thing I wanted was to have a wave sweep in from behind and fill the boat. Pumping hundreds of gallons of water from below would be almost impossible in such conditions.

This was a whole new level for me, way above anything I had ever faced. The Atlantic made everything else seem so . . . so childish, as if I'd been sailing on still water until now. But this was what it was all about. As someone once told me, sailing is not carried out against the elements but because of them. It was a matter of skill, of controlling the boat. Never, not for a second, would I ever think of giving up.

Even so, I felt quite alone – unable to call for help, nowhere near land, just me, *Cheeky Monkey* and millions of square miles of the Atlantic, doing its worst. And I was broadside to the waves, a very dangerous position to be in. A large wave could easily push *Cheeky Monkey* over on its side.

What was it? I asked myself. Why was the boat so out of control? Checking that my safety line was secure, I staggered to the front of the boat and looked over the bow. The sea anchor. I pulled its line and, to my horror, the rope came to me with no resistance. The sea anchor had been shredded!

Cheeky Monkey flew wildly down the next wave like an elevator cut loose of its cable, and I clung on for dear life.

Fear is not an emotion I normally associate with the ocean; when things go wrong or danger rears its head, I generally feel a surge of exhilaration as I turn to deal with it. To me, the ocean has never been an alien environment. Sailing is my way of life, the sea my home. I never see the ocean as my enemy, just something that is unfathomably powerful and uncontrollable which holds my total respect. After all, one false move means death. But now I faced disaster. My sea anchor was gone and I didn't have a spare. No man could hold a boat steady in such circumstances, let alone a fourteen-year-old boy.

I winced every time *Cheeky Monkey* fell off a wave but she seemed to be having a whale of a time as wind and water whirled around her. 'Do your worst,' I thought, as wind and water whirled around me too. 'I'm crossing this ocean whatever it takes!'

Problems like the sea anchor have to be solved straight away; ignoring them or coming up with the wrong answer is fatal. Outside help is usually hundreds of miles away. It is like a never-ending game of chess: problems arise when pieces are moved by an invisible opponent; the option every time is to play to win or do nothing and lose.

Keeping my line secure and grabbing on for dear life as the boat was pounded time and again, I grabbed my large bailing buckets and some rope. Forcing my fingers to work, I tied the rope to the buckets and then to the forward mooring cleat and threw them over the side. To my relief, the buckets seemed to work as a sea anchor: *Cheeky Monkey* held steady and faced the storm once more.

I couldn't stay on deck a moment longer, it was just too dangerous; there was no sailing to be done in these conditions. I clambered below into my washing-machine cabin and checked the phone.

It still wasn't working.

10

Cheeky Monkey Vanishes

Finally, the storm eased. I prayed Dad was OK. We had been blown apart, beyond the range of our VHF radios. I checked and rechecked the satellite phone, hoping that it had just stopped working because of the storm. But the antenna wasn't loose and the battery was charged; it was just dead. Dammit! I decided to stay put for the moment, for as long as Dad's phone was working Mum would be able to tell him my position so he would be able to come and find me.

After hanging about for a few hours, I pulled in the buckets. It was time to put the emergency back-up plan into action. I set sail for Lanzarote, our emergency rendezvous. I had to sail without vital information such as weather reports, so had no idea if I was heading towards a hurricane or dead air.

I sailed through the day, in fine but cold conditions, and marvelled at the setting sun on the Atlantic, truly one of the world's wonders. At sea, with nothing to break up the horizon, there was one last wink of light and it was gone. As the sun left the sky, it brought home to me that I was truly alone on the high seas.

I wondered again how Dad was getting on.

I didn't yet know it but the storm had destroyed Dad's sea anchor too; he had a tiny spare which somehow outlasted its bigger brother and he made it through in one piece. He'd been trying to call me but we were out of range on the VHF. He called home to speak to Mum and breathed a sigh of relief when she told him that both boats were clearly still sailing. She put me as being 12 miles behind him, so Dad sat tight, taking the chance to rest after what had been a long and difficult night, waiting for me to sail within range of his VHF.

Some hours later, Dad still hadn't heard from me so he called Mum again.

'But you've moved,' she exclaimed, 'and Michael hasn't changed position.'

'What on earth do you mean?' Dad asked. 'I've been sitting here waiting for Mike all day long.' Then it clicked. 'Do you think the tracker company has us mixed up?'

Sure enough, they had, and that's when Dad realized that I was sailing for Lanzarote. He was delighted to see that I was OK but now I was half a day ahead of him and that meant we'd have a few days of sailing without any communication.

Frustrated that he'd wasted so much time sitting still, he turned the boat windward and sailed after me through a fine swell. Mum then confirmed we were both moving, and that I was going to be in Lanzarote quite some time ahead of him.

Mum called Dad back a few minutes later. He snatched the phone up hoping it was me and tried not to sound disappointed to hear Mum's voice.

Clearly there was something amiss. Her voice was trembling.

'What is it?' he asked. 'What's wrong?'

'He's gone!' Mum told him. 'Mike's tracker's not on the screen!'

For Mum, seeing my signal vanish was a total shock. Fearing the worst, her heart pounded as she stared at the computer screen, willing the signal to come back. Then she realized what it might be. When she'd called the tracking company about the mixed signals, she'd asked them to broadcast the signals more often (until then they'd been sent every two hours). She rang them.

'Yes, we've reset the tracker to increase the signal frequency,' they told her, 'but we have to switch it off to do that. You have to press the reset button on the actual device to complete the change.'

Relieved and furious all at once, Mum told them off. 'You didn't tell me this before! My son is in the middle of the Atlantic Ocean with no means of communication and now thanks to you we have no idea where he is!'

11

A Flying Visit

I emerged from below to find a flying fish flapping its way across my deck. I scooped it up and chucked it over the side. I resisted the urge to try and cook it. Apparently they make for good eating, but for a solo sailor food poisoning is yet another fatal possibility. The surface of the sea shimmered as the fluttering school broke the surface.

While they never seemed to grow tired of flying fish for supper, my appetite for tinned food was already wearing thin. I dreamed of English breakfasts, fresh fruit and veg, and Mars bars. I was infuriated with myself for not bringing more snacks – something I planned to rectify the moment I arrived in Lanzarote.

Nearing the Canaries, I checked the charts and watched the seas carefully. There are numerous shallows and outcrops close to the coast, so I knew I had to remain alert.

Now that I was near to land I checked my mobile phone. Yes! It had a signal! Hoping I still had some credit, I called home.

'Hi Mum, it's me!'

It was all Mum could do to say hello before breaking out into sobs of relief; it had been a nightmare forty-eight hours for her. I laughed when I heard I was twelve hours ahead of Dad. It was funny to think that I'd 'beaten' him to Lanzarote!

I marvelled at the never-ending stream of jets carting thousands of tourists back and forth from the airport. There were many treacherous rocks here, lying just below the water, their jagged edges ready to rip the hull of a careless boat. I turned to the west, radioed ahead and sailed for the Marina Rubicon near the town of Playa Blanca.

Having guessed that I was heading for our emergency rendez-vous, Dad had called ahead to the marina, so they were expecting me. Nonetheless, I still attracted puzzled stares as I arrived in this beautiful marina full of impressive and extravagant yachts – people looking over my shoulder for the adult. I raised quite a belly laugh when I filled out the captain's declaration and had to put down my age.

An ex-Royal Marine called John came to see what all the fuss was about and went over *Cheeky Monkey*, checking and fixing my solar panels – those guys can repair anything. As far as the record was concerned it was fine for me to receive help at this point. I could start my attempt from any island in the western Atlantic and, as I mentioned, the typical launch point for Atlantic crossings is Gran Canaria. By the time Dad arrived eleven hours later I had become good friends with John, Kate and their daughter, Sophie. They even invited me to share their 'Sunday lunch' on their boat – just what I needed.

Both of our boats needed repairs – Dad's rudder needed some work – but the most pressing problem was to replace my satellite phone. Mum Fedexed one but it got stuck in Madrid customs, and despite some fairly frantic phone calls they failed to appreciate the urgency, so my uncle Iain offered to fly out with another one. While he ran for the next plane to the Canaries, Dad and I took the oppor-tunity to grab an excellent fillet steak and stock up on snacks. I bought the island's entire supply of chocolate (almost) and forty AA batteries for my iPod speakers, as I didn't want to run out of power for them.

We slept in the boats that night, and the next day Dad suggested we go on a sightseeing tour of Lanzarote's volcano, the Montana de Fuego (Mountain of Fire). Even though the main volcano,

Timanfaya, was still considered 'live', its last eruption was in 1824. I wasn't that impressed. It was all right, I suppose, but just like land-lubbers might describe the sea as a lot of water, to me the volcano was just a pile of rocks.

By the time we got back, my uncle had arrived with the new satellite phone. He hardly had time to stop as he had to get back to work the next day and was booked on the next flight back.

Finally, on day eleven, thanks to his efforts, we set sail once more.

12

Endurance Test

Cheeky Monkey rattled and shook as she rode the waves. Suddenly I was in a deep trough – a huge wave was sweeping in from behind. *Cheeky Monkey* was drawn back into a huge, curving wall of water; the stern began to rise and I held my breath as the angle increased. I was in the barrel of the biggest wave I had ever seen, let alone sailed.

Cheeky Monkey rose to meet the crest. The wave gathered its mighty shoulder under the hull and carried my 3 tonnes like a matchstick at 17 knots before rolling below into the raging wind and spray. That kind of speed was insane for a boat like this.

Suddenly *Cheeky Monkey* bucked and twisted. Everything rattled, shook and wobbled. I leapt up, my heart hammering through my ribs. What the—? I dropped out of the bunk and, palming the sides of the cabin, went to see what was going on.

Dusk was falling fast and another savage Atlantic blow was giving *Cheeky Monkey* hell. I looked up and saw the sails flapping. I had to get the boat back on track and fast, before they were shredded.

I dashed to the tiller and, what horror! The lower half of the self-steering system had snapped off. What a wake-up call. This mechanical device holds the boat on a steady course and is essential for the solo sailor. Without it I was in real trouble.

Once I'd got the boat back under control, still gasping for breath, wet and exhausted, I called Dad. He told me to 'park the boat' and get a few hours' kip before we put our next emergency plan into action. I was gutted: that meant a major diversion to the Cape Verde Islands for more repairs where we'd have to re-launch our crossing attempt (still fine as far as the record books were concerned). I'd really hoped we'd be in Antigua for Christmas, and if not then at least for the New Year.

More seriously, I'd have to do all of the steering for the entire journey to Cape Verde, which meant my hand would have to stay on the tiller for at least three days straight with hardly any breaks – an almost impossible feat. But I wanted to see this trip through to the end, no matter what. I was still going to make it, even though this was going to be as tough mentally as it would be physically. I would have to stay completely alert; no dozing and letting the wind drag the tiller from my grasp. Dad and I decided to operate on twenty-hour shifts, with four hours' rest, when we'd set the boats to drift and try to sleep. We'd then share watch, one hour on, one hour off, for those four hours.

The weather worsened so I togged up, rigged up the spray hood to keep the worst of the wind and water at bay. I crouched in the corner to stay out of the wind and spray and set up a tiller extension so I could operate the steering from a distance. I also put all the food I'd need for three days beside me in a rope bag so I could eat while steering. I looked at my selection of snacks and grimaced. 'Oh well, it'll be steaks in Cape Verde,' I thought.

Forty-eight hours later I was in quite a bit of pain. My eyes were red and sore, stung by salt. My arms were cramping and my hands were as raw as hell, worsening all the time as the merciless Atlantic tried to pull the tiller out of my weakening grasp. Huddled in the corner, my feet braced against the side for stability, every part of me was wet and aching. Everything. And there was nothing I could do to stop it. Nothing. And I still had twenty-four hours to go until I reached the Cape Verde Islands.

I stared at the wild grey sea through the eye-slit in my hood, furious at everything and everyone. I laughed bitterly at the thought of my teachers' words: 'Make sure you keep up with your school-work.' Sure! Easy for them to say. As if *they* could do *their* work in the middle of an Atlantic blow, hundreds of miles from anywhere.

I clock-watched constantly, my iPod on shuffle. I gave myself lots of little milestones, something I could look forward to, like a piece of cake. I'd decide that I could have that cake in one hour's time and that would keep me going, help take my mind off the pain and the cold.

For those final twenty-four hours I battled to stay awake. Sometimes I drifted off but woke up immediately, as soon as I felt the boat change course by the slightest fraction. Dad said that this was a sign that I was a natural sailor, as I was so sensitive to the movement of the boat.

The loneliness was awful. I could see Dad up ahead and I tried to ring him but there was no answer. I didn't know it, but now *his* satellite phone had conked out.

I steered by the compass, and I was pleased to see that I had got it spot on when the Cape Verde Islands suddenly appeared on the horizon. I had never been so relieved to spot dry land! And what beautiful land the Cape Verde Islands are. Mindelo harbour on the island of São Vicente is actually an old volcanic crater, almost per-fectly circular. Suddenly the sun beamed down on me. I tried to wipe the salt from my lips. Soon a hot shower and food!

Although this had been a real trial, I was chuffed to bits because I'd been pushed to the limit and beyond what I thought I was capable of. This gave me such a confidence boost. This and the 17 knots of boat speed had given me a taste for faster seas and sowed the seeds of my desire to sail the fastest sea in the world – the Southern Ocean.

Dad and I anchored together in the harbour and we were rowed ashore by a pair of boat boys. These lads earned about a pound a day rowing us back and forth to our boats and they were the first sign of the poverty we saw on this island. We passed by many beggars and even saw someone being robbed by a ten-year-old boy who sprinted off with his ill-gotten gains before anyone knew what had happened.

After we'd negotiated customs and immigration, which was essentially an office full of bored admin people who couldn't quite believe that I was the captain, we went into town to get something to eat. The longed-for steaks didn't materialize so we had chicken and chips, except that the chicken looked nothing like it was supposed to: it was perfectly flat and thin, as if it had been run over. It was very odd indeed, but at least it tasted OK. We also went shopping and bought some decorations as we now knew we'd be at sea for Christmas. No reason we should miss out!

Meanwhile, miracle-worker Mum had not only managed to find a new self-steering system, she'd also persuaded someone from the company to fly out with it to fit it, bunging him a new satellite phone for Dad at the last moment. He was a total star. Without him we would have been scuppered.

Now the challenge was to be re-launched from Cape Verde, and this would be our last shot at the record. There were no more islands between us and Antigua, 2,400 nautical miles away.

13

Swimming with Sharks

On 15 December, almost a month after we had first set off from Gibraltar, we left Cape Verde in a state of excitement and optimism. Once we hit the trade winds we'd end up somewhere, at some time, on the other side of the Atlantic even if everything fell off the boat. We relied on weather updates from Mum to let us know whether to drop a few miles north or south to pick up the best possible wind.

We had been going for just a couple of hours when my steering became sticky. The tiller should move smoothly but it kept dragging itself sluggishly as the self-steering tried to correct it. This was all I needed. I leaned over the side of the boat and got my head as close to the rudder as possible. It was entangled in a ball of rope.

There was only one way to fix it.

Go over the side.

Falling overboard is the solo sailor's worst nightmare, so the idea of going over the side deliberately did unsettle me. The thought of watching *Cheeky Monkey* sail away while I foundered in the cold Atlantic gave me quite a chill, but there was no alternative. I was a strong swimmer and was still only a few hundred metres off shore, so if the worst-case scenario arose I was confident I would make it back to the shore.

Looping a rope around my chest, just under my arms, I tied it very tight, fastened it to the mooring cleat, checked both cleat and rope several times, took a deep breath and slipped over the side into the cold water, my knife in my pocket.

I pulled and hacked at the rope, my legs thrashing in the water as the swell bounced *Cheeky Monkey* and me along like a pair of rubber ducks. It soon came free and I checked the rudder; there was no damage. Grabbing the rope, I quickly pulled myself aboard, job done.

A short while later, Dad, who had sailed just out of sight, called me. The excitement in his voice made it clear something interesting was going on, but the crackly line meant I missed most of it – except for one exclamation: 'Shark!' It was only then that I let myself wonder just how unlucky I might have been.

The wind had dropped and *Arcturus* had been going along at just a couple of knots. He had just checked the mainsail and was strolling aft when he spotted a large shadow in the water. Thinking it was flotsam or perhaps a dolphin, he leaned over the side for a closer look. An enormous fin cut the water. It was, at five metres, a massive shark. He watched in awe as the ancient, powerful creature shadowed the boat. Now would not be a good time to fall in. Then, after an hour or so, he called me.

'Have you taken a picture?' I asked.

'No!' he said. 'Hang on!' I could hear frenzied activity as he ransacked the boat looking for the camera. 'Damn! It's gone!'

'Daaad, now no one's going to believe us!'

Laughing about the one that got away, I hung up.

Some time after that we were sailing in some pretty good swells when there was a thump from the bottom of the boat. What now? I climbed on deck and looked out at the bright, glittering water. I'd been making great progress since untangling the rudder. I knew it wouldn't last.

I gasped in surprise and wonder when a dolphin burst through the top of a large swell at full speed. It got an incredible 30 feet into the air before piercing the water like a torpedo. Wow! Unbelievable!

They were all around the boat, dozens of them, and they came within inches of the hull. Soon I realized they were competing with one another, to see who could get closest for longest; every now and again they'd get too close and get a thump on the nose. They also loved following the rudder, matching every little change as it moved from side to side. They are truly incredible creatures, and to be sailing with dozens of them in the open ocean hundreds of miles from anywhere was one of the greatest experiences of my life. I beamed the whole time they were there. I could look over the side and stare straight into their eyes. Unlike other animals they wouldn't look away and stared back as if my equal, as if they were just as curious about what I was thinking. Every now and again they'd splash me with a perfectly timed somersault – that soon became another favourite game of theirs.

The dolphins were by no means the only wildlife Dad and I encountered during the crossing. Flying fish swarmed about *Cheeky Monkey*, scattering at the bow, glinting in the sun like flying diamonds. I was on the phone to Mum when one flapped its way on to the boat and landed with a slap at my feet. Sometimes they'd be littering the deck when I got up after a nap and I'd have to sweep the area free of their slippery scales.

On another occasion I came on deck to find a small brown bird hopping about the boat. We were halfway across, the best part of 1,250 nautical miles from land. How could this tiny bird hope to cross the Atlantic? It didn't hang round for too long before shooting off again, climbing into the sky on its seemingly impossible mission.

14

Jack-of-All-Trades

The phone rang. It was Dad. He'd spotted a school of whales, a truly tremendous sight, each one bigger than our boats. A short while later Dad was checking his boat over when he spotted a dark shape in the water a few metres ahead. With some horror he realized that the approaching object was an enormous oil drum. He dived for the wheel and just managed to miss it at the last moment.

Man-made pollution and debris were far worse than I'd imagined. When we lost the wind and the sea became still, I'd stare over the side and could see that every single cubic centimetre of water contained tiny bits of paper, wood and plastic while patches of oily film dotted the surface. The effects of human activity on the Atlantic are appalling. I, like most people, thought it was bad, but to see it like this, so visible, out there in the middle of nowhere, was a complete shock to me.

I was now ticking off the miles, desperate to make it to the finish line in Antigua as soon as possible. The boat felt great and was coping well with the big Atlantic swells. Dad and I tried to keep in sight but we'd often be blown apart in a squall. Every time the pressure fell, the wind increased and the swell rose, I felt a tingle of anticipation and excitement as I reduced sail and the dolphins vanished. The air became heavier, the clouds swelled into giants and the ocean turned grey. *Cheeky Monkey* thrived in these conditions and thundered down the faces of the deep swells. I have yet to feel a greater sensation than what I felt standing on the bow of a boat I helped to create, feeling her scud through the oceans in a Force 5, as though she could carry on towards the horizon for ever.

Once the squalls had passed, Dad and I would search for each other. It was always a great feeling when we met again and it felt like it was just us two in the entire ocean. At night, ours were the only lights on the black ocean, sea spray glittering around them like sparklers.

Problems with equipment kept on coming. I had rapidly become a jack-of-all-trades and repaired my VHF by rigging up a separate, longer antenna. My jib halyard (which holds the front sail up) snapped. Repairing this meant climbing to the top of the mast, a risky procedure at the best of times but extremely dangerous in big swells when on your own. Instead, I improvised with my mainsail and decided that this would work well enough for the rest of the crossing.

Much harder to manage on the four-week journey was the loneliness. I had the phone calls home, which always started with the question 'How am I doing?', but I missed my friends, home, even school. Oddly enough, being so isolated made me feel much closer to them. I appreciated them a lot more now that I was thousands of miles away in the middle of the Atlantic! Dad was brilliant. He missed everyone just as much as I did but kept the jokes coming.

The nights began to fall earlier; the sunsets became short spells of gloomy haziness. By Christmas Day we were still ten days from Antigua. But for our stops in the Canaries and Cape Verde we would already have arrived. Dad and I spoke all day on the 25th. In the evening he had a bright idea: grab an orange and add a collision flare to make the brightest Christingle the world has ever seen. I lit the white flare and it hissed into life and crackled like the electricity in Dr Frankenstein's lab. It was like holding the brightest sparkler in the universe – if dropped it would have burned its way straight through the deck like a blowtorch through plastic. It was brilliant. I beamed as we held them. It was about a million times better than a Christmas cracker.

Dad and I talked through the night on the VHF and we both agreed the thing we were looking forward to more than anything else was our hug! Although we could see and talk to each other, it was very frustrating not to have physical contact. That Christmas night, a hug would have been very welcome indeed.

As Antigua grew ever closer I became ever more impatient to reach dry land. I loved being at sea but I also wanted us to achieve our goal as soon as possible. I wasn't best pleased, then, when Dad called to say he had a major problem. *Arcturus* had lurched suddenly in a large swell and his rudder had snapped in two. Luckily he had a spare, but it was untested and he had no idea how good it would be once attached. Generally, rudders are fitted to within a millimetre. Dad would have to fit it in rolling seas and then steer the rest of the journey by hand as the self-steering wasn't compatible with the spare.

The next thing to snap was me, after Mum called on the sat phone.

15

Record Breaker

We had found a PR company to help us with publicity to make sure Skechers, our main sponsors, got maximum coverage. At the rate we were going we were due to hit Antigua at about three p.m. on 2 January. Kizzi, the PR guy, wanted to make sure that the papers could get the story processed on the day of our arrival in Antigua. That meant he wanted us to arrive at ten a.m. the following morning so UK journalists could meet their three to four p.m. deadlines. We would have to spend an extra night on the boat, sailing backwards, against the current.

I was totally gutted, furious, when Mum told me. 'Get stuffed!' I thought, but after some consideration I realized just how important this was. I wouldn't have been there without the sponsors, it was only fair that I delivered what they had paid for. Poor Mum took the brunt of my annoyance but was relieved to hear that I had seen sense.

I called Dad, who was shattered from steering manually. I was really fed up and I let my mood influence my sailing – a stupid mistake. I stomped around the boat barefoot as we drifted. A silly thing to do, as I managed to slip and cut my foot. I rolled around in agony, blood pouring from a deep gash. 'Idiot!' I yelled. Blood splattered all over the white boat as I hopped for the med kit. That'll teach me! I took some painkillers and stuck the gash together before squeezing my foot back into a shoe. It felt pretty sore but I could still sail.

Only one day to go . . .

On 3 January, after a six-week odyssey, we finally steered within sight of Antigua. My heart soared with excitement. When I spoke to Dad, he sounded like he could have popped with pride. We had done it. I had never doubted we would achieve our goal but to suddenly see land and know I would be there in an hour or so . . . well, I was overjoyed. I called Mum as well. She had a house full of reporters to deal with but we managed a quick chat. She was so proud, relieved, and completely over the moon.

We were right on time as we passed the Pillars of Hercules, the pale, beautiful cliffs carved by wind, rain and sea that guard the entrance to English Harbour. I spotted a launch bouncing towards us at full throttle; it was full of press people clutching cameras with one hand, the boat with the other, all looking rather seasick. My smile turned into amazement as I looked beyond to see about fifty boats chasing after them, all bearing down on me! Horns were blaring, flags were being waved, people were cheering at the tops of their voices, reporters wobbled dangerously as they yelled questions. The noise was incredible after just hearing the rattling of the boat and the churning of the ocean for the last six weeks.

As we rounded the corner that took us into the beautiful Nelson's Dockyard, full of historic buildings and tall palm trees, I could see at least a thousand people crammed on to the tiny space in front of Customs House, some dangerously close to the edge of the jetty.

'Wow,' I thought. Up until then I'd had no idea who would be in Antigua when we arrived, if anyone.

Dad had pulled back to make sure I landed first. Dozens of hands reached out to grab me as I climbed ashore. As Dad neared the dock I saw him chuck his camera at someone, asking them to take some pics for us.

Once he was berthed he joined me and we gave each other a crushing hug. Dad's eyes were wet and we half laughed, half cried with joy. That was the hug I'd been waiting for, the moment I truly realized that we'd done it, that we'd crossed the Atlantic Ocean!

We were both breathless, completely giddy and unprepared for the attention. Suddenly, a wall of CNN, NBC, BBC, Sky and ABC microphones surrounded us, all of them demanding live TV and radio interviews. Everyone wanted to film me calling Mum, so I fumbled for my phone, switched it on and waited impatiently for a signal. The journalists crowded round. After a few rings it was picked up. To my surprise, a very male, very gruff voice said, 'Yeah?' This threw me for a moment, until I realized it was Neil, a family friend who'd been fielding calls for Mum. He passed me to Mum, but with everyone shouting questions, a dodgy time-delayed phone line and fifty boats blasting their horns, it was impossible for us to hear each other.

I didn't know it then, but our house in Potters Bar was under siege. Mum had woken up that morning expecting two camera crews, but by mid-morning our quiet cul-de-sac was full of vans with satellite dishes. Dozens of cameramen and technicians were busy unwinding cables, reporters were wielding microphones, notepads and Dictaphones. Sky, BBC News 24, Five, Channel 4 and ITV – representatives from every UK news channel were packed into our house.

Lights and cameras were unloaded, dishes were jiggled into position and presenters straightened their suits. They were all very jolly, happy to be covering a good news story, especially the BBC's Caroline Hawley who'd just returned from Iraq. For some reason the BBC had sent a team of four reporters. A lively debate began about how each channel would get a live piece of the Perhams to fit in with their various schedules. Luckily, big sis Fiona took charge and drew up a plan. She did such a good job that two channels offered her a work placement.

The reporters kept asking Mum, 'So where's all the equipment then?' They were both disappointed and amazed to learn it consisted of a phone and a PC.

It was all so much of a whirl. Mum and Fiona were live on the *One o'Clock News* on the BBC while Sky TV were still setting up in our games room and ITV in the front lounge. The final interview of the day was live on *Channel 4 News* with Jon Snow shortly after seven p.m. For some reason, Jon seemed to think we were a wealthy family who could afford to do this sort of thing any time we liked. Mum soon set him straight! The following morning Mum and Fiona appeared on *BBC Breakfast*, along with the winners of *Strictly Come Dancing*.

In Antigua, after a hastily assembled press conference and once things had calmed down a bit, we climbed back into our boats. We had to strip them of all the electronic equipment and get them ready for transport, a job which took us hours.

Just as we were finishing, a silky voice asked, 'Mr Perham?' It was the Minister of Tourism. He offered us one of the island's swankiest apartments and invited us to join him and the Prime Minister for dinner the following evening. In the end the PM was whisked away on urgent business so couldn't make it, but we were chuffed to bits when we heard that cricketing legend Viv Richards was going to take his place. He proved to be great company. I was whisked off to Benetton where they kitted me out in a suit for free for the occasion.

That night Dad and I fell into bed, totally shattered, but thanks to our odd sleeping patterns we were wide awake at two a.m. We spent the rest of the night having a very cosy debrief, talking about everything we'd faced together on our record-breaking trip. It was a really special, peaceful few hours. As we talked, I realized that there was one thing I knew for certain. I wanted to sail for longer and in bigger seas.

I wanted to experience everything the world had to offer.

16

Fame!

It all felt so surreal. Wherever we went, people wanted to shake our hands. When we landed in the UK the airline crew asked us to leave the plane first and suggested we take the secret superstar exit to avoid the press. Dad and I looked at them blankly and asked, 'Press? What press?'

They were all there. It seemed a shame to disappoint them. Besides, Mum and Fiona were expecting us to arrive in the normal place.

As we made our way through the terminal, a group of girls shouted 'Well done, Michael!' and we were mobbed with barely a chance to say hello to Mum and Fiona. For a moment, just after we'd given the press a short statement, it all got a bit too much as about twenty photographers pursued us through the airport. Everybody was watching us, wondering who we were. Even the taxi was surrounded, and when we got in we were on the news on the radio – a very surreal experience! We then drove home in the pouring rain (typical!). As we approached our house, which sat past a little roundabout right at the end of a cul-de-sac, I grinned when I saw that both the house and roundabout were covered in bunting and banners. Our friends and neighbours were out in force to welcome us home.

I longed to be back with my mates and return to everyday life, so I went back to school the very next day. This brought me back down to earth, but only momentarily, as I appeared in the *News of the World*, and *The Times* (under the headline 'The Prince of Sails') and the *Telegraph*, and then on *Blue Peter* where I was given a gold badge (Dad pinched it off me and now wears it nearly every day!). A week later I was presented with the Guinness World Records certificate at the Houses of Parliament. After this I sat a science exam before I was whisked off to New York to appear on *The Martha Stewart Show*.

The investment bank J. P. Morgan very kindly paid for our boats to be returned to the UK, so I could take part in the Round the Island Race that summer, which they were sponsoring. As Dad and I rounded the Isle of Wight, I watched as *Cheeky Monkey*'s happy bow cut through the water and grinned as the cold spray struck my face.

And I wondered how long it would be before I sailed round the world.

I'd started to think seriously about the idea while I was still halfway across the Atlantic, and Dad and I had started talking about the possibility almost as soon as we were back in the UK. Taking the record for the youngest person to sail non-stop across the Atlantic was the greatest feeling I'd ever experienced, and now I had an overwhelming urge to top it by becoming the youngest person to sail non-stop round the world. Of course going solo round the world is a bit different from sailing across the Atlantic. On a scale of one to ten, sailing the Atlantic is a 'one' and the world is a 'ten'.

The sport of single-handed circumnavigation sailing was firmly established when retired sea captain Joshua Slocum sailed round the world between 1895 and 1898 on his 37-foot (11m) sloop *Spray*. His book *Sailing Alone Around the World* is still considered a classic adventure, and has inspired many others to take to the seas.

In 1966, Sir Francis Chichester set off in *Gipsy Moth IV*, which he'd custom-built to set the first speed record for a single-handed circumnavigation. With one stop of forty-eight days in Sydney,

Australia, he took 274 days overall, which meant a sailing time of 226 days – twice as fast as the previous record for a small vessel. And just to show that age need be no barrier, he achieved this at the grand old age of sixty-five.

Then, in 1969, came the first single-handed round-the-world yacht race, the *Sunday Times* Golden Globe. Of the nine boats that started only Robin Knox-Johnston completed the race, becoming the first person to sail single-handed, unassisted and non-stop round the world. This was also the race in which Donald Crowhurst attempted to fake his circumnavigation, went insane, and committed suicide.

In stark contrast, Bernard Moitessier, who was hot favourite to win, was on the home stretch across the Atlantic when he suddenly decided to drop out of the race and sail on, past South Africa, across the Indian Ocean and up to the Pacific Islands. He eventually covered 37,455 miles before finishing in Tahiti. He'd obviously enjoyed himself so much he was unable to stop – a man after my own heart! I think there is something about sailing across the sea that can drive some people on and on, and they could sail onwards for ever.

Although several single-handed circumnavigators had gone before me, they were few in number. More people have been to space than have sailed round the world, and with good reason. Circumnavigation is the Everest of sailing: it's extremely difficult and is packed full of extremely tough challenges.

British sailor Tony Bullimore caused a sensation when he was rescued during the 1996 Vendée Globe single-handed round-the-world race. On 5 January 1997, Bullimore's boat *Exide Challenger* capsized in the Southern Ocean. The media assumed that the fifty-five-year-old sailor had perished but the Royal Australian Navy found Bullimore alive. He'd managed to survive for five days in an air pocket in his upside-down boat in pitch darkness.

Another one of my sailing heroes, Pete Goss, realized his dream to compete in the 1996 Vendée Globe, despite incredible financial hardships. He was having the race of his life when he turned round and sailed into hurricane-force winds to rescue French sailor Raphael Dinelli. Against seemingly impossible odds he was successful, and he was awarded the Legion d'Honneur, France's highest honour, before being presented with an MBE by the Queen.

Many others have not been so lucky. The same race claimed the life of Gerry Roufs, who was in second place. He was in the South Pacific when his position-indicating beacon ceased to transmit. His boat, *Groupe LG2*, was later found washed up on the coast of Chile. In 1992, fifty-nine-year-old Nigel Burgess took part in the Vendée Globe and was lost at sea just three days into the race. It was presumed he had fallen overboard.

These guys were racing, however; they were pushing their boats at 100 per cent all the way round the world. I would have the luxury of time, but not as much as fellow teenager Robin Lee Graham, who set out to sail round the world alone in the summer of 1965, when he was sixteen. He left from Southern California and headed west in his 24-foot sloop the *Dove*, making many stops on his incredible journey. Almost five years later, after changing boats and getting married on the way, he sailed back on the 33-foot *Big Dove* into his home port in Los Angeles.

Only two other teenagers had sailed the globe on their own, including the Australian David Dicks, who in February 1996 at the age of seventeen set off to sail non-stop round the globe in his family's 34-foot sloop. He returned nine months later after facing knockdowns, bad weather and food poisoning, but because he'd accepted a bolt to fix his mast on the way he was denied the 'unassisted' part of the record.

Dicks was followed by another Australian sailor, Jesse Martin, who became the youngest person to circumnavigate the world solo, non-stop and unassisted in 1999. His journey in the 34-foot sloop *Lionheart-Mistral* took him 328 days and was completed when he was eighteen. Even though he said he'd taken his time, he'd still faced plenty of dangers: he collided with a whale in the South

Atlantic, he narrowly escaped being mown down by a tanker, and his boat was knocked over by heavy seas.

I wanted to become the youngest non-stop circumnavigator. To qualify for any record, a world circumnavigation has to be a passage of at least 21,600 nautical miles (40,000km) in length, which crosses the equator, crosses every meridian, and finishes in the same port as it starts.

More than anything, I wanted to sail the Southern Ocean, the seas where Pete Goss had battled hurricane-force winds. To me there was no greater sailing challenge than crossing that wild, freezing, vast body of water that powers its way around the Antarctic. With no landmasses to break the flow of water, the Southern Ocean was infamous for its huge waves and ferocious winds, and very few people dared to sail it.

By the time the decision was formally made to make my dream a reality we had a year to prepare. I planned to leave in November 2008, again the best time of year to embark on sailing round the world, when the weather should, seasonally speaking, work in my favour as I sailed my way south and then east around the globe.

For the time being, though, it was all still a dream.

17

The Dream Becomes Reality

The original plan was for both Dad and me to sail, on two separate boats, just like the Atlantic trip. We planned to raise enough money to buy the boats, which we would then sell at the end of our journey. At this stage we thought we'd need a million pounds to make it happen. Nearly all of that money would go on buying and fitting out the boats so they could be sailed by one person.

Dad set about the very difficult task of finding sponsors. He went to Business Link and got a list of the five hundred largest companies in our county of Hertfordshire and hit the phone. One of the very first calls he made was to a company called VocaLink and he managed to speak to exactly the right person. They called back the very next day, said it was just the sort of thing they wanted to be involved in and that they were putting money down straight away.

I couldn't believe it when Dad told me. This was an amazing start! Perhaps we were going to have an easier time raising money for the world trip than the Atlantic trip.

Dad had planned to call potential sponsors whenever he had a chance in between work, but after having such a huge success straight away, he took two days off and called everyone on the list. Rejection after rejection followed. It was only then that we realized he'd had an incredible piece of beginner's luck. Although many businesses were interested and supportive, they said they simply didn't have any spare cash. Several of them made grumbling noises about the economy and recession and warned us that we would struggle to raise the money we needed.

It was then that we decided I should go on my own, halving the budget. Of course we were gutted that Dad wouldn't be there with me but we had to get real. There was no way the trip would happen unless we started to think laterally.

Next, Dad approached Skechers, who'd been so generous to us on the Atlantic trip. It took a long time for them to make up their minds but they came through in the end with another generous donation.

With a good chunk of money in the bank (but still a long way from what we needed), we started hunting for potential yachts. We thought about refitting a large, spacious yacht, a 72-foot Global Challenge normally crewed by twelve to eighteen people, redesigning it so that I could sail it on my own. This would take several months of work and as we were now into the summer we realized that we simply wouldn't have the time. We needed an ocean-ready boat that was capable of taking everything the world's oceans could throw at it.

Another option, recommended very strongly by many of the circumnavigators we spoke to, was an Open 50. This 50-foot boat is known as the 'Ferrari of the ocean' because it's so fast and was used by Vendée Globe sailors. It was purpose-designed for the round-the-world solo sailor and its speed would make it easier for me to dodge storms and ride the big waves of the Southern Ocean.

I was tremendously excited at the prospect of sailing the world in such a beautiful boat. Open 50s are huge, sleek, fast and powerful; you need to be a very confident sailor to handle them. Sailing in an Open 50 is very different to sailing in a 'normal' yacht. An Open 50 is wide and flat, like a surfboard, and that's exactly how they have to be sailed. Surfing waves like this on a more traditional-size boat like *Cheeky Monkey*, which sits with much of its body below the water, is almost impossible. An Open 50 rides *with* the waves, just like a surfboard, so I'd have to get used to *not* putting on the brakes and flying along at high speeds, which is the safest thing to do in heavy seas in an Open 50.

I thought this sounded great as I'd be able to complete the trip sooner than in a large yacht. Dad reckoned that in an Open 50 the trip would take five months. I was convinced I would do the full 24,000 miles in four months.

Once again, the summer became a whirlwind of courses, outings, fitness training, sponsorship hunting, applying to Guinness World Records and publicizing our attempt whenever we could; we also auctioned *Cheeky Monkey*, for £30,000. I studied my route again and again and watched footage of sailors tackling the Southern Ocean on the internet and on DVDs. Out of all the seas I would sail, it was the South that I looked forward to more than any other. Whenever I had a spare moment to myself – which wasn't often – my mind filled with thoughts of the Southern Ocean.

One of the other many things I needed to do was tell my girl-friend, Beckie, about the trip. We'd first met through mutual friends in July and had hit it off straight away. We were inseparable, like best friends. When I told her she was pretty surprised and she asked me if I was serious. When she realized I was, she quickly came to accept the idea that I'd be away for four or five months. It would be tough, but we felt our relationship would survive this separation.

As time went on and our sponsorship pot failed to fill up, we decided that rather than buy an Open 50, we'd charter one. This would save us about 80 per cent of the cost of a boat. Of course that would mean we wouldn't get most of the money back at the end of the trip by selling the boat, like we did with *Cheeky Monkey*, but it at least made the trip more likely.

We started looking for Open 50s on the internet, even though at this stage we still weren't sure if we would raise enough sponsorship money. We eventually found a likely candidate in the north of France. The boat was called *Etoile Australe*, but that would change once we found a sponsor prepared to pay for the privilege of renaming her. She had a fine pedigree. She'd already recorded one victory with French sailor J. P. Mouligne in the 1998–99 Around Alone solo race round the world, just beating veteran Japanese sailor Minoru Saito. (I couldn't know it yet, of course, but Minoru and I would have our own encounter during my adventure.) She'd logged almost 70,000 nautical miles, had made ten Atlantic crossings and, with Mouligne at the helm, had set a speed record from Newport on the Isle of Wight to Bermuda.

In July, Dad and I travelled to France to see her for the first time. I felt a rush of excitement when I saw her 70-foot orange mast in the distance. When we turned the corner and I saw her in her entirety, I was seriously impressed.

'Now that,' I said, 'is one beautiful boat.'

Sleek, with a wide, flat hull, a 4-metre bulb keel and a low cabin, I could see she was extremely quick and powerful. She was super-strong as well, tougher than she needed to be in fact. The Open 60s that take solo sailors round the world today are, in terms of build strength, right on the edge when it comes to the physical abuse they can take from wind and waves. The Open 50 had a decent margin of error built into her design to allow for some seriously hefty abuse, and I was very pleased about that.

As I mentioned earlier, you had to have a lot of confidence to sail an Open 50, and I was confident I could handle her. You've got to be physically fit but not fanatically so. You don't need to be an Olympic triathlete, or a long-distance runner or a weightlifter; you just need to be a good all-rounder. You have to be able to put your back into winding the winches for about fifteen minutes at a time and sometimes you have to be able to do that many, many, times a day, which is tough for sure, but I knew I could handle it.

We talked money, and eventually Dad and the charterers brokered an agreement. Now we just had to find the money to pay them.

It was a hell of a lot of work. Every night was spent sending proposals to dozens of potential sponsors, trying to mock up designs of their logos on to the boat sails to show them how good it would look. Dozens of small companies and individuals offered everything they could, from life-saving equipment to tool sets, but we were still desperately short of the £200,000 we needed in cold, hard cash. We'd barely raised half of that. One company director told us he loved what we were trying to do and said they were prepared to offer us some money with this proviso: 'If Mike dies then we want our money back.' That was pretty harsh! We said no way.

We had a piece of luck when Channel 4 came on board. They wanted to make a film about my journey and that meant we'd get a bit of money from that. But it was starting to look like the dream would remain just that. It was the end of August and we were still £100,000 short. If we didn't get the money now, we wouldn't have enough time to charter and kit out the boat in time for November.

Then, the TV producer who was making the film set up a meeting with a potential sponsor – TotallyMoney.com. Dad and I travelled down to London with butterflies in our stomachs. This was our absolute last chance and we pushed this fact home during our well-rehearsed PowerPoint presentation.

At the time, TotallyMoney.com was quite a small company, run by a young and enthusiastic team, so this was a massive investment for them. They were keen to get involved but we were asking for a lot from them so it wasn't too surprising when they offered us just under half of what we needed.

'That's not enough,' Dad said. 'The trip won't happen with that amount. How about Mike and I go out and grab some lunch? That will give you a chance to think about it. We really need to know today.'

We went back in an hour later and they told us they were prepared to raise their offer by another £10,000. This was still short. But we took it, and gave my boat the official name *TotallyMoney.com*.

Dad thought there was a chance that we could save another £25,000. He'd had some last-minute interest from someone who was prepared to sponsor my insurance – not many companies will insure someone my age for anything, let alone to sail round the world. 'If we can make the insurance happen, then we're on our way,' he said. Amazingly, Dad worked his magic and a syndicate agreed to provide the insurance in return for sponsorship.

A charitable fund gave us £10,000 and we were given another £15,000 from private and corporate sponsors.

Suddenly it was real, not a dream; it was actually going to happen! It was financially tight but we had £200,000 in cash and equipment sponsorship, just enough to cover everything I needed for the trip, although this would leave us with no real contingency, just credit cards and overdrafts. We thought that if we spent as much as possible on the boat and its contents, it would reduce the chances of us having to spend any more once I'd left, especially as the trip was supposed to be non-stop.

We really needed to get moving. We had to pay the charterers and get them to start refitting the boat to my requirements. They would have to examine every nut, bolt and wire, every square inch of her body and the rig. She also needed repainting, and we had to arrange for sponsors' logos to be put on.

Dad and I were in the midst of arranging all this, and 1,001 other things, when Mum dropped a bombshell.

18

Doubt

Mum didn't want me to go.

Up until this point she hadn't worried about it because she really thought that the trip wouldn't happen. Dad had kept giving himself ultimatums along the lines of 'If we don't have enough money by the end of this month, then that's it, the trip's off.' But when that deadline passed, Dad would extend it to the end of the following month and redouble his efforts to raise the money. By the time we reached late August, Mum really thought there was no way we'd make it.

Mum was all too familiar with the idea that her son and husband were very likely going to spend much of their lives chasing adventure and excitement and in a sense she had become acclimatized to this. After all, she'd let us sail across the Atlantic! What made it especially hard for her this time was that Fiona had left home on a gap year at the start of September, just days after Dad and I knew we had enough money to make the trip happen. Having Fiona around had made the Atlantic trip easier for Mum to bear. They were girls together and had lots of long chats as they ran things from home. Now, suddenly, Fiona was gone, and here I was telling Mum that after all these months of trying, right at the last possible minute, I was going to sail round the world, and I would be leaving in just eight weeks' time.

There was no way I was going to leave without Mum's blessing.

A fractious weekend followed. Dad had to give Mum a deadline. He needed to transfer the money to the charterers on the Monday so all the work could go ahead. He needed to know with 100 per cent certainty by then because once he transferred the €30,000 deposit there was no getting it back. Although Dad understood Mum's viewpoint, this was the last obstacle he'd expected to face, and the question on his lips was 'Why now?'

Dad and I spent the weekend making our case for the trip while Mum spent a couple of sleepless nights trying to decide. We talked, argued and debated, then we decided to invite about half a dozen of our long-term family friends, most of whom had known me nearly all my life, to join in. They asked me every question under the sun before deciding that I was prepared and capable enough to achieve my dream.

Our arguments were pretty persuasive. The charterers would train and test me and make sure that I understood how everything worked on the boat. There was no way they would let me take their very expensive, beautiful boat unless they were wholly confident that I was completely capable of handling it.

Dad and I had also spoken to twelve people who had sailed round the world and they had been very supportive, agreeing with our choice of boat and recognizing my ability and experience. Only one person came out against me, Mark Turner, who was Dame Ellen MacArthur's business partner. He said that I needed more experience of the Southern Ocean. But how was I supposed to practise sailing in the Southern Ocean? You can't just go out to some special centre for a practice sail. All you can do is sail in the Southern Ocean; there is no warm-up for that. You sail it, that's all you can do.

We also planned to hire the charterers as project managers of the trip. Dad wasn't that familiar with the Open 50 so we thought the charting company would be the best possible people to advise us when things went wrong with the boat, as they inevitably would.

After another sleepless night, Mum told us her decision early on

Monday morning. She didn't want to stand in the way of my dreams because, she felt, I might hold it against her later in life. She would then come to regret not having let me go, especially as the whole trip rested on her decision. It wasn't as if we were still in the early stages of planning.

We hugged.

'Thank you, Mum,' I said.

It was happening. I was going to sail the dream.

19

Full Steam Ahead

I finally got to sail the boat 'on my own' when we took her from St Malo in France to the Southampton Boat Show. Although Dad, Stan and Servanne (from the boat charterers) were on board, they made sure I did everything myself. This was my first 'test' and I was determined to show them I could handle her. Feelings of excitement mixed with a dash of nerves as we entered the English Channel, one of the busiest shipping routes in the world. All that traffic made for exhausting work, but I had a big grin on my face the whole time. I could feel my boat wanted to fly and I simply couldn't wait to begin my journey round the world. Once we were safely moored in Southampton, I was delighted when Servanne told me I was a natural sailor and that I would have no problems handling the boat on my journey. At the show, I received lots of advice and encouragement and many exhibitors offered me free or greatly reduced prices on equipment.

It was as if the floodgates had opened. We had absolutely no time whatsoever to hang around; we had everything to do and only a few weeks in which to manage it.

I zipped back and forth to France on the ferry to oversee the refitting, and to train. I'd head over on my own for at least four days every week to work on the refit with Stan and Fred, a pair of crazy but highly experienced circumnavigators. We'd start work at dawn, and as we raced through the French streets in Fred's car he'd hoot his horn and shout, 'If I have to be awake then everyone else should be too!' When he wasn't honking his horn he was eyeing up every single woman we drove past. He just couldn't help himself!

I'd also started college, studying Sports Performance and Excellence at Oaklands Athletics Academy. They were right behind the trip and even provided me with a sports psychologist.

At the Southampton Boat Show we met Mike Broughton, an internationally renowned professional navigator and weather specialist. He'd helped round-the-world sailor Dee Caffari on her voyage. We hit it off straight away. Mike is one of those guys who is a genius at everything he tries and who packs every second of his life with adventure. He'd seen action in several war zones as a 'special forces' Commando helicopter pilot and was one of a very select few able to 'loop the loop' as part of his flying display. Mike's also qualified as a Master to captain huge superyachts.

Mike got right behind us straight away, offering us a special discounted rate as a weather router. I was delighted to have him on board; his experience and knowledge were invaluable to me. His advice would enable me to make informed decisions and safely maximize my progress, helping me strike a balance between safety and performance. We would be in touch via email on a daily basis, more often if the conditions proved to be particularly difficult. In the end he went far beyond what we were able to pay him for, and for this we are eternally grateful.

At the start of October I went to France with a camera crew. We saw my freshly painted boat being lowered into the water and then spent two weeks test-sailing and prepping every last piece of equipment. I had precious little time to sail the girl on my own, thanks in part to my hectic schedule, but as strange as this might seem, it's not the sailing bit that's the hardest.

I'd been sailing all kinds of boats for over a decade; I'd lived and breathed boats all my life. The hard part is being an all-rounder, being able to deal with all the problems that will arise – and being able to deal with them on your own. By the time I left I knew every nut, bolt and cable and wire on that boat, and all the equipment that went into it.

The other hard part of a trip like this is the endurance, toughing it out through the inevitable fatigue and loneliness. There is no way to practise for tiredness like that and being away from friends and family. You can prepare yourself mentally to a certain extent, but in the end all you can do is go for it.

Once again, I'd have to follow all the stringent rules that apply to single-handed records. The voyage had to be completed under sail, operated and powered by wind and muscle power alone (although laptops and electronic autopilots were allowed). The Royal Yachting Association said they wouldn't endorse the trip. In fact they actually wrote to us, advising us against it, saying that I was too young – which was exactly what they'd said about my Atlantic trip.

We begged, borrowed, bought and rented tonnes of equipment, including two satellite phones, two GPS trackers, and a four-man life raft equipped with a satellite phone and an emergency beacon. We received wonderful sponsorship from Kemp Sails, who had some magnificent sails made for us, stronger and thicker than for any other Open 50, so much so that special fittings and attachments had to be custom-made for them.

Dad persuaded Tesco to let us go on a free trolley dash for supplies, so Mum, Dad and I took off round our local superstore and piled up five trolleys with batteries, chocolates, other snacks and tinned food until they were completely overflowing. The checkout girl nearly had a fit when she saw us coming. The till receipt was twice as long as I was tall.

Apart from snacks and tinned food, my main food supply would be dehydrated meals. These were cooked by adding boiling water. The range of dehydrated meals was impressive and included curries, spicy mince, shepherd's pie, Lancashire hotpot and potato hotpots – and this is just a small part of my dinner choices.

This time my food intake was carefully planned and we took

advice from a nutritionist. We weren't going to make the same mistake as we had with the Atlantic trip where I'd just helped myself in any order and ate all my snacks right at the start of the trip. Ten days before my departure date, with the help of friends and neighbours, we spent the night packing twenty-four bags, each containing a week's supply of food and snacks. It was a military operation. We worked as a chain gang, gradually filling each bag. They were numbered in the order that I'd eat them and arranged so that my calorie intake would increase, from 4,000 to 5,000 calories per day, as I headed further south to allow for the extra work dealing with increasingly difficult seas and the much colder climate. Each bag contained fourteen dehydrated meals, eight tins and lots and lots of snacks, including chocolate and Pringles. About a quarter of my total food supply was made up of snacks.

Once again, Mum made sure I had a ridiculous amount of medical supplies. I couldn't believe it when I saw the eight enormous boxes, but Mum insisted that I have everything I could possibly need. The watertight plastic boxes were packed full of needles, thread, splints, bandages, surgical tape, scalpels, creams and pills. In fact, there was so much stuff I thought that in an emergency I wouldn't actually be able to find what I needed, until I noticed each box had been carefully labelled by Mum. I called the section of the cabin where they were stored 'the hospital'. My first port of call in case of injury would be my small general first-aid box, which had pretty much everything I'd need in an emergency.

Eventually, all the boxes we needed to tick for the preparation were ticked, and the day of my departure was imminent. I couldn't wait.

20

Leaving

On the afternoon before my departure, Mum, Dad, Fiona, Beckie and I drove down to Gunwharf Quays in Portsmouth. It was then that I realized that if I was going to be at sea for four to five months, I was going to need a good haircut. But I'd left it a little bit late in the day, and those hairdressers that were still open didn't have any free appointments before they shut. The only option was to buy some scissors and let Fiona cut my hair.

I spent the early part of the evening with my head over a sink while Fiona chopped away. When I saw the finished result I wasn't pleased at all. 'That,' I said, 'is the worst haircut in the world!' I looked about twelve years old. 'Great,' I thought, 'just in time for the world's press.'

There was nothing I could do about it now, so we went out for dinner at an American steak restaurant. The evening was full of love and laughter. We were all in high spirits and talked about everything but the trip. It had dominated our lives so much it was nice to change the subject for a while. Dad clowned about as usual and tested his new camera by taking pictures of other diners.

As we left the restaurant, my thoughts returned to the trip. I could hardly believe that we had finally reached this point after all these months, that I was about to live my dream. Of course, that didn't make saying goodbye to everyone any easier.

After dinner, Beckie and I went for a last walk together along the

71

promenade. It was a still night and we could just see my boat sitting quietly on the quay. We felt so close to each other at that point. Although I couldn't wait for my adventure to begin, I was going to miss Beckie so much. We climbed on board the boat in the dark and stuck up about a dozen photos of us in the cabin. I promised to call her from the satellite phone whenever I could.

This was a huge moment for me. I was sixteen years old and about to leave my family to sail round the world, crossing the world's most dangerous oceans, without ever touching land. But we'd made it happen. After all the work, stress and worry we'd been through over the year we'd been preparing, finally the dream was about to become reality!

PART TWO

THE ATLANTIC

Days at Sea: 48
Distance Covered: 8,385 nautical* miles

* 1 nautical mile = 1.15077 miles

21

Sailing the Dream

Leaving was a truly bittersweet experience. Sunlight broke through the clouds as we coasted out of Portsmouth harbour. I let the tears of joy flow freely, as did Mum, who was being interviewed by the BBC on the dock. Dad was staying on board with me as far as Falmouth in Cornwall, where I planned to drop him off.

'Stay safe,' Mum had said, 'I love you, come back soon, and remember to be careful.' She told me she was so proud and totally confident that I would succeed. Mum tried to make parting a bit easier by pretending I was going to university, as if I was just going away for a few months, like a gap year.

After Mum, I hugged Fiona, and then it was Beckie's turn. God, this was difficult; I wouldn't see her again for almost five months.

Once Dad and I were a hundred metres from the dock, he hugged me. 'We've done it!' he yelled. I couldn't answer him. I was speechless, overflowing with emotion. We turned and waved to the cheering crowds as we made our way out of the harbour and out of sight, into the English Channel.

I was glad to have Dad with me as we sailed out into the Channel. It's one of the world's busiest seaways and was therefore packed full of traffic. We had to be constantly alert to avoid collisions.

As we sailed towards Falmouth, Mike Broughton emailed to say that one of the best weather windows he'd ever seen would be opening up in thirty-six hours. 'If you catch it you'll be at the equator in a couple of weeks,' he wrote.

Now that was good news! I was determined not to miss this chance and was so excited to have the weather on my side right at the start of the trip.

After a smooth 200-mile sail along the south coast we berthed at Falmouth's famous harbour, where Sir Francis Chichester, Sir Robin Knox-Johnston and Dame Ellen MacArthur began their world-record-breaking voyages. Now here I was, at the start of mine. I had an enormous task ahead of me but I was ready. I couldn't wait.

Except that I was missing one thing – a large screwdriver! Dad and I strolled past the Georgian buildings, many of which were now B&Bs, to the local well-stocked chandlery where we quickly found a suitably enormous round-the-world screwdriver.

Now I was ready!

Dad and I waited in Falmouth for the best time to catch the weather window and then we sailed out together. Dad was followed by a rib (rigid inflatable motorboat), which would take him back to Falmouth.

Finally, once I was totally happy that the boat was ready, the moment came.

Dad looked at me. 'I think it's best if I step off now.'

'All right,' I said quietly. I really didn't want to see him go. I really, really hate goodbyes at the best of times, and saying farewell to Dad, my best mate, the man who had done everything to make my dreams come true, well, it was extremely tough, one of the hardest things I'd ever had to do.

I took a photo of us both at the moment of parting.

We hugged.

'I love you.'

Then Dad stepped off.

'Now you take care,' he said. 'Put on the power and go for it and get home soon cos we'll miss you, all right?

I waved at Dad as the launch took him back to Falmouth. Saying goodbye now, away from all the pomp at Portsmouth, was much harder than I thought it would be; it was far more final. I wiped away a few tears, grabbed my binoculars and watched Dad's boat disappear.

By a tremendous coincidence it was 18 November, two years to the day since I'd set off to sail the Atlantic, aged fourteen. How long ago that seemed! I reminded myself of the euphoria I'd felt when I successfully crossed the Atlantic. I was going to recapture that feeling; in fact I was sure it would be magnified a hundred-fold once I made it back to the UK in about five months' time.

I also thought of the feelings I'd experienced on the Atlantic crossing, the sense of adventure, the independence, the thrill of sailing alone over an entire ocean. I'd had so many adventures on that trip; I wondered what was in store for me now that the whole world was ahead of me.

I continued on my own in a drizzly Force 5 wind, sailing another hour along the coast to reach Lizard Point – where the challenge, as far as the record books were concerned, officially started.

I checked my emails. Mike Broughton had written saying I was perfectly lined up to catch this amazing weather window, adding, 'Now go out there and have some fun!'

'Right,' I thought, 'this is it, I'm across the start line. Here we go.'

I sailed on in my beautiful boat and one majestic moment followed another as she raced gracefully forward, full of excitement and purpose. The sun peeked out from between the clouds and lit the spray that flew before me; stepping into the cockpit left me soaked but feeling fantastic. The bow showed no resistance at all as the boat stormed ahead happily at 11 knots. Suddenly the sun broke right through and turned the water a dazzling blue.

I wanted my first night to pass as uneventfully as possible, so I played it safe, stayed slow and hoped the weather window I'd been promised would open up the next morning. I wanted to ride those

20-knot northerly winds all the way past the Bay of Biscay and into warmer air.

The sun was sinking and I'd just flicked on the cabin light as I was working on the chart table when I heard something breaking the water. I stepped outside, grinning at the familiar sound. Six beautiful dolphins had decided to join me. Their skin gleamed in the twilight, and I watched them until the sun had set.

'Now that's what I call a good omen,' I thought.

22

Mikeworld

I didn't have much time to reflect. The radar, which had a 24-mile radius, sounded its warning almost constantly. I was in the world's busiest shipping channel and traffic was everywhere.

There was no time for sleep, I had to keep my eyes peeled, so my beanbags, which were stored in the cabin, went unused. I didn't dare take my eyes off the horizon. Just a few minutes' inattention could spell disaster.

The girl gave me all the speed I needed to dodge any oncoming traffic. I was on constant alert, though. I was travelling at 10 knots and ships were coming towards me at 10 to 20 knots, so a 3-mile gap between us could be eaten up in just a few minutes. It was not unheard of for fatigued sailors to sleep through the radar alarm, even though doing so can be fatal. A ship will very often assume that you've seen them and that you will change course to avoid them, the bigger craft. But if you're not watching then evasive action may come too late and you run the risk of being hit and dismasted or sunk. Besides, you can't rely 100 per cent on the proximity alarms; smaller fishing boats just show up as flotsam, for example. I used binoculars with a glow-in-the-dark compass inside, which helped me to work out the direction ships were approaching me from.

A welcome sunrise brought some warmth back to the boat and gave me a much clearer view of what the surrounding ships were up to. After munching down some breakfast I had a big tidy up.

I was so incredibly happy. I was free, in total control. This was my world, Mikeworld. I had complete control over everything I wanted to do; I simply sailed just as I wanted to (within the limits of the weather conditions, of course). This is something that I think is extraordinarily rare in life – especially for a teenager.

I knew I was going to be hit by the unexpected during the trip but I was confident that I'd be able to cope with everything the oceans were going to throw at me. The hardest part by far, as I mentioned earlier, would be the loneliness. I already missed everyone terribly. It would be such a long time before I saw friends, family and my girlfriend Beckie, or anyone, again.

As soon as I became overly reflective I told myself to snap out of it and to keep smiling. I *had* to enjoy this, otherwise I shouldn't be doing it. I couldn't live my dream and feel bad, that would be crazy.

The boat and I found our groove straight away. I knew I'd made the right choice, opting for the faster boat. The sensation of speed came through so strongly; I marvelled at her beautiful wake as she flew over the water. I wasn't even pushing her at this stage; I was perhaps sailing at about 80 per cent of the speed she was capable of. But that was my plan. There was a long way to go and I needed to keep my own pace.

The wind picked up to a healthy 20 knots, and with the centre starboard ballast tank pumped full the boat leapt forward and held at a pleasantly fast 11 to 12 knots.

Around 5.30 p.m. on the second day I was on deck when four or five dolphins joined me and kept pace effortlessly. Just like in the Atlantic a couple of years earlier it was as if they were playing a game, seeing how close they could get to my bow, every now and again a slight bump telling me they'd got a little too close. They were such good company. Whenever I was able to I stopped whatever I was doing to watch them. Taking this time out often helped me put the day into perspective.

Just as it fell dark I switched on the generator. A few minutes later it switched itself off and came up with an alarm saying 'Exhaust Overheat'. Incredible how these days your generator will actually tell you what's wrong. Shame it doesn't tell you how to fix it.

This was Problem Number One, an incredibly important moment. Dealing successfully with problems like this would give my confidence a boost. I was going to have to sort out many unexpected problems during this trip and there would be no one I could call on for assistance, especially once I was in remote seas.

I worked through what could be causing it to overheat, checking the impellor, the water filter, seacock – aha! There it was, a blocked seacock.

Job done, I sailed on, hoping that the generator was successfully repaired and that it wouldn't suddenly conk out again. Much to my relief, the shipping traffic had eased off. I was shattered and wanted to catch up a little on lost sleep. Choppy waters and low winds made this pretty difficult; though; it was like trying to sleep in a washing machine. Nonetheless, I was exhausted, and once my head was down . . .

My eyes snapped open. An alarm was ringing through the boat and it wasn't the one that was supposed to wake me up.

First thought: 'Not good.'

Second thought: 'Which alarm is it?'

It was the autopilot. I just had time to register this as it reset itself. Suddenly I was without steering, and with no one at the helm I was probably just seconds away from a crash gybe.

Yikes! I scrambled up, flicking off the switch that killed the power to the autopilot and then back on again before dashing towards the helm, just as the boat started to swing off course. The sudden change in position meant the wind would be able to 'flick' the mainsail to the other side of the boat with so much force that it could bring down the mast.

My heart racing, I grabbed the helm, brought her back on track and on she flew, as if nothing had happened.

Now what was that all about?

My autopilot (AP) was completely fundamental to the trip. Without it I'd really be in trouble, particularly on such a fast boat. There's no way I'd be able to hand-steer my way round the world.

The alarm sounded again. This time I was right by the helm and I had no trouble retaining control as the AP reset itself.

'Not good,' I thought glumly.

I now had to spend the whole time watching the damn thing as I crossed the Bay of Biscay. I eased back on the boat speed a touch, so she wouldn't dive into a crash gybe so quickly if I were away from the helm.

The AP continued to reset itself about three times a day. Each time I had just seconds to get to the helm. There was simply no way I could continue sailing like this. I had to pull in for repairs.

I called Dad and told him the bad news. We decided that the best and nearest place was Cascais, near Lisbon in Portugal, so while Dad got on the phone to Cascais Marina and then booked himself on a plane to come and meet me, I climbed below, set the course and deciding to hand-steer. I upped the speed. I wanted to get there quickly, get this sorted and get out again. I would restart my non-stop attempt from Cascais, meaning I would have to finish there to get the non-stop record, before carrying on home to Portsmouth.

The boat tugged at the leash, she leapt forward and surfed the waves at 16 knots. I was delighted with the way the girl zipped onwards – this was more like it!

Everyone had said that my first week would be the toughest, and they weren't far wrong. After a nervous night's sleep with one ear open for the AP alarm I struggled to warm up as the dawn appeared, a growing grey light on the horizon. Suddenly the generator decided it had had enough and refused to start at all; this time the problem was a melted seal. I managed to get it going again but this was something that would also have to be sorted once I reached Cascais.

I was up on deck around lunchtime when the sun came out. As the rays came through and I felt the warmth on my skin, I sighed with pleasure. Determined to enjoy the slight increase in temperature, I sat on the helm and steered for about two and a half hours in just my T-shirt – not bad for November. This was just fantastic. No worries about the AP, just me, the boat and a few million square miles of sea.

The boat really was like a 50-foot surfboard. While I was helming, she just took off, happily rushing over the water at around 14 knots, surfing in the high teens every now and again as she caught a large wave just right. Then, as she surged forward, the bow dug into the water and *whoosh*, the spray flew everywhere.

Helming is hard work at this pace but I just loved every moment. My grin grew as my tiredness was forgotten. The hull hummed happily as it slid through the rushing water so quickly and effortlessly. I might have been heading for land after less than 1,000 miles after leaving the UK but at least the sailing was fantastic. This trip was going to teach me to take the good with the bad.

As evening approached and I neared Cascais, the wind was blowing about 8 knots more than forecast. This makes a world of difference in an Open 50. The wind steadily increased, and before long it was up to 38 knots.

'Uh-oh . . .'

Sure enough, the boat took off like a rocket, shooting off the tops of waves and sending spray everywhere before shooting off the end of another wave, all without slowing. Although this was just fantastic, waves were now constantly sweeping over the boat. Definitely time to reduce sail!

I went up on deck to quite a sight. I love a good old ding-dong in strong winds and I was thrilled to see large rollers and the bowsprit kicking up a huge spume of hissing spray. Despite having dressed for the conditions and made sure all the cuffs on my clothes were sealed, I still managed to get thoroughly wet as I furled away the solent (the second biggest furling foresail) and moved over to the foredeck to raise my small, virtually bulletproof staysail. This would give me just enough wind to have control over the boat but not so much that we would be flying into the backs of waves. Once that was done I was thoroughly exhausted. I climbed back into the cockpit, out of spray's way, and tried to get some much-needed rest.

The following morning was clear and, as the sun rose, it got pretty hot. I ditched my thermals, fleece and waterproofs and soon I was in thin trousers and a T-shirt. It felt great to be out of the full gear.

The boat was cruising nicely when the wind suddenly shifted round to the north much more than I'd expected and I took the helm, bringing her round to meet the headland. Perhaps sensing the excitement on board, about twenty dolphins popped up beside me and kept pace with little effort. I couldn't have been happier.

And then came the really exciting part . . .

I knew that just before rounding the headland to come into Cascais I would pass a wind acceleration zone just to the west of Cape Raso. Mike Broughton, my wonderful weather router, had warned me that the winds could increase by as much as 50 per cent for a short time.

The wind was blowing at 23 knots when I cautiously sailed into this area with fairly reduced sail, two reefs in the main and the solent. I'd decided that this would be OK for up to around 30 to 35 knots of wind.

I was just thinking 'So where's the wind then?' when it shot from 23 knots to 46!

'Yeee-haaaa!'

The boat responded immediately. She sat up in the water as if to say, 'What's this? You want to see me fly, do you?'

She took off at 16, 17 and then 18 knots, so I grabbed hold of the helm tightly to keep her under control. Spray rained down across the deck as she flew over the pale blue waves.

I was scanning the horizon when I spotted a familiar sight, something I'd seen often enough while sailing off the Dorset coast. A lobster pot marker! Then another and another, and soon I could see dozens dead ahead, scattered across my path. I started swerving

Left: My sister Fiona and me (aged four) aboard *Blue Jay*, the first family boat and my 14-foot piece of heaven.

Right: Sitting on our new boat, *Arcturus,* parked in our drive. If I wasn't in the house then everyone knew where to find me – on the boat.

Below: Sailing a 40-foot yacht with Dad, which we chartered in the Solent.

Arcturus

My boat *Cheeky Monkey* in Gibraltar. Our lorry driver had a terrible accident when the trailer separated from his lorry, sending the boat crashing into the central reservation of one of Spain's busiest motorways.

Dad and me walking the short distance from Gibraltar airport to the marina. We used the airport trolleys to wheel our bags all the way there.

Left: Loading *Cheeky Monkey* with drinking water.

Below: Joined by my friends the dolphins. They were wonderful company and if I could I'd stop what I was doing and watch them until they took off again.

Above: I love this picture. It reminds me of the feeling of freedom you get when you lose sight of land, the thrill of the boat moving through the water...

Below: The grey seas of the Atlantic: On my way to the Cape Verde Islands. I had to sail for three days straight with only three hours' rest after my self-steering failed. The weather was hardly brilliant either!

Mindelo, Cape Verde: It was so fantastic to enter this barren harbour, and to know I was going to get some decent sleep that night!

Arriving at Nelson's Dockyard in Antigua. I had no idea so many people had come to welcome me; I wasn't expecting anything like this!

Mum, Dad, Fiona and me having a quiet
family lunch after we landed back in the UK.
I went back to school the very next day.

Record breaker:
Shadow Sports
Minister, Hugh
Robertson,
presenting me with
the certificate,
along with Craig
Glenday from
Guinness World
Records.

Left: *TotallyMoney.com* being lowered into the water in France. Note her flat underside – she's essentially a 50-foot surfboard, designed to ride with the waves. I was looking forward to flying along at high speeds – and I wouldn't be disappointed!

Below: Hours of fun: It took all night to pack my twenty-six food bags full of dehydrated dinners and snacks. I would be on the solo-sailor diet – eat as much as you want, whenever you want!

Below: Beckie and me trying out some of the film equipment that I would be taking.

Below: In the Atlantic with an unreliable autopilot, hence the hand steering.

Right: Happy Christmas: My dodgy autopilot meant I spent Christmas in Las Palmas – still, at least Mum, Fiona and Beckie came out to see me, so there's always a bright side!

Below: The Equator: Well, not quite... I managed to sleep through the actual crossing, whoops!

Equator
09/01/2009

Cape Town: Dad and I made sure to take some time out to explore Cape Town whilst the boat was being worked on. We even had a race up the Lion's Head and Table Mountain. I won, which was a surprise, considering I hadn't walked very far in the last thirty-seven days since leaving Gran Canaria.

Below: Dolphins provided me with real companionship and entertainment. They'd play around the bow and I once saw one leap out of a large swell 30 feet in the air.

round them at 17 knots. I grinned and whooped as I cut through them, my first experience of slalom sailing in an Open 50! I tried not to think about what would happen if I became entangled in one. I definitely didn't want to end up dragging a large pot full of lobsters into Cascais Marina.

The wind vanished as fast as it had arrived, just minutes after I'd rounded the headland. Much to my relief the boat speed dropped to 9 knots as I approached Cascais Marina. I was tied up in no time, and although I was disappointed to be on land so soon, my sail here told me that many amazing adventures lay ahead.

23

Bad with the Good

'God, I love this boat,' I thought as she caught a wave perfectly and surfed on ahead.

The generator and autopilot fixed, I'd left Cascais to be met with a strong 19-knot northerly wind. The log climbed, 8, 11, 13, 14, 15 knots, as the wind really started to blow. Soon it was over 40 knots and still climbing, eventually gusting in the mid-40s.

White spray flew back from cresting swells as I raced onwards. This was what it was all about! I was in the middle of a good strong blow in a very fast boat. These winds really made the boat surf like she was made to. She was magnificent, only slowing for a moment when she hit the back of a wave before thrusting forward once more.

Always at the back of my mind was the Southern Ocean, that mass of wild sea circling Antarctica. If it was like this here, then what on earth was it going to be like down there? I couldn't wait to find out.

My exhilaration was cut short in one fell swoop when the dreaded, sickeningly familiar sound screeched across the boat once more. The AP again! Surely it couldn't be malfunctioning already, after having the experts look at it in Cascais? Nightmare. I should have been passing the Western Sahara by now, on my way to round the Cape of Good Hope, but instead I was battling my way through a storm off the coast of Portugal with a faulty AP.

The stop in Cascais had at least been short and sweet. My first shower in five days – and a freshwater one at that – had been fabulous, and while in port a few people had come up to wish me well. I'd even given a whole family the grand tour. I was so proud of my boat. She looked amazing, so powerful when berthed, and she gave me such confidence.

It was great to see Dad again. He'd found Alfonso, a marine electronics engineer, to help us. Alfonso was short, round and jolly, everyone's favourite uncle. He quickly managed to get the autopilot working again, but replacing the generator cap took a while longer than expected. We drove with Alfonso all over Cascais looking for a replacement, searching boat yards and garages until we found someone who had the next model down and was generously prepared to let us pinch his cap.

We zipped back to the marina and got everything ready as quickly as possible. I still had a chance of catching these fantastic winds that would take me all the way to the equator and I didn't want to miss them, especially as Mike Broughton had warned me that a wind-hole was right behind them.

I took the helm and once again reset the AP. Once it finally seemed to have control of the boat, I called Dad on his mobile. No time for 'hello', just: 'The AP's malfunctioned again!'

Dad, who was at the airport about to get on his flight home, immediately called Alfonso, who in turn got the manufacturers on the phone. I can imagine that was quite an interesting conversation; Dad would have stressed the urgency of the situation in no uncertain terms. We really needed it fixed right away. I couldn't just switch off the pilot and hand-steer twenty-four hours a day.

Eventually, after a painfully long analysis, the AP guys reached a very interesting conclusion. The AP had two secondary control units and they thought that these were interfering with each other and therefore couldn't configure with the master control. This was causing the master to reset.

'Mike, they want you to cut one of the wires to the secondary control unit,' Dad said.

'Which one?'

'Well, believe it or not, they don't actually know. Just choose one!'

'OK, fair enough.' I took my pliers, clipped one of the white wires and reset the AP.

The winds faded away and I sat there waiting through the night for the dreaded alarm to cut through the quiet. After four hours I got quite excited, as it seemed to be working beautifully. Then, with perfect timing, the piercing scream caused me to jolt in shock.

'Sod it!'

I stared at the autopilot in disbelief and frustration. The thought of having to pull in and stop somewhere *again*, something that would really add time and money to the trip, was a lot to bear. We had no contingency funds for such stops and they were very expensive. Every week I was delayed added thousands to the cost of the trip in terms of charter fees alone.

All I could do now was get on with the job in hand.

The pilot continued to malfunction. On one occasion I was getting changed into a fresh set of clothes and had to race to the helm in just my thermals where I got a good freezing-cold soaking for my trouble.

The stress of not knowing when the AP was going to reset was very hard to handle; it made it extremely difficult to rest. As the sun rose, the problems with the AP continued. I was really raging, as were the guys on shore, who felt just as helpless to do anything else to fix it. I disconnected and reconnected everything and spent hours reconfiguring the rudder alignment, all for nothing. I started to feel really down, and as time went on I struggled to be my normal positive self.

But then I had lunch. I boiled up some fresh water – produced by my miraculous desalinator that turned seawater into drinking water – and rummaged in my food bag for one of my favourite hot meals, chicken curry. I cut open the foil bag, poured in some boiling water, waited for ten minutes, and *voilà*, dinner was served.

These on-board meals were truly fantastic; 800 calories later I was firing on all cylinders again. In situations like these, food – something we all pretty much take for granted at home – is such a morale booster. One moment I was feeling awful, then *bam*, I was so much better.

Building on this, I treated myself to a quick call home to speak to Mum, Fiona, Beckie and a few close friends. This topped me up with another healthy dose of positivity.

I reflected on how my emotions had shot up and down over the past twenty-four hours. Bad comes with the good. It's inevitable. I'd been forgetting just how incredible this trip had been so far. I was the luckiest teenager in the world to be sailing round it on this fantastic boat.

I'd set myself the challenge of completing this journey and, come hell or high water, I was going to achieve my goal. 'No matter what problems I'm going to face,' I told myself, 'I *am* going to see it through!'

24

Las Palmas – Coming and Going

The AP kept quiet for several hours, so I finally turned to the south-west and sailed towards Madeira.

Of course, as soon as I did that it malfunctioned.

My whole world was once again tipped on its head.

This time I solved the problem by changing over to my back-up pilot. This was nowhere near as good, as it steered by compass only. This can be quite dangerous if there's a sudden and substantial change in the wind (which is pretty common): the back-up AP would try to over-correct, making for a bumpy and dangerous ride.

There was no way that I could sail quickly and safely around the world without a reliable AP looking out for me; it had to be fixed. After a chat with Dad on the good old satellite phone, we agreed I should head for Las Palmas on the island of Gran Canaria. Gran Canaria is the starting point of the ARC (Atlantic Rally for Cruisers) Race and was therefore chock-full of boat mechanics and suppliers, so we reasoned if it was going to be fixed anywhere then this was the place.

After such a stressful couple of days on board, I took advantage of the calmer weather and slowed down a touch so I could get a good amount of sleep. I fastened my vibrating mobile phone to my chest, set the clock alarm (essentially a car alarm) and slept for twenty minutes at a time. These two devices never failed to wake me from the deepest slumber.

That night, I managed a wonderful five-and-a-half-hour sleep overall. Beautiful. Nothing beats a full stomach and a good night's rest.

The morning brought with it some variable winds, from 9 to 26 knots. This was pretty hard work as it was virtually impossible to find the right sail set-up. Too much sail area in strong winds and the boat will lose control, especially when it's only being steered by the back-up autopilot. However, a fantastic lunch of spaghetti bolognese kept my morale well and truly boosted.

After lunch I gave the back-up AP a rest and took the helm. This allowed me to up the speed. I wanted to get to Las Palmas as soon as humanly possible and this was the only way to do it.

The iPod was on full blast, I grinned madly whenever the boat was lifted by a gust, and our speed climbed into the high teens. This was just amazing. I was in control of one of the fastest sailing boats in the world, zipping across the great grey Atlantic on an epic mission. Imagine living your dream and listening to your favourite song or album, knowing that you are master of all that you survey. I hadn't felt a more wonderful feeling than this in my life so far.

By the time I reached the end of my first week of sailing I was coming to realize that no two days on board would ever be the same. That night the wind fell and the sea flattened; there was a mild 12-knot breeze and a warm blanket of cloud covered the sky. Life on board the boat until then had been one of constant noise, with the hull slapping the water, equipment rattling on the shelves and the sound of the never-ending rumbling, hissing and roaring ocean. But now the boat rocked gently, and to add to the feeling of quiet isolation, not a single star was in sight. Now I understood the words 'pitch black'. It was as if a huge blanket had been draped over the boat.

After sunrise it was time for me to gybe east-southeast. It was the easiest gybe so far, as there was very little wind at the time. Then the wind started to pick up, rising to 22 knots, bringing a scattering of squalls with it. At one point three of them had me surrounded but I managed to steer my way through, getting really close to one to pick up some extra wind.

I almost wanted to be hit by one, as the boat needed a good clean, although I was getting a little concerned about the amount of rust I was seeing. I had no idea why this was happening; I certainly hadn't expected it and neither had Dad. It was a real head-scratcher, that one. Rust on a boat is never a good sign!

As it was the start of my second week, I eagerly opened my next food bag. There were always a few 'bonus' surprises Mum, Dad, Fiona and Beckie had slipped in, including a couple of Yorkie bars and some packets of crisps. Each food bag also brought a morale-boosting personal message from someone, sometimes a silly gift (Fiona was really good at choosing the most bizarre of these – she even gave me a grass skirt and a fake flower necklace, which put a big smile on my face). I ate a Yorkie, then had a tidy up as the sun came out, fastened another bin bag and stashed it in the aft compartment – my very own rubbish tip.

Once that was done I was baking hot so I changed into the long-dreamed-of shorts and T-shirt and dried out my clothes, which were still soaking from the gale at Cascais.

I was chased by a couple of squalls later that afternoon. It was very weird knowing that while I had blue sky above me and 11 knots of wind behind me, a mixture of torrential rain, gales and calms were less than a mile either side. I looked at them through my binoculars. Now, which way were they headed?

I couldn't tell their exact direction, and this was just a tad worrying. To be caught in 35 knots with full main and genoa would be pretty hairy, especially with no ballast in the tanks to hold me steady in the water.

I sailed further west, searching for better winds to take me down to the Canaries. Sailing in light conditions was horrible as the sails just flapped back and forth. It felt as if I was getting absolutely nowhere.

I cooked up some curry for lunch and ate it outside, sitting on the beanbag in the sunshine. Yum. I was in shorts, T-shirt and shades. It was a little chilly but I didn't care – I was outside in the sun! And I knew that it would continue to get warmer as I headed further south.

I had now spent almost two weeks at sea. Everyone told me that the first week at sea is always the hardest. Well, these last two weeks at sea had been two 'first weeks' thanks to my stop at Cascais and now I was going to have to endure a third once I'd stopped at Las Palmas. These starts were so incredibly tiring as I had to struggle back into the routine of napping for short periods and get used to the motion of the boat again. Even seasoned sailors have trouble with seasickness.

For the moment at least I was back in the routine and I enjoyed the warm weather and worked on my tan. I also enjoyed the chance to have regular showers, which for me meant a few buckets of sea-water over the head and a wash in special saltwater shampoo. I'd then rinse off the salt with a litre of fresh water and drip-dry in the sun.

The boat constantly surged forward, making the most of every knot of wind. I could tell she loved to fly and I was desperate to test her in fast conditions. For the moment, though, with steady winds and smooth water, I had plenty of chances to rest.

These came to an end as I neared Las Palmas and my AIS radar beeped into life. The Marine Automatic Identification System was fantastic, alerting me to vessels that were in close proximity and giving me their position, speed and course. Now it was telling me it was time for a bit of ship dodging. At one point I was right behind a tanker when it stopped dead and threw its engines into reverse. I eased off the sheets and shot round its leeward side. I wondered what on earth he was up to as I skimmed past.

By ten a.m. I was stern-to in the marina and ready to crack on with the repairs. From my berth, I looked out to sea longingly. The northerly winds were still holding steady. If I could sort this out quickly there was still a chance that they'd get me a flying start down the African coast.

Besides the dratted autopilot I'd found some other little problems, including a small fuel leak, a few damaged seals and a problem with the main engine impellor. I also wanted to sort out the rust problem. The boat was thoroughly covered now and neither Dad nor I had a clue what was causing it. Then, as I inspected the boat, I spotted a tiny hairline crack in the carbon mast! This looked pretty serious.

I was feeling pretty down about all this when a familiar voice said, 'Hiya, Mike! Good to see you, mate!'

John was a shipwright and the former Marine who I'd met in Lanzarote during our Atlantic crossing. He was now based in Las Palmas. Dad had arranged for him to meet me to help with the boat and he immediately proved his worth by sorting out the rusting problem. It was down to an ill-fitting wire connected to the strobe light. Excess electricity was passing over the surface of the wet boat, causing electrolysis, which had produced the rust.

I was so relieved to have that sorted that my spirits climbed, so much so that I decided to give my climbing system a test run. This was the equipment I would use when I climbed to the top of the mast in an emergency, if the mainsail was caught on one of the spreaders or if the lazy jacks, which hold the bottom of the sail in place when it's reefed, were broken.

I had a full set of body armour to try to minimize injuries in case I was bashed against the mast in heavy weather. It took me fifteen minutes to get up to the top and twenty-five to get back down again. 'Phew,' I thought afterwards, 'I don't ever want to have to do that in bad weather and rough seas.'

It was then that I noticed that one of the lazy jack lines needed to be repositioned. It was just catching ever so slightly when the third reef was in.

All these little jobs had to be sorted out as soon as they were spotted; ignoring them or putting them off was simply never an option.

Dad had flown down to meet me and called the boat charterer straight away. They blamed us for the cracked mast but Dad had taken some photos of the boat at the Southampton Boat Show and when they were blown up you could clearly see the crack, which thankfully turned out to be cosmetic, the result of a bit of dodgy filler which had been used to hide an old long-gone winch attachment. I found this a little worrying. Just how well did they know their own boat?

They also pleaded ignorance over the AP and said they couldn't help. We'd asked and paid them to project-manage the boat but now they weren't doing anything. We felt betrayed because we'd put our heart and souls into getting the boat ready but it was as if they didn't take us seriously. We were quite surprised to encounter so many problems with the boat so early on in the voyage.

I also wanted to fix the clutch on my ballast pump, and Dad and I ended up at the biggest shipbuilders on the island who worked on some enormous projects. They smiled when they saw my tiny clutch and quickly machined me a new part free of charge! This was typical of the sailing community; people always wanted to help a fellow sailor if they could.

Waiting for the AP repair was agony. Experts flew back and forth from Spain until finally we thought we had it fixed. But, after sailing out of Gran Canaria for ten hours in a 20- to 30-knot wind under a beautiful moonlit night, the autopilot suddenly miscalculated by 70 degrees and almost sent me into yet another crash gybe. I felt like I'd been kicked in the stomach. So much time, money and effort spent on this problem already – I simply couldn't believe I was going to have to turn round, sail back and do it all over again! Tears of frustration overcame me despite reminding myself to keep smiling, that I was sailing the dream.

Well, the dream had become a nightmare.

These delays wore on me heavily, especially as Christmas

approached and Dad had to fly home. He couldn't afford to take any more unpaid leave. He was worried that if he left it too long he'd lose his job, and the recession was now in full swing and the charter fees were pretty expensive, not to mention the repairs, berthing fees and my accommodation.

I was so happy when Mum, Fiona and Beckie said they were coming over. Although Mum and Beckie could only come for a couple of days, Fiona was going to stay with me over Christmas. Fiona brought a load of photos of friends and family with her and we stuck up about fifty of them inside the cabin; suddenly the boat felt a lot more homely and colourful. They would be there with me whatever I went through, they would bring me strength, memories of good times would come pouring in and would keep a big smile on my face.

Beckie's visit was wonderful but all too short as she had to go back to the UK just two days after she arrived. Another tough goodbye, but I was so grateful for any extra time with her.

Finally, after yet another expert flew out to look at the AP, we thought we'd finally cracked it. It seemed as though a simple mechanical device that switched control between the two rudders as and when the boat tacked had caused the problem. Once it had been replaced, it looked as though everything was in order.

It had taken an incredibly frustrating four weeks but I finally sailed out of Las Palmas in the blistering sunshine. This latest restart of mine would mean I'd now start and finish in Las Palmas to claim the non-stop record before heading back to the UK. As I left the marina, people shouted 'Good luck!' and waved; some boats even tooted their foghorns. I was so grateful for everyone's help, especially all the top-rate mechanics who had turned around all my repairs so quickly.

This was my third goodbye and proved to be the easiest so far. Despite the fact it was my third first week at sea, it felt so good to be on the water again. After I made it out of the port, I hoisted the sails close to where around thirty small sailboats were racing. I swept past several tankers all at anchor and made my way down the southeast side of the island, only to land in a wind-hole. There was nothing I could do but take down the foresail as it was just flapping about and wait patiently until I finally managed to drift out of it. A 12-knot breeze eventually rescued me and I tacked towards the African coast in search of wind. I watched as the Canaries gradually disappeared beyond the horizon.

Finally, I was at sea once again.

25

Happy New Year – Not

My eyes snapped open. I had the feeling that something was wrong. It was pitch dark. My watch said midnight. I peered outside. A fishing boat with its lights on, heading straight for me.

Fishing boats are harder to avoid than large ships. They're usually in a hurry to get to their fishing grounds or to deliver their load back to port and don't always keep a lookout. They also tend to be quite small, and in this case the boat was tiny, so my warning system hadn't sounded the alarm. This just showed me how collisions are possible, even out here.

Could they be pirates? Although most pirates seemed to operate off the Somalian coast there was pirate activity off the coast of Western Africa, where (according to the BBC) the International Maritime Bureau stated there had been at least a hundred attacks in just twelve months.

At that moment I was more worried about a collision. I immediately steered away. It was a calm moonlit night but there was just enough wind to sail me out of trouble. I tried to call the boat on the VHF but there was no answer.

I was twenty-four hours in and overjoyed to find that the pilot was working perfectly. I was still drained from acclimatizing to life at sea but I knew I just had to keep pushing on and I'd get back into my rhythm soon enough.

By seven the next morning I was coasting southeast, towards the

African coast, in a 12-knot breeze. Soon I was within 50 miles of the Western Sahara, hugging a ridge of high pressure. I climbed out of the cabin on a baking hot morning to hardly a breeze. I looked up to see my beautiful white sails were now ever so slightly stained: I was sailing straight through a cloud of Saharan sand carried here by the high pressure and southeasterly winds.

Some rain would have been nice but the gentle conditions seemed determined to hang around. So, making the most of the quiet seas, I cooked up some apple pancakes. After a few miserable lumpy failures and badly timed flips, I eventually got the hang of it and managed to fry some beauties. I piled a stack on a plate and went to sit on the coach roof with the music playing.

As I sat down to eat, whoa, what a sight! At least a hundred dolphins decided to join me. All I could see was foam and fins.

I didn't get much of a chance to enjoy their company, however.

Something wasn't right.

I could hear a strange noise, so I scooted round the boat. It was coming from the forepeak, the area where I kept my spare sails and all my food bags. I went down to have a look.

I stopped in shock. In front of me was the most worrying sight for any sailor: water sloshing about inside the boat. Thoughts about leaks, cracks and holes rushed through my mind. I searched around, looking for the source, and discovered that the forward starboard ballast tank was full.

'That's odd,' I thought, 'I never filled it.'

At least I'd found the source of the problem, and it wasn't a hole. I looked more carefully at the ballast system and realized that something had pushed the bailer into the water, which had caused water to run up into the system. If none of the other tanks was being filled or emptied then the water would go straight into the forward ballast tank. Now the tank was full, it was spilling out into the boat via an access hatch on the top of the tank that had gradually come loose with the vibrations of the boat. I'd need to check these more often!

I closed the ballast and set to work pumping it free of water, and once that was done I began the long process of bailing out all the water that had collected in the forepeak. I did this wearing just my trousers and T-shirt – a bad idea as I was immediately drenched. Despite the boiling weather I got changed and threw on my dry-suit. I began shifting the water out bucketful by bucketful. I literally bailed about a tonne of water out of the boat.

I took a ten-minute break to grab some chicken curry for lunch, and while the kettle was boiling I looked over the side and there they were again! The dolphins were grouped into three packs and there were so many of them that at times it was hard to pick out individuals among all the foam and fins. I wondered if I'd disturbed their lunch and was sailing over a huge school of sardines. I could have watched them all afternoon but I had to get back to work.

I eventually finished just as it fell dark. Exhausted, I tidied up all my gear and changed back into some normal clothes. It was eight p.m. and time for a very welcome dinner.

The following day was New Year's Eve, and after my busy day's bailing I was pleased to have a chance to rest in the morning. I sat in the sun and took some time out. At around ten a.m. I put up one of my spinnakers and furled away the genoa, which brought the boat speed up by a welcome 2 knots.

As the sun set I took down the spinnaker and put up the genoa as the winds were forecast to increase very early in the morning.

But then it happened again.

By now I was back into the swing of things and hadn't even thought about the dreaded AP for a few days. So when the alarm sounded across the deck my heart jumped with disbelief.

Not again!

I ran for the helm as the boat began to swerve massively. I was ready to rescue her from a crash gybe but this time the AP didn't reset and instead successfully auto-corrected, bringing the boat back on course.

I looked at the display. Some of the numbers were fluctuating randomly; it simply couldn't tell wind direction and speed any more. This took the phrase 'incredibly frustrating' to a whole new level for me. To have spent four weeks testing and fixing this one item and for it not to be working perfectly was really beyond belief.

My satellite phone rang. It was Dad. Great timing once again.

'Hi, Mike! Happy New Year!'

They were in Trafalgar Square and on good form, obviously enjoying the New Year celebrations and about to join in with the countdown to midnight. I could barely hear them over all the noise going on around them.

'Dad, the autopilot's gone!' I sobbed.

'What?' he replied in disbelief.

'Dad, this is the worst New Year ever.'

After a bit of fiddling and resetting it seemed to be OK once more. 'Sod it, on we go!' I thought, my spirits lifting. It wasn't perfect but it did at least seem to be steering the boat in the direction I wanted, and that was good enough for me.

By the time Dad called me back I was in better spirits. 'It just blips a wrong reading but then manages to sort itself out,' I told him. 'It's not forcing me into a gybe any more.' Dad suggested I keep a log of all the errors to send to the manufacturers to see if they could tell what was wrong.

He and I then had a serious chat. 'We can still stop it Mike,' he said, 'you're not too far to stop. We can return the boat and we'll sort this out.'

He knew that this was unbelievably frustrating for me. All these hold-ups and the stress that went with them were a very unpleasant psychological burden, something I really hadn't been expecting. Bad weather, yes, high seas, yes, freezing and dangerous conditions, yes, loneliness, yes, but sitting in port while other people failed to come up with solutions to an impossible problem, no.

But Dad had brought it home to me. I wanted to do this more than ever now. The time was right. We had come this far and I was utterly determined to see it through. I couldn't go home now, I just couldn't.

At the end of the day it was my call, and I didn't have to think about my answer.

'No way,' I said passionately. 'I'm not going to give up now, not after all we've been through to get here.'

26

The Doldrums

Just as the pilot was sorted, a very painful rash appeared on my back, which made sleeping almost impossible. On top of this, my right eye had become infected. Red and raw, it stung every time I blinked, and soon I could barely keep it open. I'd just cleared the shipping lanes to the west of Africa which meant I should have been able to rest for longer, but now I couldn't as it was just too uncomfortable.

I changed course slightly, following southwesterly winds, which took me further out into the Atlantic. My speed picked up and I averaged 9 knots although I regularly surfed at 11 or 12 knots.

The heat was still pretty intense, and I guessed that it was this combined with only washing in salt water that had caused my painful rash. As I moved over to the southwest, the boat was shaded by the sails, which brought me some precious relief.

My course took me right through the middle of the Cape Verde Islands.

When I went up on deck I found six flying fish. As I mentioned before, quite a few sailors see them as a gift from the ocean and eat them. I wasn't about to throw them on to my frying pan and cook them. I wasn't exactly the best cook in the world and there was no way I was going to risk food poisoning. My freeze-dried add-water meals were perfectly fine and didn't need supplementing by anything other than my snacks as far as I was concerned.

Once I was through the Cape Verdes, I headed southwest to my waypoint that would mark my entry into the tricky Doldrums. The Doldrums are spread out within the catchily titled Inter-tropical Convergence Zone and are known for their light and variable winds which can make for very troublesome sailing. They can trap boats for weeks as they wait for the wind to fill their sails. I had my fingers crossed this wouldn't happen to me and I was counting on Mike Broughton to help steer me through.

Even though I felt quite rough, it didn't mean I could take a day off or ignore any jobs that needed doing. Every problem that arose needed to be tended to straight away before it developed into something significant. During my daily boat inspection I spotted that the very small cleat that's used to adjust the leech lines (which tighten the sail to improve the shape) had come away from the foot of the genoa, thanks to a spot of loose stitching, so out came my needle and thread. The only problem was that the cleat was right on the bow, which was plunging underwater quite regularly.

So, despite the fierce sun, my sore back and one good eye (if only I'd had an eye-patch I could have looked like a proper pirate), I threw on my bottom oilies (breathable oilskins) and my boots, went right up to the end of the bow (after hooking myself on with my harness, of course) and spent an exhilarating twenty minutes doing some extreme sewing while being regularly dunked in the ocean at 10 knots. 'I knew I should have brought my thimble!' I joked as the bow ducked below the cold, clear water for the tenth time. I had to wait until she lifted clear for a few seconds and then sew like mad before bracing myself for another soaking.

I returned to the cabin wet through but pleased I'd taken care of this problem. It was only a small thing, but if the cleat had gone unrepaired, there was a real danger it could have torn itself free of the sail and then my beautiful genoa would have been left without control of its shape, which could have cost me a knot in boat speed.

I also set about creating a system to fasten the hatch door more securely and started working on one of the extra protective rope covers on the mainsheet, which had come loose. I always found it extremely satisfying to see these jobs done well and early on, before they snowballed into something unmanageable.

Of course, that applied to my body as well as the boat. I decided to call home to see if I could get some medical advice for my eye and back. 'You've given me four huge chests of medical supplies, there must be something in there that can help,' I told Mum, but there wasn't so much as an eye-patch.

I took pictures of my sore back and my eye – labelling it 'eye' with half a dozen arrows pointing at it, just to give the doctor a hand – and emailed them home. I tried not to overuse the email system as this was again very expensive. We paid per kilobyte and it soon added up.

The sea stayed pretty calm. I could tell it was like this for some distance as the AIS picked up ships that were over 200 miles away, telling me their heading, speed, call-sign and current coordinates. Although I wasn't so pleased about the lack of wind, at least I knew I was going to get plenty of warning before I came too close to anything.

As the temperature continued to climb, reaching the low thirties, more and more dolphins decided to join me until hundreds of them were swimming leisurely alongside. They were always curious, sometimes swimming side-on to the surface so they could have a good stare at me staring at them.

By now the boat was covered with a thin layer of grime, and the satellite dome had a coating of the type of muck you get on cars that have been parked on a city street for a week or so, the kind you can wipe your finger along and pick up a sticky layer of dirt. I wondered when some rain was going to come and wash it off. No time soon, it seemed. But at least I was able to have a bucket-over-the-head shower. The seawater was freezing cold but oh, so utterly refreshing. It didn't last long; I was a sweaty mess again within the hour.

Of course, I'd soon be missing this lovely hot weather once I moved into the South.

The South.

These two words sent tingles down my spine. I knew I was going to be tested to the limit once I'd gybed around the Cape of Good Hope. I couldn't sodding wait. For the past two years I'd dreamed about sailing the waves of the Southern Ocean. I thought about all that video footage I'd watched over and over on YouTube, recorded by a handful of other sailors who'd been there.

Soon it would be my turn.

I'd been umming and ahhing all day whether to put up the gennaker, my largest furling foresail. It felt like the boat was telling me she was a tiny bit underpowered. I didn't want to race the boat. That was the main difference between the Vendée Globe sailors and me: they were pushing their Open 60s at 100 per cent all the time on their single-handed round-the-world yacht race, and almost two-thirds of the thirty-strong field would drop out as a result; I was more than happy to be sailing at 90 per cent, which was at a steady 10 knots, although there were regular surfs when she'd shoot effortlessly up into the teens, causing my pulse to race and my heart to soar.

The AP was still misbehaving, so I switched off every single bit of electronics on the boat, except for the pilot to see if anything was interfering with it. But no, the gremlins were still there. Despite this, my spirits remained high. I was bonding to the boat more and more. The further south we sailed the more confident I grew and the happier I became.

I thought about friends and family a great deal and would carefully plan my calls home. Our budget meant I could only have five minutes so I had to make sure I said everything I wanted to say within that time. Invariably we'd end up talking about the weather: home was freezing, the South Atlantic was roasting. The cabin had turned into a pizza oven; there was no ventilation apart from my small entry door and a tiny 12-volt fan. I could've fried an egg on the black surfaces on the deck. I spent as much time as possible in the shade, especially as I'd misplaced my sun cream.

I didn't want to think about being stuck in this heat for weeks on end. I was right into the Doldrums now, and after a chat with Mike Broughton I aimed the boat WSW, hunting better wind.

As I sailed west I climbed atop the coach roof and perched there, watching the setting sun disappear with a wink over the horizon. I stayed there for another hour, just taking everything in. The way the boat moved, gliding over the water so gracefully, as if there was no resistance; the way the sun lit the clouds it had set behind with a soft pink light. I watched as a small wisp of candyfloss cloud turned pink just above me, as if it had been placed there especially.

I had another chance to take stock around noon the following day as the sun blazed down. I was in the shade of the mainsail, sat on my beanbag, reading a book and listening to music, when I stopped reading and stared out to sea. The boat was flying along effortlessly, as if she knew exactly which way to go. After what felt like no time at all I checked my clock and was amazed to see that two hours had flown by without me noticing.

It's incredible how you can just lose yourself in something so beautiful.

27

The Equator

The sun scorched the deck until it stung to the touch. Forget the eggs, I could have fried a half-pound steak on its surface, no problem. I still couldn't find my sun cream either, and to add insult to injury, there was no one around to see my tan.

Then I saw a squall heading straight for me. A dark, low blotch on the horizon, growing rapidly.

'OK, now that's a big one,' I thought.

I guessed that it was about 8 miles wide, and bearing down pretty fast. Suddenly it was all noise. The rain came down so hard that visibility dropped to nothing and in an instant the wind spun round to the south. I was soaked pretty much straight away as I took in one reef, after which we made slightly more relaxed progress.

As soon as the first one had passed I spotted another. This was followed by a third, just twenty minutes later.

'Oh well, could be worse!' I told myself.

Around an hour later the wind dropped back off to 20 knots and I unfurled the solent so we'd keep on moving at a reasonable pace.

Sailing in this area really kept me on my toes. No boredom in Mikeworld, just squall after squall. Another one rolled in as night fell. Suddenly, a bolt of lightning lit up the sea.

Now *that* got my attention. If there's one thing I didn't want to see, being the tallest object in the ocean for hundreds of miles around, it was lightning. And this squall was full of it. Huge white flashes lit up the night sky. The wind rose to 35 knots and then dropped to 4 knots, then back up to 35, then down to 4 as the squall rumbled over me like an angry car wash. Luckily none of the lightning bolts wanted to make contact with the boat.

The following day I decided to drop the mainsail just after lunch. One of the mast track car fittings that joined the batten and sail to the mast had broken. The sailmakers had put rings in the sail by each of these fittings, so if one of these broke it was just a case of using a simple lashing between the ring and the car instead of the normal fitting.

This small job only took five minutes; getting the main back up proved to be the hardest part. Sailing downwind, the sail just refused to go up without catching in the lazy jacks. Usually, anything from three reefs and up she was completely fine, but getting the sail up all the way from the bottom can be quite an exercise. Eventually I decided to put up the genoa, furl the gennaker, sail closer to the wind and then finally hoist the sail right up. After this I bore away, unfurled the gennaker and put the genoa away.

This took a while but it was well worth it, and once it was done I popped into the cabin to try to grab a quick snooze. This was rudely interrupted when another big fella decided to drop by and say hello. When I poked my head outside I saw a dark line of clouds on the horizon and felt the electricity in the air. I guessed I had about ten minutes before it hit so I took down the gennaker. This done and with one reef in the main I was happy that I'd be fine in the squall.

I squinted at the horizon. It looked peaceful from here but I knew it was going to feel anything but that as soon as it swept over me. In fact it looked like it was really going to throw a serious amount of water over the boat.

Suddenly inspired, I ran inside, stripped off, and grabbed three buckets and some normal freshwater shampoo instead of the special saltwater one I'd been using. I jumped up on to the foredeck, being careful not to stub my toes just as a wave of rainwater swept over the boat. I soon filled the three buckets with fresh water collected from the reefed part of the mainsail.

I was delighted they'd filled so quickly. I took the first one, emptied it over me, then put it back under the mainsail. I could feel the salt leaving my dry skin as bucket after bucket went over my head. Six buckets later the squall had passed me by. As I towelled off, I looked at the boat and saw that I wasn't the only one who'd benefited from that amazing downpour. She glistened as the sun came out and we dried off together in just a few minutes.

It was definitely time for a clean set of clothes, so I got dressed and savoured the feeling of fresh cotton on my skin. My back felt so much better. I grabbed something to drink, put the music on and curled up on the beanbag in the slowly setting sun, one contented sailor.

The following day began pretty busily, to say the least. The sails went up and down over and over again as several squalls passed through. Soon I found myself caught between two of them.

'Sod it,' I thought, 'this time they're staying reefed.'

It was hard to resist the temptation though. I was nearing the equator, a major milestone, and wanted to cross the line as soon as possible. One minute I was crawling in 6 knots of breeze, the next I was in 29.

I stayed heading southwest, towards South America, on Mike Broughton's advice as there was simply no wind due south. I was delighted to see I was almost out of the Doldrums and I was looking forward to the arrival of the South Atlantic trades, some steady winds at last that would help me make good progress south. The wind continued to blow all over the shop and it became a real battle to try to push myself further in the right direction.

I was due to cross the equator at around midnight UK time, about two to three a.m. Mike time – not really when I'm at my best. I found the champagne and set up the cameras to record on the computer the zero-latitude moment when I crossed from north to south. Dad was watching my progress on the computer back in the

UK, wanting to share this milestone with me. He called to check everything was set to record the moment. I told him I was all set and then decided, as everything was quiet and as there was still a half hour to go, there was enough time for a nap. I'd had precious little sleep these past few days, what with all the squalls.

I set my alarm and shut my eyes . . .

. . . and opened them forty minutes later. I'd slept through the alarm!

Bugger!

I leapt up and looked at the computer.

Bugger! I'd missed it! I'd slept through crossing the equator! I was gutted, totally gutted. I must have been the first ever single-hander to miss this moment. But there was no way I was going to turn round and sail over the equator again. 'Oh well,' I told myself, 'next time!'

I popped the champagne for the on-board cameras in the morning, a little sip for me and the rest shared between Neptune and the boat.

Even though I'd missed the moment, I had passed a major milestone. I'd sailed a massive distance now and had ticked a big box on my list of milestones. Fortunately, the conditions continued to provide me with lots of wind, although I was still being pestered by countless squalls. I raced southwards to escape them, to get to those wonderful trade winds that would take me south and then finally east.

The following evening I stood outside on deck, just lost in the moment. The clouds were high and puffy, the sky was a sharp bright pink and the boat was already careering along upwind when a gust came through, giving the girl an extra turn of speed. I thought it was the most beautiful thing I'd ever seen. I didn't want to go back into the cabin so I just stayed outside, soaking up the atmosphere. This I quite literally did, as five minutes later a largish wave swept over the side and soaked me completely.

I stayed up through the night because my routing was taking me straight to the island of Fernando de Noronha and I wanted to make sure I didn't sail too close. This island, part of a very small archipelago, used to be a prison for the worst Brazilian criminals but now it's a national park attracting a sprinkling of tourists.

I eventually managed, after a little bit of pinching, to clear Fernando de Noronha by a respectable 10 miles or so as the sun rose. This meant I managed to get a good glimpse of her on the horizon, and I could see rugged tall peaks piercing the skyline.

I was distracted by a sudden squawk. I looked up to see a pair of birds circling the boat. They kept me company while I tidied up and then decided to hang out with me for the rest of the day.

I also invented a new bucket for collecting seawater. It wasn't a good idea to use a normal bucket as the force of the water at the speed I was travelling would just rip it out of my hands. So I adapted one of my small dry bags, created some straps for it and put it all together to make a fantastic new bucket, one that I was even able to fold away.

Unfortunately, a short time later it was hanging from a winch when we hit a wave quite hard and the bucket flew away over the side. I was gutted to lose it so soon.

This didn't stifle my inventiveness. Like many ideas, my next came while I was in the middle of a shower. By using a load of duct tape and adapting a large pot of moisturizer I was able to create a solid platform for my small fan so I could place it anywhere inside the cabin.

That evening brought with it yet another fantastic and totally unique sunset. As the horizon glowed with the last light of the day, the boat was filled with a gorgeous warm orange colour. I'd never get tired of watching these amazing sunsets, never.

I was now just 100 miles away from the coast of Brazil and past the huge city of Recife, still heading south, waiting for the wind to veer, enabling me to turn SSE.

The next day dawned cooler. The heat had until then been pretty unbearable but suddenly the clouds started to thicken and the temperature fell slightly, just enough so it was bearable to be inside while I boiled the kettle for lunch. After studying the charts on the computer screen and talking with Mike Broughton I calculated I had about two days left before the wind would take me towards the southeast and back over towards Africa.

That done, it was time for my daily boat inspection, so I clipped on my safety line and took a walk around the deck, checking over every piece of equipment. I then walked to the bow and back on both sides, checking all the rigging. This was followed by a careful look inside, checking the aft compartment and the forward sail locker. Every couple of days I ventured into both the watertight compartments forward of the sail locker, looking for cracks.

'A pass with flying colours,' I thought proudly. The boat was in tip-top shape.

But when I looked at the cabin . . . oh dear, what a mess. Thanks to the steady conditions, I'd started to let my high standards slip ever so slightly. A towel and a collection of clothes of varying dampness were draped over the chart table and seat, a few bags were rolling around on the floor, and the rubbish bin was packed to the brim. I flicked on the iPod, set it to shuffle and cleaned everything away, sealing the rubbish into a watertight dry bag. I was rewarded with the discovery of a not-too-melted Dairy Milk bar hidden among the mess – hurrah! Time for a quick break.

Once I resumed the house, I mean boatwork, I couldn't stop and cleaned and wiped every square inch of the cabin until I was satisfied it was spotless. To reward myself I stretched out on the beanbag and spent a long time eating lunch. Food stays hot for ages inside the foil packets so I was able to stop midway through lunch for a quick nap and come back to it half an hour later.

Once I was fresh and rested I rigged up my routing laptop with a foam cushion and Velcro to hold it very firmly in place. That way it would be protected if I was caught out by any unexpected gybes and wouldn't go flying across the cabin.

The wind was blowing me in the right direction, the sail set stayed the same; it didn't get much better than this. The spray flew before the bow as the boat stormed ahead at 11 knots. It felt as if she could go on like this for ever. The ocean, lit by the bright sunshine, was a dazzling blue crystal.

'God,' I thought, 'I wouldn't swap this for anything.'

I sat back near the helm.

Then the autopilot died.

28

The Autopilot Strikes Back

Oh no! Why the hell wasn't it steering? There'd been no error, no alarm, it'd just gone dead.

Then I realized. It was me! I'd accidentally hit the off button by leaning against the autopilot. I laughed at myself, switched on the pilot and sighed with relief as it snapped back into life and took the helm once more.

This straight run had lasted a week, and both the boat and I were more happy and relaxed than we'd been on our adventure so far. I felt more than ready to meet the challenges of the South and I couldn't wait for the faster running conditions.

The autopilot was still behaving itself several hours later, so I decided to clean out the forepeak, the storage area at the front of the boat in which I kept the spinnaker and gennaker sails. This sounds easier than it is as it meant I had to crawl through various compartments inside the boat and squeeze my way through a tiny hatch into the forepeak while the boat bounced over the sea.

I removed both sails to create some room and set about bailing out all of the water that had collected on either side of the forward ballast tanks.

After this I had half an hour's break and wolfed down another 800-calorie freeze-dried curry. Then it was back into the depths of the forepeak once again. This time I tidied up some of the fenders and mooring ropes and made sure the spare rudder was still securely lashed to the hull.

I stopped when I saw the gennaker, and thought for a moment. Hmm. Well, why not?

I would be needing the gennaker soon enough, once I turned ESE and made my way back across the Southern Atlantic to the Cape of Good Hope, with the prevailing winds running behind me.

The gennaker is raised at the bow end of the boat and balloons out in front when it's set. To hoist and fly a gennaker on an Open 50 on your own is quite a feat, taking anything between twenty minutes and an hour depending on the conditions.

First, I dragged the sail to and through the hatch before laying it on deck. Next, I had to pull it out of the sail bag and get it unlashed, which took a while as it was very tightly packed to save space in the sail locker. It was harder than I thought. 'Oh well,' I thought, wiping the sweat from my face, 'no going back now.'

I attached the foot of the sail to the bowsprit then ran the furling line to the back of the boat where I attached it to a snatch block using a piece of elastic, which keeps the line taut. Then it was back down into the sail locker again to grab the sheets (ropes). These are attached using the clew (corner) of the sail, which needs to be run round almost every part of the boat.

After I'd zigzagged my way round the deck, I attached the halyard (the rope used to hoist the sail) to the head of the sail and, gradually, up it went, to the top of the rig. I was careful to make sure it didn't catch on anything. After this it was back to the cockpit to tighten up a little on the downhaul line to make sure the sail was taught.

Finally, after checking everything once again, it was time for the best part. I pulled on the sheet and gradually let the furling line travel, letting the sail come out quickly but steadily. The gennaker filled with wind, and the boat soared onwards.

'Job done! Yee-ha!'

I trimmed the sheet until I was happy it was as perfect as it could be before furling away the genoa. What a beautiful sight. I was breathless with excitement. There's no sound better than that of the sail billowing full of air and the sound of rushing water as the boat sails happily onwards making the most of her new sail.

I was delighted that today was the start of a new week, for that meant it was time to drag out the next food bag from the forward compartment.

This one was noticeably heavier than the last. As you may recall, they'd been stored in the order I was supposed to open them. As I was now heading further south and the air was about to get colder and the seas heavier, I had to eat more. I was on the special solo sailor's diet: eat what you want and not put on any weight. I scrabbled around inside until I'd found what I was looking for, and with a triumphant 'Aha!' I pulled out a packet of cookies and sat on the deck munching away while sailing along and watching the spray.

I generally ate my favourite meals first, but I always tried to save a curry for the last day. I also had to fight the temptation to eat all the snacks straight away. After all, I wasn't planning to pass any corner shops on my way round the world.

Although things were going great, I'd not seen any rain for ages and the deck had become pretty salty. Just touching anything or sitting down anywhere left me covered in sticky crystals which caused my skin to itch no end.

'Some rain would be nice,' I thought, looking skywards.

As my gaze returned to the horizon I spotted a dark cloud in the distance. I watched as it drew close. The wind increased steadily from 21 to a healthy 29 knots and we really started powering along. The boat just loved it and she leapt away without any resistance, raising her speed from 10 knots to a steady 15. What a boat! It was a shame the squall brought almost no rain but I was hardly going to complain, the day had pretty much been perfect.

I was feeling pretty pleased with the way things were going generally. The sails were full of wind, the weather was fair and warm and we were flying along at 14 knots as the sun was setting—

Beep-beep-beep-beep-beep-beep-beep-beep-beep.

Oh no! Not again. Please, not again.

I scrambled to the helm as the boat started to turn and grabbed it just in time. Nothing like a potential crash gybe to set the pulse racing. I reset the AP but it simply cut off again.

Aaaargh! Would my pilot problems ever end?

I restarted the system a few times but it seemed to have come down with a major headache this time.

This was hardly the best time for this to happen as darkness was just about to fall. After a few more resets it suddenly started working again and I spent an anxious hour sat by the helm, praying it wouldn't cut out.

Fortunately, it held up throughout the night with no problems at all, although I was still pretty annoyed as I had spent a stressful, sleepless night with one eye firmly on the autopilot. I did some more tests in the morning and disconnected a malfunctioning display, which seemed to solve the problem. 'Just keep it together from now on,' I told it, patting it very gently at the same time. I remained on 'edge of my seat' mode, always expecting a crash gybe to happen at any second.

Then, an email from Mike Broughton had me grinning from ear to ear. 'A fast-moving tropical low is travelling southeast, just to the west of your location, some great winds are going to fire you east across the South Atlantic.'

Excellent!

To celebrate the good news I decided to do some extra fitness work on the foredeck, something I always found amusing.

I got down to do some press-ups. 'One, two, thr— Whoops!' I rolled across the deck, laughing. The rocking motion of the sea had scuppered my first attempt.

I didn't fare much better with sit-ups. I found a taut rope I was able to slip my toes under for stability. The problem was, every time I sat up my wonderful boat tried to help me by tilting me in the right direction. It was just like having a friendly hand lift me back up. After a few abortive attempts I eventually managed a few sets on the coach roof. I also worked on some bizarre leg exercises which involved me stretching out my legs in turn in the air and writing out the alphabet.

Exercise was pretty important as I didn't actually move around that much on the boat. I would spend most of my time sat in roughly the same position and most things were within reach or just a couple of steps away. Exercising was important for me psychologically, too: fitness in body = fitness in mind.

Also of great psychological benefit were the regular checks on my progress, something I obsessed about. I was loving my sail but I wanted to get back to my family as soon as humanly possible. I'd study the charts meticulously and check my position relative to the whole world. It was always great to see that I'd travelled a little bit further every day.

My exercises and chart checking done, it was time for more food, so I cooked up what was possibly the mildest curry in the world. Out of my pretty comprehensive range of freeze-dried meals curries were my favourites, but I was less than impressed with this one. It didn't really deserve the title 'curry'. More like chicken and unidentifiable red sauce. Ugh.

As I finished I noticed a group of birds sitting in the water, watching me as I passed by. I wondered what on earth had brought them all the way out here. Then again, here I was sailing in the middle of the ocean hundreds of miles from land, so they were probably wondering the same thing. They were around 15 metres away and I was unable to identify them as anything other than birds. Never been much of a twitcher, I'm afraid.

During our brief nightly call Dad told me I was within 60 miles of Michel Desjoyeaux, the leader of the Vendée Globe yacht race in his Open 60. Sadly, I was too far away to be able to communicate via VHF, which was a shame; I would have loved to have a chat with another solo sailor. For now, it was just me and the birds – and they weren't the best conversationalists.

That night the temperature started to drop and the wind started to climb. Time to dust off the oilies. There really was a change in the air. I was definitely in colder waters now and the boat surged forward with a sense of seriousness and urgency.

I treated myself to a winter feast of sausage casserole and tidied the boat yet again. It never ceased to amaze me just how quickly it turned into such a mess. I packed away my personal stuff including books, spare batteries and camera and placed them in some water-tight plastic boxes, which I wedged in really well so they wouldn't come loose even if the boat was knocked on her side. I then checked the other side of the boat, where I kept my tool bag, a sail repair kit, more batteries, as well as my shoes and clothes. All my clothes were packed into dry bags so there was no chance of them getting wet whatsoever – that would be very bad news indeed.

I was in the middle of all this when I stopped short and grinned. I'd found a very bizarre present someone had given me for Christmas while in Gran Canaria. I'd forgotten all about it. It was a nodding Scooby Doo. I plonked him on the edge of the chart table. He made a great barometer: when he nodded a lot I knew it was rough outside.

Scooby Doo's head almost fell off the next morning as I approached 40 degrees latitude, aka the Roaring Forties, so called because of the boisterous prevailing westerly winds. With little landmass to slow them down, these winds are especially strong in the southern hemisphere.

Although I was still in the thirties, I had a bumpy and sleepless night. With the full main and genoa up the boat flew along, delighting in the high winds. But I became slightly anxious. I knew I was pushing it now by sailing ever closer to the limit. As dawn broke I changed down from the genoa to the solent and it made all the difference. The average speed dropped from 14 to 12 knots. That was a heck of a lot more comfortable and I was able to get some rest.

When I got up I decided to have a look at my rudder, which had started making a very tiny grinding noise. A close inspection revealed that one of the rudder shafts was moving around in the top bearing. The movement was very slight, only about 2mm, but if it was 2mm now, how much would it be by the time I made it to the Southern Ocean? I knew I couldn't go into the Southern Ocean without total confidence in the steering system. I decided to keep a close eye on it and review in a few days' time.

The temperature dropped another couple of degrees as the wind speed continued to climb. As it reached 32 knots the waves climbed, and so did the boat speed. The sense of movement and power in the ocean was just incredible. I was just a tiny, insignificant piece of flotsam trying to make my way across this unimaginably vast, wild, living thing – at great speed.

The boat really was like a surfboard. Every so often a large wave would pick us up and prime us, and we'd pause, sitting at the top for a moment; it was a bit like looking down a giant, very steep slide, full of the anticipation of the stomach-lifting feeling that's about to come. As we started each descent the speed picked up to 12, 13, 14 knots; then came the flurry of spray as the bow was lifted into the air above the water and she really came alive, shooting down the wave at 15, 16, 17 knots, slowing up as we ploughed into the trough; and then the next wave was already there, and we were at the crest, ready to do it all again.

It was a sign of what was to come. I knew I had to brace myself for much heavier conditions and higher speeds. This boat was designed to go fast, it didn't do slow, it just wouldn't happen. Whatever wind and sea threw at me, we would be forced to sail it at speed.

That evening I decided to reef down in the main to increase the chances for a fairly restful night. As I eased off the main halyard two of the lashings on the cars that held the main fast against the mast decided to part with the sail, creating a big loose section which got caught on my lower spreader.

That was a real pain in the backside. A snagged sail was usually pretty difficult to sort out. There was always the risk of a tear in this situation, something that didn't bear thinking about. The smallest tear could spread very quickly, and if the wind was strong it could end up splicing the sail in two.

Eventually, after two hours' work, playing with all the reefing lines, bringing the boat upwind twice and moving the sail around in every possible way, it came free. I sighed with relief. I finished reefing and replaced the missing lashings. Exhausted, I gratefully stepped into the pleasant shelter of the cabin where I suddenly realized I was dripping wet.

I started to shiver. Enough was enough. I'd earned a total change of clothes. And once I was changed, I felt fantastic. I squirrelled down into my beanbag, oohing and ahhing at my new clothes' softness.

29

Life, the Universe and Chocolate

It was now late January. I was way south of the equator, the following morning was cold and cloudy. The winds were light, and as the day wore on I predicted that the next twenty-four-hour run would be the worst so far. I had to be patient. Mike Broughton had told me another very strong front was due in just two days.

As I pottered about the deck, fiddling with the battens, my best deck knife slipped through my fingers and, just as the butter-side-down rule predicts, it bounced along the deck and hopped over the side. Now that was very, very annoying. I had two spares but that one was by far the best of the three.

I sensed movement from above. I looked up.

My deck knife was forgotten as I gazed with wonder at the sight of my first albatross.

These giants have the longest wingspan of any bird, up to 3.5 metres, and are the undisputed airborne kings of the Southern Ocean. They use their huge wingspans to ride the ocean winds and glide for hours, flying up to 10,000 miles at a time, coasting for hundreds of miles without flapping so much as a feather.

I watched as the beautiful bird demonstrated her grace in just 5 knots of wind. She glided effortlessly around the boat, dipping in and out of the air currents, never faltering for a moment.

I watched in awe as she gradually began to coast away.

I took a nap on the beanbag in the cuddy (the area between the helm and the cabin), and was awoken by the pleasant sight of the sun breaking through the thick cloud, filling the boat with life-giving warmth. It lasted for just a few minutes before vanishing.

There was something I'd been meaning to do for a while, and now, while things seemed fairly quiet, there was no reason for me to put it off any longer.

A slightly unpleasant job, but why the hell not?

I hadn't had any rain to wash the boat clean so I did it myself. I got out my deck brush and gave the whole stern of the boat a good scrub down. This done, I stood back and took a long look. 'That's better, now the girl's looking beautiful and clean again!'

Of course, as soon as I'd finished all hell broke loose, weather wise. I was in the cabin when I glanced at the routing software on the laptop and stopped dead. That couldn't possibly be right, could it? It said I was heading north. Two minutes earlier I'd been head-ing east!

Suddenly the boat leapt forward; the wind was blowing wildly. Poking my head out of the hatchway, I spotted an enormous pair of violent-looking squalls rumbling towards me.

Uh-oh!

I dashed for my oilies and pulled them on in record time. I then clipped on my safety harness and jumped outside. There was no time left to reef or furl away the headsail and I grabbed the helm just as the squall hit and 35 knots of wind shot through the rig. We took off in a fantastic flurry of spray.

About two minutes later the wind dropped off to 5 knots, but just as things began to calm down I heard the hiss of an approaching wall of rain. I turned to see a grey waterfall advancing slowly but steadily towards me. It spent a good ten minutes giving the boat a thorough rinse before passing by, taking what little wind there was with it and leaving me with an oh-so-fantastic nothing.

'What on earth's going on?' I demanded as the boat performed its second pirouette of the afternoon. The wind had come back and circled again before suddenly picking up to 17 knots, which took me completely by surprise as by now I was sailing upwind to try to get myself east. Suddenly we heeled right over, overpowered by wind and water.

I held fast and waited for five minutes to see if the wind was going to change its mind again, but for once it stayed put. I left the helm and quickly filled the starboard ballast tank. The boat swung upright and picked up a little speed.

'May the fun and games continue,' I thought, and continue they did.

Good old Mike Broughton emailed to tell me that I needed to take some drastic action: 'You need to duck south as soon as possible to avoid being totally becalmed by a high-pressure system.' I wasted no time tacking and headed SSW. I found myself sailing straight into the waves. I cringed as the boat's lightweight flat hull flew off their crests and landed with a sickening *slap* in the trough of the next one. Everything rattled furiously with each slap; it felt as if she was going to shake herself to pieces. I tried everything I knew to ease the pounding but it was impossible. I forgot about getting any sleep and just sat there, cringing with every single crash, bang and wallop of the bow. Finally, about ten hours later, the wind started to back right round, before settling on a NW direction, which was great news, and I managed to get some kip.

Despite the recent heavy shower, the boat had become even saltier. I couldn't touch anything on deck without rubbing salt. Even the guard wires were covered in a thick crust, and the winch handle had become totally encrusted. It had started to whine, which was incredibly annoying as it was one of the most used items in the cockpit. As soon as I got the chance I bathed it with some of my precious fresh water, and that seemed to fix the problem.

Also making an unpleasant noise was my rudder. The grinding, groaning noise seemed to be getting worse. Fixing it would be simple – just replace the bearing – but of course that would mean stopping again.

When Dad called, the wind had dropped away, although every

now and then a teasing breeze of around 4 knots appeared for thirty minutes or so, blowing ever so slightly southeast. I told him that I'd decided to stop at Cape Town. Of course, the downside to that was that I would no longer be eligible for the record of non-stop sail round the world.

For a short while, I felt bitter and frustrated. My goal to become the youngest person to sail single-handed around the world non-stop was no more. There still remained the record for youngest single-handed around the world 'with stops' – but it wasn't quite the same.

I drew consolation from the fact that this was no fault of my own; it was simply down to faulty technology. My spirits lifted when I thought about seeing Dad again – and I was pretty excited to visit Cape Town. 'Yes,' I thought, 'despite the setback, I'm still sailing the dream.'

The quiet weather meant my deck brush made another appearance, and I scrubbed the cockpit until it gleamed, rinsing away every tiny speck of dirt that I could find. As I studied my handiwork I noted that a few of the screws weren't looking as attractive as the clean white bulkhead below them; they were a little rusty in fact. I dug out my rust remover and a short while later they were glinting in the sun.

Another job well done, so it was time for a snack and a listen to the iPod.

As I lay on my beanbag, munching some chocolate and quietly coasting along in the orange sunset, I came to realize that records were by no means the be all and end all. I was sailing the dream, and life was pretty damn good. 'If I could just have a bit more wind,' I thought, 'it'd be perfect.'

30

The Need for Speed

My eyes snapped open. Something had changed, but what was it? I sat up and looked out of the cockpit.

Wind! We had wind!

I grinned, and that grin hardly left my face all day as the boat surged forward and flew at speeds of up to 18 knots. In no time at all we were power reaching – sailing at around 110 degrees to the wind – and with the ballast full and the boat set for full speed ahead, we turbo-surfed eastwards. It was such a majestic feeling whenever the boat took off in a strong wind. She came alive. It was almost as if there was no water beneath her, yet she remained totally under control, balanced and happy. I was now able to enjoy it so much more. I felt totally at ease with the boat and now knew exactly when she was feeling a little too pushed or when she wanted a little more sail.

We were flying at 14 knots when a whale broke the surface just 15 metres away and ploughed on alongside me.

Wow!

I was delighted to say the least. This was the first whale I'd seen. With her rectangular head and her blowhole sending a spray of water high in the air, she really was a spectacular sight. It was wonderful to see her keep up with the boat, creating her very own bow wave. She was only with me for a minute and I couldn't tear my eyes away from her, so I didn't get a picture, but I knew I'd never forget her.

After such a long period of quiet I was ready to rock and blasted eastwards, covering a fantastic 300 miles in just twenty-four hours. This was more like it!

As the sun set behind a line of grey clouds on the horizon, it turned the sea silver. My heart was full of so many strong emotions, mainly joy at my progress tinged with loneliness and the pain of missing my friends and family.

With a last glint, the sun disappeared and the lights went out. There was no moon, but just a short while later the night was lit up by thousands of stars, as if bright silver glitter dust had been thrown right across the sky. Potters Bar felt like it was a million miles away. Out here it was just me, the boat, the sea and the universe.

I had clambered up on deck for my regular night-time check for any ships and to cast a torch over the boat when I noticed that the bottom of the mainsail was really slack.

That was weird.

I grabbed my powerful spotlight and had another look, and discovered there was a problem with the outhaul at the end of the boom. The outhaul is a line used to extend and control the mainsail. Tightening or slackening the outhaul can flatten or fill out the sail, for example. Sorting it out meant a trip to the end of the boom.

It had started raining, so I threw on my oilies and, with my head-torch on, shinned along to the end of the boom in the pouring rain. With perfect timing, a proper little gust arrived. 'Just what I needed, thank you very much!' I thought as I swung precariously over the Atlantic.

I quickly found that the original Dynema (rope) lashing had chafed through somehow. It needed replacing. So, after shinning in reverse back down the boom I jumped down into the forepeak, cut myself a length of Dynema and shinned back up the boom. Then, after cutting away the remains of the original lashing, I quickly attached the new one between the end of the outhaul and the ring at the clew of the mainsail before shinning back. I winched on the outhaul and trimmed the main.

Job done! I was pretty pleased with myself, especially as doing this had enabled me to check all the other lashings at the end of the boom. I jumped below, grabbed a quick chocolate bar and a drink, and climbed into the bunk for a well-earned power nap.

I really wanted to stock up on rest. If these winds kept up I'd be drawing close to Cape Town in just a few days and this would mean a sudden increase in shipping. There'd recently been early signs of this when two ships popped up on the AIS, one of which was heading in my direction.

BANG, CRASH!

I leapt out of 'bed' in a flash, clambered up on deck and immediately saw that the top half of my iridium antenna had dropped off. Uh-oh. I needed my satellite comms! I did wonder how I was going to reattach it, then remembered my ever-reliable friend: duct tape. I strapped it back together and it seemed to work perfectly. Another problem solved.

To celebrate, I grabbed some snacks, turned on the iPod and cranked the music right up to maximum, some very bass-filled tracks blasting into the twilight. A giant grin spread across my face as I realized I must be one of the very few people in the world sailing across the ocean with the music at max volume.

I now had just 300 miles to go to Cape Town. Dad was already there. Never one to waste any time, he'd got to grips establishing new contacts. There were a few tricky things that he needed to find, including a diver to check the hull and every underwater fitting. I really couldn't wait to see him.

When the sun rose it brought a very pleasant warm morning with it, and I decided to set myself a challenge: to climb halfway up the rig to check out my mast-climbing system while at sea. Wind and sea were both moderately calm, so I reckoned it was the perfect opportunity.

Going up the rig while at sea rather than on the dock is a very different experience. For a start, the sails are up and the boat is moving up and down while the wind shoves her from side to side, so I had to be prepared to sway about a fair bit.

I used a rock-climbing system that allowed me to climb up and down a taut rope using two jummars – supports that hold you while you haul yourself up the climbing rope. I also had a back-up fail-safe jummar, which was pulled up the rope just below my climbing harness, so if one of my jummars failed I would only have to slide down around half a metre. To ascend, you slide one jummar up, put your weight on that, slide the other one up behind it, change over the weight, then repeat this process over and over again. It's tricky, but becomes much easier with practice.

I called Dad to let him know what I was up to. He'd stay by the phone until I called him back. If he didn't hear from me soon then he'd know that something was seriously wrong – either I was stuck, unconscious, badly injured or in the water.

I donned my protective upper-body pads and helmet (there's always the risk that you'll be thrown around the rig and there's lots of things to crash into). I climbed up a couple of metres at first then came down again, just to make sure I was happy with the system. I then grabbed the camera and the remote control for the autopilot and hooked myself back on to the rope for the climb up to the halfway point.

Going up was fairly smooth and uneventful, and I stopped briefly at the first set of spreaders to have a glance around at the now much broader horizon. Not a single boat in sight, so I continued up to the halfway point.

I looked down at the boat. It was a fantastic angle to watch her from but I don't like heights at all so I decided not to hang about any more and began my descent.

This was much harder and took me twice as long, but I eventually reached the bottom, happy that I'd really tested the system while at sea and that it worked like a treat. I was now confident that I could use it if I had to.

I let Dad know it had worked beautifully, and he sighed with relief.

After all the excitement I chilled out for a bit, spending some time on deck lying up against the coach roof with a book in hand and the gennaker flying, giving the boat a little extra sail area to quickly bring me into the final stretch for Cape Town.

It was soon starting to get dark, and I was washing my saucepan outside in a bucket when I noticed that the wind had really shifted round much more to the south. She was pointing too far north for Cape Town.

Not good.

I quickly finished washing up and set about dropping the gennaker before darkness fell. The sail furled and came down in record time, and once I'd pushed it through the forehatch I set about getting the sheets together and shoved them into the forepeak. It was so dark by the time the genoa came out that I needed my headtorch.

The radar leapt into life as soon as I came within 10 miles of the continental shelf and started on the home straight for Cape Town. The edge of the ridge was a popular fishing area, and sure enough, just one hour after I'd spotted the first fishing boat, I had twenty-eight more in my sights. It was nerve-racking, seeing all those lights up ahead, moving in all sorts of directions. The count continued to increase: '30, 35, 40, 45, 46, 47!' They all seemed to be travelling at around 10 knots. Then I spotted some tankers. One was more or less on the same course as me and I watched as the 500-foot-long monster powered past.

As dawn broke, I scanned the horizon looking for the 1,000-metre-tall Table Mountain. Eventually I spotted a blur on the horizon, which gradually turned rectangular and sharpened as the sun continued to climb. There it was, the distinctive shape of Table Mountain. I was almost there!

All the traffic funnelled into the same bay. I weaved one way and the other. It was stressful but I enjoyed the challenge, as ever. I was now handling the boat with far more confidence than at the start of the trip.

I carved my way through the traffic and sailed into the bay where I was caught by a wind shadow, so I ghosted towards the Royal Cape Yacht Club at just 1 knot. I was totally shattered. Just then I saw a small rib racing towards me.

'Dad!'

'Mike!'

He leapt on board as I entered the marina and gave me a crushing hug. My tiredness vanished as I did my best to crush him back, laughing happily.

31

What Were the Odds?

As soon as I was berthed in the Royal Cape Yacht Club it was time to meet Zac Sunderland and his dad Laurence. Zac was just three months older than me and over halfway round the world. He'd always planned to stop on his way round and wasn't trying to go as fast as I was, but he was closer to finishing.

We had lunch together – my first meal on land since leaving the Canaries – then Zac showed me round his boat *Intrepid*. It was beautiful but, at 36 feet compared to my 50-foot surfboard, she was quite a bit shorter and slower.

I know which boat I preferred.

Zac had faced pirates in the Pacific and kept a pistol on board to deal with them. Luckily for Zac, they'd just followed him for a while before losing interest and hadn't tried to board.

As I showed Zac round my boat, I felt so lucky. Sure, it was perhaps a little more cramped and not as cosy as his – after all, she was built for speed, not comfort – but my goodness she looked so beautiful in the water, and boy, could she move.

I also met up with Jean-Baptiste Dejeanty, the youngest Vendée Globe sailor that year. He was in Cape Town after retiring due to autopilot problems. I told him I knew just how he felt!

I was in awe when I took a look round his fantastically powerful boat, a 60-footer that he had personally customized. It looked like a Stealth Bomber.

Jean-Baptiste very kindly donated some of his food, as my trip was taking a lot longer than I'd expected. It was French food and it didn't look nearly as tasty as my own supply. Still, they would make fantastic emergency rations and I accepted them gratefully. 'Maybe I'll have a French week for a bit of fun,' I thought.

Then, even more amazingly, the world's oldest circumnavigator sailed into the harbour. I mean, what were the odds? It was such an amazing coincidence that we all crossed paths at the same place at the same time. Seventy-five-year-old Minoru Saito was on his eighth solo circumnavigation, except that this time he was going the 'wrong way round'. Zac and I met him for lunch.

He was also in Cape Town to repair his autopilot. What is it with autopilots?

'I'm desperate to get moving,' he told us. 'I want to be out there.'

All three of us turned and looked out to sea. It gleamed at us from under the burning hot sun that sat low in the sky.

'I know that feeling,' I said, thinking of all the repairs that needed to be done before I could get back out where I belonged.

All three of us were pretty exhausted. I'd stayed up for twenty-hours straight as I'd sailed into Cape Town and been too excited to grab much sleep once I'd seen Dad and then met my fellow circum-navigators, so it was definitely time for an early night.

The bad news was that Dad had lost his job with Hackney Council. They'd been amazingly patient with him, as very often he'd had to spend a lot of time at work dealing with all things Mike-related. Dad always had to make sure his mobile was close to hand and would explain at the start of meetings that he would have to drop everything and answer his phone if I rang. It was a bit awkward for him when I rang up for a 'quick chat' during one of these meetings. Now, in the middle of the recession, Hackney Council's budget had been slashed, which meant they had no money to pay Dad so they had to let him go. This was a real financial blow and we were now seriously concerned about the family finances.

Trying to save money, Dad had hired the cheapest car he could find. It had over fifty dents (I counted them) and was a wreck. When I pulled open the passenger door, the handle came off in my hand, just like a clown car. The 'apartment' wasn't much better. As we entered we were hit by a damp and musty smell. The place hadn't been lived in for some time. Plaster was crumbling off the walls. It wasn't pretty, but it was cheap and suited our purposes just fine.

My first, instant thought on waking the next morning was: 'Time for repairs!' First job was to examine the rudder bearings, and because this was a highly technical task there was precious little for us to do.

Dad had an idea. 'How about a trip up Table Mountain?'

I hadn't even thought there would be time for sightseeing, but it made sense.

'Why not?'

Dad thought he'd easily outrun me on the way up as I'd been sitting on a boat for the past few weeks and hadn't had much in the way of cardio-vascular exercise, but in the end I outran him easily. I'd done a lot of fitness training in preparation for this journey, much more than for the Atlantic trip.

We climbed the mountain in a couple of hours and spent some time admiring the breathtaking view of the Cape. The sun was ducking in and out of the clouds, lighting up the ocean. It was doing a pretty good job of keeping us nice and warm, too, despite the fact we were 1,000m above sea level.

'The wind is looking pretty wild,' I said, watching the surf.

'About forty knots, I reckon,' Dad said. 'We won't be craning the boat out today.'

He was right. We wanted to check the underside of the boat and her keel was 4 metres long, meaning she would need to sit high and secure. Hoisting her out of the water in high winds was not an option.

So, with the lift called off, we made our way down to the beach.

It really was stunning seeing the rocks offshore kicking up huge plumes of spray as the sea shot across them. There were about fifty kite-surfers and windsurfers storming along, pulling off some great jumps and tricks.

I couldn't wait to get back out there again.

Dad then took a call from the British Embassy. Someone had been in touch with them questioning whether I was fit for the voyage I was undertaking. Dad spent an hour on his mobile phone before they were finally reassured. Dad was pretty annoyed as that was all on his roaming charges.

Besides this, Dad was worried that the French boat charterers might try to seize the boat from us, as it was a well-publicized fact that this trip was taking a lot longer than we'd planned. That meant they'd want more money for the hire of the boat.

Just as we were talking about this, the French Embassy called, which caused our hearts to jump. It turned out, however, that the ambassador was a sailing fan who wanted to hear all about my adventures!

Dad had found local help in the form of Manuel, a rotund uncle-type character who knew everyone and anyone in Cape Town and had booked all the teams of workers we needed.

Once the boat was out of the water, various teams of specialist workers descended on her. One team checked the mast from top to bottom, another removed the rudder, and Dad and I inspected the hull and the antifoul, a special self-cleaning paint that protected the hull from the degrading effects of plankton, barnacles and so on. It was in superb condition. The people at Blakes Paints who'd provided us with the antifoul had done an amazing job.

We then spent a sleepless night thanks to the sudden arrival of 70-knot winds. My boat was sat high in her cradle and we worried that the ropes holding her in place wouldn't hold fast, but they were well used to high winds here and we needn't have worried. The boat was held extremely securely.

The summer heat in Cape Town was extraordinary, averaging

about 30 degrees in the shade and peaking at 38. About ten forest fires had started and the flames were fanned by the high winds, making them very difficult to extinguish.

The guys who were fixing the rudder discovered that the problem was a lot more complicated than we'd thought. The steel sleeve around the carbon shaft that held the rudder bearings had worn away slightly. A replacement had to be machined from scratch.

While Dad and I waited, we took the chance to go on safari for a day. It was amazing to drive out of Cape Town and join a safari just like that. In no time at all we were ticking animals off the list as we saw them: giraffes, tick; rhino, tick; zebras, tick; and so on. It felt quite surreal.

We eventually fixed the rudder back on, craned the boat back in the water, craned on the mast, tuned the rig, attached all the sails and set about getting her ready for sailing.

Then, when I took her out for a test sail, the autopilot conked out again.

Dad decided to deal with the autopilot once and for all. 'I'm going to ask the main sponsors to chip in three grand each for a new one,' he said, and got straight to work. As soon as the first sponsor said yes, Dad ordered a new system. In the end, one of them refused to give us any more money, so another £3,000 had to come from Dad's pocket.

I was delighted when the dreaded autopilot was removed and replaced with a brand-new one. I sat with Peet the technician and studied both machine and manual until I knew its workings inside out.

That night I sat down on the marina dock, about 100 feet away from the boat. I couldn't take my eyes off her. The sun was coming down, giving way to the late evening. With Table Mountain in the background, she was quite a vision to behold, more beautiful than ever.

I'd already been through so much and I'd been feeling pretty up against it with the various equipment failures. But everything had been turned around again with amazing support from the people we'd met in Cape Town, our sponsors, family and friends. Now I could look at the boat and dream of circumnavigation once more.

I was desperate to sail her again and get into the business end of the Southern Ocean. I imagined the boat surfing down huge long waves, brilliant and unstoppable. At the same time, I hated the thought of leaving Dad behind. We'd had such an amazing time in Cape Town. Just being together was fabulous.

I'd been getting a little flak from some people who were criticizing me for attempting to cross the Southern Ocean when winter was about to set in. Our own research showed us that we would see only a small increase in average wind speed for this time of year. It was going to be a little colder, for sure, but the risk of ice was low. I'd been given lots of advice from very experienced sailors in Cape Town who'd sailed the Southern Ocean all their lives, and they agreed the end of February was still a good time to set off. There was, however, one critic in Cape Town who told as many people as possible behind our backs that I was mad to set sail into the South.

Dad and I had one final magical day together before I set off on the next stage of my adventure and he had to catch his flight home and hunt for work. We went to Blue Rock Lake, just outside Cape Town, and spent the day wakeboarding and water-skiing. Dad had some really spectacular crashes as the wind was howling across the lake at around 30 knots. I laughed so much, it was the kind of laughter where you can barely stand any more.

We then had a long, leisurely dinner in our favourite restaurant, Cubana, a lively place where the waitresses tried to sell us cigars. These evening meals were wonderful, treasured moments between father and son. Very often we'd worked from dawn until late at night on the boat, and eating at one of Cape Town's many restaurants was a great way to wind down, make plans and fool around.

We talked for many hours that last night. Dad told me what a great sailor I was, how well I'd coped and how proud he was of me. I knew that I was putting Mum and Dad through an awful lot.

They'd allowed me to live my dream but they were paying a high price, spending months on the edge of their seats, never knowing whether the next ring of the phone was going to bring bad news. It was tough for them to bear, especially as the trip was now taking much longer than we'd predicted. Dad was very good at covering up his feelings and putting on a brave face for the TV cameras and papers and giving great quotes, but his emotions ran deep and he was so worried for me – and now for our family's financial security.

When Dad and I hugged goodbye at ten the next morning I didn't want to let him go. After all we'd talked about I felt closer to him than ever before and I didn't want to leave him. I'd been looking forward to the South more than any other part of this trip and I knew I had to do it, there was no other way, but Dad couldn't come with me – although that would have made for an interesting call home!

I'd be lying if I said I wasn't scared. Of course I thought about the storms, the high boat speeds and the fact that there would be no one down there to help me if I got into a pickle.

It was impossible to put all we felt into words as Dad prepared to step off. 'Mike,' he said, 'why don't you make a chart of a hundred days? That's what you've got left before you get back to Portsmouth. I'll make one too, and every day we'll tick one box at the same time. We'll do it together, OK?'

I nodded. 'One day at a time.'

It was a great idea. When it came to heading closer to home I needed to think in terms of the days left, not in terms of the distance yet to sail – because 70 per cent of the journey still lay ahead.

We hugged again.

'I love you.'

Dad stepped off.

PART THREE

THE SOUTHERN OCEAN

Days at Sea: 39
Distance Covered: 8,315 nautical miles

Total Days at Sea: 87
Total Distance Covered: 16,700 nautical miles

PART THREE

THE SOUTHERN OCEAN

32

Into the South

That first half-hour alone was pretty damn hard.

Ask any single-handed sailor and they'll tell you that the worst part of long-distance sailing is the first week or so after you leave land. I was now on my fourth start. Out of eight weeks of actual sailing, four of them had been spent getting used to life on board, and here I was restarting yet again. These starts had made the trip incredibly tough, physically and mentally. It's not easy reacclimatizing to the extreme isolation.

'Come on, Mike, keep smiling,' I told myself as Table Mountain disappeared in the fading light. I reminded myself I was living the dream, that I was going to succeed and that I'd be seeing my family again soon enough. I was finally here, in the South at long last, the ocean of my dreams!

As I sailed away, a whale surfaced with a blast from its blowhole. A good omen if ever there was one. The whale was then joined by a good-sized pod of dolphins, and as I looked over the port bow a pair of cape seals blinked at me.

'Nice of them to come and see me off,' I thought.

I started short-tacking every hour down the coast, heading further offshore, as I knew I'd find better wind there. After hand-steering through a lull until two a.m. I caught a good 10-knot breeze and managed to squeeze in a ten-minute catnap outside on the beanbag – a much cooler place to rest than the humid cabin. As I lay there I started to feel a little seasick.

The Cape of Good Hope was ticked off not long after dawn, although I was feeling too tired and queasy to really enjoy it. I sailed along the edge of the Agulhas Bank where the waters of the warm Indian and cold Atlantic Oceans meet. This collision point means the seas can get pretty wild, making it one of the most treacherous parts of the world for sailors. I steered clear of the edge of the bank, avoiding the 2km-deep abyssal plain because the waters there were short and unruly, and plotted a course to the south east for the Prince Edward Islands, just as the wind filled the sails, pushing me into the Southern Ocean.

My spirits lifted with the wind. 'This is it,' I thought. 'Here we go!'

Soon I was sailing upwind, the boat slamming into each and every wave with a nasty thump. As the boat fell off each wave my stomach retched and groaned. I was feeling pretty weak, tired and fairly miserable and I hardly dared to risk a smile in case I retched again. The waves had lengthened slightly and I reefed down before dark to try to give myself an easy ride through the night, so I could grab some precious sleep.

I felt a lot better in the morning and, to match the much colder temperatures, I cooked up a lovely hot soup. The soup stayed put and my stomach continued to growl with hunger so I prepared a large helping of chicken and pasta with white sauce for an early lunch. Once that was done my thoughts turned to dinner, a nice curry. Yup, my appetite was most definitely back in action.

My ability to nap for twenty minutes at a time returned not long after I regained my appetite. As I awoke from one such nap in the early evening I saw that a couple of curious albatrosses had dropped in for a visit. I sat on deck, snug in my oilies, staring at these incredibly graceful birds as they whirled around the boat in the fading light. An hour passed without me even realizing.

They were still there in the morning, coming and going as they pleased. I grabbed my camera but they flew away as soon as they saw me lift it to my eye. Camera-shy, perhaps? Many years ago albatrosses were hunted for their feathers so perhaps they'd learned to be wary of humans pointing things at them. They eventually regained their confidence and I was able to get a couple of great shots as they swept in close for a good gawp at me.

A high-pressure system overtook me later that day and I was disappointed to find myself stuck with some pretty light conditions that forced me head-on into the waves. The boat took the brunt and got slapped around quite a bit. I hated the sound as the boat charged into each wave: the mast shook, the cabin rattled, and the engine, which was positioned just below the cabin, rumbled ominously. It was agony to sit through; it felt as if she would fall apart at any moment. I moaned and grunted as we thudded into each wave. Of course, I knew the girl was tough enough to handle these conditions, but even so I simply had to bear away until the wind backed round to the north a little and I was able to take it fairly easy with an average speed of 8 knots.

I was even able to grab a break and read a book. This gave me a chance to be 'somewhere else' for a little while, to escape the boat. Although I loved every moment, occasionally I'd think it'd be nice to stop the boat, to press a magical pause button, so I could get out for a stretch and a bit of peace and quiet. The boat was constantly surging forward, she was always looking for speed, and there was always noise, always movement. It was never-ending, unrelenting. Reading was a great way to take my mind off the boat and travel to another world for a little while.

The heat of Cape Town was forgotten after a week of sailing. I'd soon dug out my thermals. Although I had a heater in the cabin I preferred not to use it: I worried that I'd become addicted and use up my precious diesel supply. Far better to just wrap up well and keep moving, I thought.

The albatrosses continued to come and go as they pleased. Every now and again I'd glance up through the cabin window to see them whizz past. Their gracefulness never ceased to amaze me. I could have watched them for hours but I had important jobs to attend to, like applying Velcro to all the items that lived on the chart table, including my keyboard, mouse and my brilliant glow-in-the-dark clock. This would make it a lot easier for me to work at the laptop in heavy seas.

Just as darkness was about to fall, the wind dropped for two hours. It was time to knock out my second reef. As soon as this was done, the wind immediately picked right back up again. Typical! I waited half an hour to see if it was just a long gust, but the wind held steady. I applied the old saying 'If you're thinking about reefing, then you should go ahead and do it!' and put the reef back in while there was still a bit of daylight. This was always harder than shaking it out, but after twenty minutes the boat was all trimmed up again with all the lines tidied away neatly, and she was much happier for it.

I woke after a great night's series of naps and decided to call home for a quick morale-boosting chat. 'Tell me what's been happening,' I said.

'Not much really,' Mum replied, 'just as crazy as always.'

'Tell me everything!'

I loved to receive updates from home; even the smallest news items about family and friends were pure gold to me out here. I now kept better track of all my family's daily life than I had done at home. It made me appreciate how wonderful life is, even the routine day-to-day stuff.

By lunchtime I was starving, despite having attacked a tube of Pringles. I examined the contents of my galley, aka Chez Mike. There was nothing else for it, I had to have spicy beef sauce with rice, most definitely not one of my favourites.

After the washing up was done – this consisted of the scrubbing of my trusty fork – I decided to put some fresh towels to good use and had a really good wash. I braced myself as I dropped a bucket of cold water over my head.

'Aaaaaargh, freeeeeeezing!'

I then towelled myself dry at the speed of light. I decided that shower was going to have to last me for quite a while now.

That evening I pulled out my snug, thick woollies and curled up in the cabin. The temperature was falling fast but I was still warm and cosy.

The following morning I went through my mental checklist and ticked off every part of the boat as part of my inspection. All that was wrong was that the cap on one of the fuel tanks had vibrated slightly loose.

The weather had stayed fairly stable, but the winds had been much lighter than I'd been expecting. 'Come on,' I thought, 'aren't I supposed to be on a rollercoaster ride by now?' The wind was blowing at 9 knots so I bedded down, nice and snug, in the bag on my bunk next to the chart table. I stayed there for several hours, forcing myself outside every hour to check the boat over. My mind never let me rest for long. I was always thinking of jobs that needed to be done, one of which was to sort out my forepeak and make sure my spinnakers were securely lashed. I also bailed a little water out of the aft compartment – just one and a half buckets in total, so nothing out of the ordinary.

Then Mike Broughton emailed. He'd been watching the weather like a hawk, as usual. 'Surf's up, Mike! Some fun stuff is heading your way.'

Aha. So it wouldn't be long now before the South gave me my first real test. We always knew it was inevitable. We were going to try to dodge them but you can't help but get caught by storms in this part of the world. There are too many lows moving too fast, you can't avoid them all.

My pulse raced at the thought of some strong close-reaching conditions; I was really looking forward to ticking off the miles.

The wind climbed and was soon blowing at a steady 25 knots; the boat leapt forward and really started to enjoy herself. With Mike Broughton's help I managed to dodge a mean-looking tropical storm that was sat just to the northeast of me. Forty-five-knot easterlies were just 200 miles away from my current position; I really didn't want to have to deal with those if I could help it. Luckily, it moved eastwards and I was able to follow as it dissipated, heading towards my next waypoint, north of the Crozet Islands.

I celebrated my storm avoidance and my good progress by cooking up some apple-flavoured pancakes in my tiny frying pan. Belly full, I raised the 'full stack' – main and genoa – and a large group of birds decided to fly along with me. I counted nine albatrosses among them; they were quite amazing to watch. One tiny little bird kept trying to land on the bowsprit, despite the fact that it kept plunging into the drink.

These thoughts were interrupted by an alarm. What the hell? It was the autopilot! My heart racing, I checked the screen. 'Drive system error'. I scrambled into my oilies and harness in record time, dashed outside and quickly took the helm before we gybed.

I was aghast at the thought of losing the autopilot now, ten days from Cape Town; I couldn't survive without it here. I looked down at the helm and out of the corner of my eye I spotted that the rudder sensor had come off. That meant that the pilot wasn't able to detect any movement on the rudder. The day-to-day vibrations must have shaken it loose.

I laughed with relief. Thank goodness!

I lashed the tiller, grabbed a couple of spanners and had the rudder sensor reattached in no time. 'Here goes . . .' I pushed the reset button and held my breath as I waited for the pilot to come on.

I looked over the side at the growing seas and got a sudden sense of just how big an area of water I was in. There were millions of empty square kilometres of ocean out there. There was simply nothing out here, no sign of life, nothing at all. It was just little old me and my boat, that was all.

The pilot beeped back into life and took control of the rudder. Fantastic!

I switched on my pump to move my ballast from the middle tanks to the aft. I wanted it at the back of the boat so the bow would be lifted clear of the water to better suit the high winds and long, fast seas I was expecting to arrive soon. I needed to be ready to surf.

It was pumping away when it suddenly let off an ear-piercing shriek. I dived over, hit the off switch and went into Mike the Mechanic mode. I fetched my tool kit, thinking this was going to be an interesting operation. I took the pump off the main engine and its mountings and gave it a thorough inspection. I soon discovered the problem: the clutch had come loose. With a bit of tinkering here and there and some wedges to help me tighten it up I had it mounted and back working in no time. It was a small job but vital as I needed to be able to move my ballast. I had a good portion of porridge with sultanas to celebrate, and just in time, as the winds started to pick up, giving me some decent downwind conditions.

Yet more birds came to join me as I neared the Crozets, six small and inhospitable volcanic islands. It was time to keep lookout. I wanted to give these islands a fairly wide berth as they're surrounded by shallows, meaning lumpy and unpredictable seas. So many ships sank off their coasts in the nineteenth century that the Royal Navy would send a frigate to look for survivors every two years or so. People ventured to the islands in search of seals and slaughtered them for their skins. These days the islands are protected and are a sanctuary for seals and penguins, and are surrounded by killer whales that hunt them.

I passed them without any incident and spent the day in sunshine with good winds behind me. I took the chance to air some clothes, and hung them on my washing lines. By the time darkness came the temperature had dropped pretty drastically so I did a load of press-ups and sit-ups to warm up and thought about a hot supper.

Someone had slipped a Pot Noodle into one of my food bags so I thought this was a good moment for a hot snack. Afterwards, despite preparing it, eating it and putting the packaging away fairly quickly, the cabin retained a rather interesting chicken noodle aroma. I couldn't really air the place so I was stuck with it. That was the last time I was having one of those.

'And after aaaaaaaaallll!'

My iPod had been on shuffle all evening, and when Oasis's 'Wonderwall' came blasting out over the speakers as I reefed I couldn't help joining in at the top of my voice.

'You're my wonderwaaaaaaaalll!'

I kept my iPod permanently on shuffle so I never knew what was coming next. Music was tremendously effective at boosting my spirits. It was great company, and I was able to get lost in it and have a break from this sailing business.

Also key to my mental wellbeing were the calls home. I was able to tell Dad everything and he understood exactly what I was going through.

'It's so bloody annoying,' I told him that night. 'I should be racing along with downwind conditions, instead nothing's really happening.'

'Come on, Mike,' Dad said. 'You're halfway between Africa and Australia and you haven't seen a single Southern Ocean storm. Count yourself lucky that Mike Broughton's doing such a fantastic job.'

This was true, but I did want to experience a good Southern Ocean blow.

Of course, one should be careful what one wishes for.

33

Ding-Dong Time!

Possible 50-knot winds were forecast to arrive so I spent most of the day preparing, making sure everything that could be lashed down was lashed down. I also climbed into my dry-suit. As the wind picked up I reefed, once, twice, and then for a third time, after which I hoisted the staysail. With a 28-knot wind, this left me feeling very under-canvassed, but I knew it was the sensible thing to do. Far better to reef now while it was still light rather than have to do it after the winds hit, in the pitch black with waves regularly sweeping across the deck.

Once I was happy with everything on deck, I retired to the cabin to stay warm and waited for the winds to arrive.

They climbed steadily. Spray lashed the cabin windows above my head as the seas rose. I was wide awake and felt the boat surging down some pretty heavy waves. The wind speed quickly moved into the mid-thirties before peaking at 40 knots, so not as bad as forecast – a pleasant surprise. It was mainly thanks to our routing that we'd managed to avoid the worst of the weather, and the boat emerged the following morning looking just as great as when the front had arrived.

'Happy birthday to me, happy birthday to me . . .'

I was now seventeen! Mum and Dad had stashed away a few treats for me in the birthday week food bag, and there were some presents from back home. I tore at the brightly coloured paper and threw it around the cabin as I worked my way through the gifts: CDs, which went on my music player straight away; books; some DVDs; and a huge array of random but brilliant items such as a mini aquarium, some giant chocolate bars, a miniature bowling set and a frisbee from Dad. Typical Dad, he called it the one-shot frisbee as I could only throw it once. I decided against using it as it made me smile every time I saw it. I was also delighted to receive a CD for the theory part of the driving test.

But of course nobody could give me what I really, really wanted for my birthday: HUGS!

As it was a special occasion, I decided to 'treat' myself to a full body and hair wash. Got to be smart for one's birthday. My reward for washing was a clean set of clothes.

Just as I finished changing into them, the phone rang. It was Mum, Dad, Fiona, Beckie and various other family and friends. They all sang 'Happy Birthday' with the phone on speaker, which felt quite surreal. There they were in the peace and quiet of Potters Bar and here I was coasting along in the mighty swells of the Southern Ocean. Beckie blew out the candles on the cake for me. I held a lighter and blew out the flame at the same time.

'Make a wish, Mike!'

I wished for fair winds that would blow me safely home.

I then talked to everyone over the speaker for a few minutes. It was quite wonderful and brought a tear or two to my eyes.

'We're so proud of you, Mike,' Mum said, 'you're doing amazingly well.'

I hated having to hang up the phone. Even though it was short, my birthday party had been very, very sweet – one I'd never forget.

Not wanting to dwell too much on home, I climbed on deck. I couldn't help but think just how lucky I was to be in this incredible place, a place seen by few people and sailed by even fewer. 'I'm in the middle of the Southern Ocean,' I told myself, stating the obvious somewhat, but it took moments like this to make me appreciate what an adventure I was having. The albatrosses constantly circled overhead while the grey, cold and foaming sea rushed past the hull. To be able to celebrate my seventeenth birthday down here was really special.

The end of the day was pretty spectacular as my kicker/preventer line (the kicker flattens the mainsail) chafed through which meant I had to climb to the end of the boom, harnessed on, of course. Jobs like this were always a little heart-pounding. If something happened, like hitting an unknown object, then the boat could go into a crash gybe, lean over and dunk me in the water, pinning me there. Fortunately this job went about as smoothly as it possibly could and I celebrated by listening to my new CDs while sat on the beanbag, munching chocolate.

I'd had a couple of days of fairly slow wind speeds and wanted to get a bit more of a move on. This wasn't what I'd been expecting from the Southern Ocean at all. Sure enough, the new day brought 20-knot winds with it. The boat leapt forward, gleaming in the cold grey morning light. We rocketed eastwards as the winds continued to build. A fast and explosive low pressure was sweeping under me at the pretty spectacular speed of about 50 to 60 knots, giving me chilly winds of up to 35 knots.

It was time for the solent to go up. Spray flew across the deck as I wound the sail out and the boat felt so much more relaxed as she slid gracefully along, the only indication of our speed the rushing hum of water racing past the hull. With the increased speed, the boat was able to sail in the swell as the surfs became longer. I laughed and whooped as I chased the wave in front for absolutely ages on my amazing surfboard.

I had to reduce sail and then raise the genoa again as the wind dropped off to 26 knots. I took my seat at the helm. Whenever I made drastic alterations to the sail, I always sat on deck for a good half-hour, just to make sure everything was just right. It was twilight by the time I finished all my changing and it was great to see the bow continually kicking up a load of white spray as we flew into the waves.

When I went in I checked the chart and saw that I had crossed the halfway point. I was now closer to Australia than South Africa. Yes!

It was now getting into the last third of March and I could tell winter was on its way, thanks to the freezing cold rain I woke up to the following morning. It rattled down on the cabin windows. Many people who've sailed in the Southern Ocean have described the conditions down here at this time of year in one word: grey. They were absolutely correct. 'Rain, rain go away,' I sang through a yawn and tried to nap through the noise. It seemed as if there was no end to this murky world that had suddenly enveloped me. The mist, caused by the rain bouncing off the water, sometimes became really thick, reducing visibility massively.

The other, much more unpleasant side effect was the dampness. I had to be very careful to keep my clothes as dry as possible as once they got wet it was nearly impossible to dry them out. My boots were a case in point. They'd been wet pretty much from day one; it was impossible to dry them out.

Despite the rain, I still managed to clock an amazing day's sailing, covering 280 miles in twenty-four hours. Now that's what I call progress. That really was quite something. The 280 miles were measured point to point, as the crow flies. I didn't sail in a straight line, the boat moved in a very slight zigzag motion as she moved with the wind and the waves, so I actually covered many more miles than that.

The good news was that these fast conditions were set to continue. Finally, the Southern Ocean was behaving as she should.

It was time to gybe again. I needed to change course from NE, which I'd taken to avoid a nasty windless ball of high pressure, to SE. It was drizzling, so I climbed into my wonderful dry-suit, which always kept me snug and warm, and set to it.

By now I'd become a real expert at handling gybes and I could do the whole thing in about fifteen minutes, even though it was a pretty complicated operation. This was how it went.

First, I tidied up the inside, making sure everything was in position and ready to lean on the other side of the boat and that nothing was going to topple over. This done, I headed outside, clipped on and then bore away a little more. I then furled away the genoa, making sure that the sail remained taut and didn't flap at all as a flogging sail would soon beat itself to bits.

After this, I adjusted the lazy jacks, adjusted the preventer, brought the traveller up to the centre, and got the leeward backstay ready to be winched on. I then went down and dumped the ballast to the other side, which involved opening two valves and letting the water flood the lower tank before shutting off the valves again. Then it was back outside again and, once clipped on, I winched in the mainsail until it was almost at dead centre, which slowed the boat right down. I then winched on my leeward backstay as much as possible and bore away a little more so that we were almost dead downwind.

Once I was happy that everything was ready and all the lines I needed weren't in a tangle, I slowly took the boat down round in a gybe until she was sailing downwind on the other gybe.

After I was happy that we wouldn't gybe back again, I immediately winched the now windward backstay on tight, and after doing so I eased off the leeward backstay and put it away. I then eased off the main sheet a fair bit so that the boat was happier, before easing off the traveller to the right point and putting on the preventer/vang which I then winched on fairly tight to flatten out the mainsail. I then wandered up to the mast and adjusted the lazy jacks to hold in the sail I'd got reefed in. After making my way back to the cockpit I unfurled the genoa, trimmed this, and once I was totally happy with this I tidied away all the cockpit lines into their relevant bags and made the cockpit nice and organized, just how I liked it.

And that's just the brief description!

I was feeling pretty pleased with myself, and I knew how to celebrate yet another successful gybe – with the opening of a new food bag, yay! I went below to the forepeak and started to drag the heavy bag out to the main cabin.

As I crawled back into the main cabin the boat thudded into a wave and the hatch swung shut with a *clump* on my right forefinger. Ow! I wiggled the now throbbing finger. Not broken. That really would have been inconvenient. I'd gotten off lightly, with just a bit of bruising.

After gorging on a lovely kingsize bar of Toblerone, I went outside to check on the sails and as I glanced across the grey ocean I gasped in surprise. Just 10 metres away was a seal. He seemed to be taking it easy, lounging about quite contentedly. I hadn't expected to see a seal all the way out here. At the time I had no idea if this was a normal or exceptional place to find a seal, but apparently they do swim up to 1,500 miles from their mating grounds in the Prince Edward and Kerguelen Islands to feed on krill on the edge of the Antarctic seas.

The sun popped out from behind the clouds. The seal and I watched each other for a few moments in the warm light before she decided she'd seen enough and dipped her head below the water.

She made me reflect on my own long journey. I'd come so far now, although I still had two and a half oceans to cross, and I had grown in confidence enormously. I was sure I could do it. I was in love with my boat – after all, she was my world! We'd formed quite a bond. I was able to hear her whenever she was trying to tell me something; I could tell immediately by listening to her as she glided through the water if something wasn't quite as it should be.

In the last week of March a strong front roared through with 40-knot winds. The boat went into surfing mode and the sailing was breathtaking, with some very, very long surfs. I'd just sit there as the boat squared herself inside a wave and sailed along with it, keeping pace tirelessly until it seemed as though she'd had enough and wanted to try another one. The sea kicked up a fair bit and the distance between waves was surprisingly short. Many people had told me to expect much longer swells down here, but so far this hadn't proved to be the norm.

The speed was really hard to get used to. I'd sometimes sit in the cabin willing the pilot to put the helm over a bit more so we'd come out of the wave, but it fearlessly held the boat right where she was. It knew no fear and would happily drop into a hollow between two waves and shoot off again without a moment's pause.

I felt there was always a chance that the autopilot speed would register too high and produce an error, forcing the pilot to reset. The autopilot nightmare from the start of the trip still haunted me. Over time, I gradually became more confident that the pilot could hold the boat steady while we sailed at these serious speeds.

The fast storm front passed through, after which the wind steadily declined, back off to 15 knots, so I knocked out my reefs and changed up my foresails. The short, ugly swell stayed with me, which made for pretty hard sailing as the heavy, choppy waters caused the boat to slew about a fair bit. Not an easy time to heat up dinner, but it was a good time to call home, especially as today was a very special day.

'Hello, Mum! Happy Mother's Day!'

I told her she was the best mum in the world.

'Thanks for letting me do this, Mum, I'll never forget it.'

I knew that she had found it very hard to let me go on this trip. It was understandable, of course, and although I would never have gone if she hadn't wanted me to, I realized I'd put her in quite a difficult position. She could have put a stop to my dream but she didn't, and for that I shall be forever grateful.

After the all-too-short call was over, I stood in the cockpit for an hour, leaning over the coach roof, just feeling the boat cut her way through the short, steep waves. I ducked as a wave of spray whipped over the coach roof. The boat was devouring the miles like I did Pringles.

It was inspection time. I climbed down through the deck hatch into the aft compartment. It only took a minute for me to check so I left the hatch open. Just as I turned round to climb back out, the boat suddenly ploughed into a large wave. I felt the boat dig down into the water.

Uh-oh.

I tried to get to the hatch but I was too busy just trying to keep my balance. I heard the rushing sound of water storming across the deck.

'Oh no!'

Gallons and gallons of freezing seawater came pouring in, right over my head. I'm sure my expression was priceless. I wasted no time bailing out before returning to the cabin where I attempted to dry off.

An email from Mike Broughton brought news of my third low pressure to arrive that week. This one looked to be the strongest, up to 45 to 50 knots.

'Well, my girl, looks like you and I are set for a fair few more days of really trucking along!'

That evening the sky turned a vivid deep dark grey. The sun just managed to crack through the clouds as we flew east, lining them with silver. A few hours later the new front hit and the sea soon turned into one enormous washing machine. I was both frightened and delighted as a huge wave lifted the boat up and up. I watched the display climb and it bounced between 43 and 47 knots of wind, strong enough to blow the tiles off roofs.

I had wanted to sail in a proper Southern Ocean blow, and now my wish really had come true.

The remnants of a breaking 10-metre wave thudded on to the coach roof above my head. I could tell I wouldn't be getting any rest for a while yet.

While the wind strength didn't worry me too much, it was pretty hard to handle the huge swell and breaking waves. I'd never seen anything like it. Suddenly the boat looked and felt very tiny. She was designed to race, so I had to screw up my courage and race with the ocean, keeping the power on so I didn't get caught in the barrel under any breaking waves. Our speed climbed, and climbed, and climbed. I was soon surfing over 20 knots, outrunning waves. I was untouchable! In a smaller and slower boat I would have been really knocked about, but with the Open 50, speed was my friend.

It was like being on a giant log flume for hours and hours. The surf begins, the boat edges forward at 14 knots or so as I begin the descent. As the waves are both long and steep, the bow drops away and I feel the boat accelerate beneath me very quickly. I look left and right and see the face of this huge, roaring wave of pure power on either side of me. I feel the boat really lift up on to an incredible plane, the bow slightly above the water, ballast keeping her aft in the wave, and still the speed increases – 15, 16, 17 knots. It's dark and I wonder what's going to happen when we hit the bottom of the wave travelling so fast. Still the speed rises – 19, 21, 24 knots! I see the trough below and brace myself for the deceleration. But the boat simply ploughs straight into and over this wall of water barely slowing, sending waves and spray cascading across the deck and over the coach roof, 20 feet in the air. I grab on to the handholds to prevent myself being washed backwards and . . . here we go again!

Dad sent me an email: 'Tracker clocked you doing 24.6 knots. Everything OK?'

'I'll get back to you on that!' I thought.

That was a new top boat speed. To say spray was flying everywhere would be one hell of an understatement!

As morning broke we were still flying at breakneck speeds and I changed down from solent to staysail as the wind and spray tried to blow me off the slippery deck. Job done, the boat relaxed a touch, but still came close to maintaining those same 20-knot-plus speeds.

Mike Broughton emailed to say there was no avoiding what was turning out to be one hell of a storm.

It had to happen sooner or later.

I charted my position in relation to my next waypoint, Cape Leeuwin, the most southwesterly mainland point of Australia. Now we were really moving I thought I'd be across this ocean in no time.

I was still awake at midnight as the boat flew through the darkness. The noise was more intense than ever. Everything rattled and shook as she shot over waves and cut through swells.

I checked the wind speed. Still in the mid-forties. I worried about my mast but I had three reefs in the main and this, along with my tiny bulletproof staysail, was the ideal set-up. I reminded myself my boat would outrun most breaking waves and she was built to sail in the wildest seas imaginable.

I looked outside. I could make out streaks of foam stretching across the sea, turning it white; I could see breaker after breaker, huge waves that collapsed under their own weight with a tremendous *whump*.

We shot over a huge wave and the boat surged forward as she passed the crest, picking up speed as she dove downwards. I held my breath as we accelerated and I began the incredible 'routine' once more. Looking ahead, the boat was angled down at 20 degrees, pointing at the wave's trough.

The speed rose to 18, 19, 20 knots as we plummeted down its front. I continued to keep an eye on the speed: 22, 24, 26 knots! Another new record!

Again, into the wall; waves and spray 20 feet in the air; grab the handholds. Her bow rose at 20 knots and we were already on the crest of the next wave.

'Here we go again!'

The speed! It was just amazing. I was setting new fastest boat speeds by the minute. Twenty-six knots in these lumpy seas was just insane. But not for one moment did I wish I were on dry land. I was scared, for sure, but not panicked. The ocean is where I feel most at home.

During the first few weeks after leaving Portsmouth I'd had good reason to doubt this trip, thanks mainly to the equipment failures, as well as the sheer magnitude of what I was attempting. Despite everything, the fatigue, the loneliness, the frustration, I'd kept going; I'd kept plugging away, no matter how bad I felt. I had my dream. And in those times when it became a nightmare, all I could do was carry on, keep pushing forward, keep dealing with every single problem, no matter how big, painful or frustrating.

I knew that if I made it through this storm then I'd see this journey through to the end. I was physically and mentally tougher than when I'd left; in fact in many ways I was a different person. I wondered if Mum would recognize me by the time I made it back home.

Home. 'God,' I thought, 'now I really understand what loneliness is about.' Here I was in my tiny boat, thousands of miles from any land, let alone the UK. My heart sank when I realized that it was close to impossible to be any further from home than I was now. The nearest humans to me were actually in space, 200 miles up in the International Space Station that passed over this area of the Southern Ocean every ninety minutes.

I looked at the 100-day calendar – still so many boxes to tick. After an incredibly tough day like this one, it really felt like I'd earned my tick.

34

Knockdown!

Wedged inside the cabin at the chart table, I tried to work on the chart, bounced every which way by the broiling sea. Every time the boat charged over a wave she landed with a deafening *thump*. This constant battering was pretty tough to deal with.

I was in the cabin when the freak wave came thundering through the darkness from the port side. I didn't see it coming, but I heard its roar. It scooped the boat up and slammed it flat on its side in an instant. There was no time to react. All I could do was hold my breath and somersault with the boat as my world was flipped upside down. The noise was just insane. It sounded as though the boat was being ripped apart.

The fear was immediate. I knew this could be the end, not only of the dream but of me. Time seemed to slow as we went further and further over, objects flying past my head. As they did, I thought, 'That's broken, and that's broken, and that's broken . . .' Suddenly a 20-litre jerry can of diesel flew through the air and cracked open as it smashed into the side of the cabin.

The boat turned further on to its side, past 90 degrees. I skidded as I fought to keep my balance and realized I was steadying myself with my feet against the roof.

'Oh crap,' I thought.

This was about as bad as it could get. The boat was on her side, keel out and mast in. I'd heard stories of sailors being trapped like this for ten minutes before they were righted. Speed had dropped to a few knots. A wave could sweep in from behind at any moment, turning or flipping the boat fully, ripping the mast from the deck, bending steel as if it were rubber.

I was in a Force 10 storm in the middle of the ocean, somewhere between Australia and Africa, hundreds of miles from any shipping lane. Not a good time to be sailing over 90 degrees to the water.

As diesel fumes filled the cabin, I thought about the mast. I guessed that it was underwater. There was no way it would survive the strength of these waves. They would bend, twist and snap it off the boat like matchwood.

I felt the boat dip in the water as the back of the rogue wave finally passed underneath. Then the boat strained to right herself.

Come on!

I held my breath as I felt the boat start to come the right way.

Come on! Come on! You can do it!

Gravity gradually took hold of the keel and I felt an enormous wave of relief as the boat flipped back up with another tremendous crash, almost as quickly as she'd fallen.

She took off immediately. I gripped the table, terrified. I looked around me and saw so many things scattered and broken but I didn't care about that, I was just relieved to be upright again.

No time for shock. Deep breath. Damage report. First, I was in one piece. Nothing broken – so far so good.

The mast. I had to check the mast. I needed my torch. I carefully crossed the cabin, which was now covered in diesel and bilge water. Luckily, I'd strapped everything down and the torch was just where I'd left it. I switched it on with trembling hands, stuck my head out of the hatch and checked the mast – and almost fell over as the boat shot through another wave. It was still there, sails still attached. More relief. Unbelievable! What a boat! She was sailing at over 20 knots as if nothing had happened; we were back on the log flume.

I guessed that when we were almost upside down the mast must have been pointing down the front of the wave and hadn't gone in the water at all. From my data readings, I could tell that the various instruments attached to the top of the mast were still there, so there was no way the top of the mast had gone in the water otherwise they would have been gone.

That meant the wave must have been over 70 feet tall, as high as a six-storey building.

Bilge water was everywhere; I could see where it had left a water-mark on the ceiling. It had taken out most of the electrics. Right. Not the end of the world. I couldn't see any cracks in the hull; there was no water rushing in anywhere. Diesel, too, was everywhere. The fumes were so strong they made me retch.

To my great relief, the laptop and the satellite phone were still working. Unfortunately, the charging equipment wasn't, so I switched off the laptop to save power.

We flew down the front of yet another huge wave. This was far from over.

Tiredness gripped me. I wedged myself back into the chart table and held on tight.

Time to call Dad.

'I've been knocked down. I'm OK. The mast is still up but I've lost my electrics.'

Dad told me to conserve battery power by switching everything off, then to get myself sorted and call back in an hour, after I'd checked and rechecked the boat. 'Drink some water,' he added, 'and have some chocolate.'

Good idea. My adrenalin had been fired sky-high by the knock-down; the exhaustion was already hitting me. I needed fuel.

I quickly cleared the floor of the bits and pieces that had pinged about the place, being careful not to slip on the diesel – easier said than done in these conditions. After a few falls, I had everything put away. But I couldn't bring myself to munch on some chocolate just yet thanks to the diesel, which was still making me retch.

I called Dad back. Thank goodness for satellite phones; it was wonderful to be able to talk to Dad now. It was lunchtime back in the UK. Mum was at work and Dad had held off telling her for the moment, at least until he had all the latest information from me, so he could give her the full picture. He knew it could have been much worse and I could hear the relief in his voice.

I was still flying when dawn came, although the pace was less drastic, under 20 knots. Now I could really take a good look round. I hoped I wouldn't find anything too serious.

As I did so, I tried to take some pictures of the current sea state for the folks back home. They really didn't do it justice. It was simply impossible to capture the waves' sheer power and size in a photo.

I searched the boat from top to bottom, dreading what faults I might yet find. Amazingly, apart from three significant problems, she appeared to be in absolutely perfect condition. The first problem was that the lazy jack line had come away and had managed to wrap itself tightly round the main halyard (the rope used to raise and lower the mainsail). The lazy jacks form a cradle of lines which help guide the mainsail on to the boom when it's lowered – pretty essential for solo sailors. This meant my mainsail was stuck with three reefs, leaving me drastically underpowered. I'd be in danger of being swamped by fast waves, which would now constantly overtake me.

Damn. To fix that, I'd have to climb the mast – a real high-risk operation. I didn't fancy being bounced around 30 feet or so above the boat in these seas. It would have to wait until the conditions improved.

Another pressing matter was the 20 litres of diesel that had poured from one of my spare tanks. It had turned the floor into an ice rink. I grabbed some cloths and mopped it up as best I could. The diesel fumes were overpowering, but eventually the worst of it was gone.

Finally, my battery chargers were frazzled, temporarily at least. These cost £1,000 to replace. It was just bad luck that they were on the side of the boat that tipped towards the water, meaning they were both hit by the bilge water.

I took stock. I was at least six days' hard sailing from Hobart, Tasmania, the nearest place I could put in for repairs. My body ached; my hands were sore and blistered from the seawater and from holding on so tight; but I was dry and warm, if exhausted. When had I last slept? I couldn't remember. My neck was taut with stress and apprehension as we hit wave after wave in the lumpy ocean, all the while surfing along at up to 20 knots. *Thump* went the bow, *thump . . . thump . . . thump*. It was like being inside a huge bass drum being constantly walloped with a baseball bat. How long was I going to have to endure this? What else was still to come?

Plenty. The Southern Ocean wasn't finished with me yet.

35

The Tough Get Going

It was time for the tough to get going, as it was mast-climb day. The seas were still pretty wild but I needed to fix the lazy jacks that had snapped three quarters of the way up the mast after I'd been knocked down. That meant I only had a tiny amount of my total sail area available – brilliant if I was sailing in 55 knots but not so great in a more typical 18 knots.

I got everything ready, checked and rechecked all my gear for the climb, and put on my helmet and body armour. Then I called home. Dad quickly double-checked everything with me.

'Be careful, mate,' he said. 'Talk to you when you get back down. I'll be right by the phone. Love you lots.'

'Love you too.'

I set off, up and away. As soon as my feet left the ground I was slammed against the mast – the first bruise of many. The sea was still pretty dicey but I had no choice, these repairs couldn't wait. I stopped for a quick rest at the first spreader. I looked around at the sea and couldn't see any nasty surprises headed my way so I climbed on. Twenty minutes later I was 40 feet above the deck, beside the broken lazy jacks, and covered in bruises, despite my armour.

The sea continued to throw me at the mast as I wrestled with the lazy jacks. I looked down in wonder at her. She was moving so quickly and I could see the autopilot working really, really hard in the fast and lumpy seas. I tried not to think about what might happen to me if she was hit by another rogue.

But this was no time to enjoy the view, especially as I hated heights, and I cracked on with the job in hand. I untangled the lazy jacks, set up a new line and, job done, started my descent.

Going down was much harder and took a lot longer. Every few seconds the boat jerked and *bang* I'd slam into the mast, another bruise to add to the collection. As I descended the climbing harness became more and more uncomfortable; it chafed everywhere. I sang a few random songs at the top of my voice to take my mind off the pain.

Thirty minutes later my foot touched the deck and I whipped off the climbing harness.

Elated that I'd ticked off this kingsize box, I rang home to let Dad know that it was all done and dusted. Again I heard the relief in his voice; it was as if he'd been holding his breath and could finally breathe again. Mum had spent the past forty minutes cleaning the house to try to stop thinking about what her crazy son was up to deep in the Southern Atlantic.

As ever, we kept the calls as brief as possible as the comms on the boat were costing us £2,000 a month. It's pretty difficult to pay bills like these when you're unemployed. Dad had tried so hard to get the comms sponsored and he was still trying desperately.

I celebrated with a quick chocolate feast and by hoisting the main all the way up from fourth reef to the top. She went up as smooth as anything. It was wonderful to see her up there, nice and happy, and, of course, to be moving as fast as the waves we were sailing over once again.

My eyes snapped open. Most of the time I didn't remember my dreams, if I dreamed at all, but this time I did. I'd been at home in Potters Bar, with my friends and family. I quickly forced those thoughts away as the boat was broaching pretty spectacularly. It was as if I'd been running along and someone had suddenly grabbed me by the scruff of the neck and pulled me back.

By the time I'd dashed outside, the boat had virtually turned round and was pointing towards the 25-knot wind. Something was dragging her back. Trying to keep my balance, I grabbed the guide rail and looked over the side.

My heart skipped a beat. I'd sailed over an enormous 10-inch-thick rope. It looked like a never-ending serpent as it weaved in the water behind me over the next set of swells, further than I could see. It was caught round the keel, which is shaped like a double-sided hook, so the chances of it coming loose were minimal. The rope, probably a towline for supertankers, weighed tonnes and was holding me fast. I'd never make it to Australia as long as it was strangling my keel.

I was stumped. I couldn't believe it. I'd seen and expected to see lots of flotsam and jetsam near land, but not out here. Totally at a loss, I didn't have a solution. I shuddered at the terrifying thought of diving in and trying to saw it free with my tiny hacksaw; I was in Antarctic waters, being tossed about by a lumpy sea. All I could do was furl away the solent before it was torn and the boat came to a complete standstill.

Feeling desperately thirsty, I went inside for a bottle of water. I took a long swig and then shut my eyes.

'Please, please, make the rope go away,' I prayed.

I stepped back on deck. The boat suddenly lurched forward, causing me to stagger. Suddenly, she took off downwind again. I ran to the side. The rope had dropped off the keel.

I stared after it in wide-eyed disbelief as it drifted away on its never-ending journey round the world. I didn't dare breathe until I was certain that the entire length had passed beneath the boat.

Massive waves of relief swept through me. I'd had a lucky escape. Imagine what might have happened if I'd been up the mast when the boat had hit the rope.

Inspired, I set to repairing the engine, which had been overheating. I needed the engine to drive the ballast pump. About an hour later I'd managed to use the water maker and a separate water pump to push seawater through the engine to keep it cool.

I followed this with a huge and very thorough tidy up. I was delighted to discover that the only thing I'd lost in the chaos of the knockdown was one fork! I had a couple of spares so that was no problem at all.

Afterwards I sat down, totally exhausted, and took stock again. I was emotionally and physically drained but I'd come through a storm in the Southern Ocean and the girl had bounced back from a knockdown like it was nothing. I looked at the wild and huge rolling waves with a newfound confidence, and smiled.

It was now the end of March, my fifth month of the trip. If everything had gone to plan I would've been on my last leg by now, approaching the south coast of England. This trip was turning out to be a lot tougher than anyone had expected.

'Yes, this is tough,' I thought, 'but I am tougher.'

A few hours later the boat was happily zipping along in 24-knot winds. I'd filled the aft ballast tank so the bow would sit high in the water and she charged along, cutting through the waves with a real sense of purpose.

I'd finished cleaning at the forepeak and had started to crawl back into the main cabin area when the boat suddenly went very quiet. The music stopped and the general hum of the electrics faded.

'Uh-oh.'

I looked about me. Every item in the nav area had simultaneously gone dead, including the autopilot.

Then it suddenly clicked. 'Idiot!' I scolded myself as I realized that I'd knocked off the main domestic breaker switch. I ran back, switched it on, ran back again to the cockpit to position the tiller dead centre, then set the pilot back up again. Two minutes later all was calm and it seemed like nothing had happened.

I took the helm for most of the day and just took in the

incredible seascape. It was grey and desolate but I found it quite beautiful and powerful. There was something about it that made my heart soar.

I was standing in the cockpit, contemplating this amazing world I was in, when I heard a bit of a commotion at the bow.

'What the—?'

A huge albatross suddenly lifted straight out of the water right in front of me. She must have been sleeping – what a rude awakening! She wasn't at all happy. She ignored my apologies and flew for the horizon as if her life depended on it.

I ducked back in to check my emails. Mike Broughton had written: 'A low-pressure system has formed to the northwest of you heading SSE, so the wind is set to increase quite considerably over the next 24 hours. You're going to have to face some more strong northerlies.'

Here we go again!

It was exhilarating and terrifying all at once. Every now and again the moon broke through the clouds and lit up the great untamed beasts, and little old me hurtling down them in my tiny boat, which reminded me that speed was my friend. I rode the log flume for at least six hours straight, my heart and stomach in my mouth for most of it. There was no time to speculate about rogue waves or be thankful for my dry-suit. The boat loved every moment and flew over the surface without a backwards glance, sending water everywhere. My hands were raw and my palms turned to slippery white mush from grabbing the handholds in an effort not to get washed overboard.

After the worst of the front finally passed through I was able to have a rest. When I came back out on deck I was pleased to see that two magnificent albatrosses had joined me.

The following twenty-four hours proved to be a typical Southern Ocean day: wind, rain and never-ending greyness. I had the genoa in and out and in and out as the wind dropped off for a few hours. The albatrosses kept on whirling overhead;

they seemed completely oblivious to all the commotion below them.

Once things calmed down a bit I started to have a bit of a tidy up. I was rearranging some of my gear in the cabin when I stumbled across a packet of chocolate digestives. I sat down and devoured the lot in one sitting. I'd bought them in Cape Town and had forgotten all about them. This unexpected discovery lifted my spirits no end – not that they really needed lifting – and it suddenly hit me just how long ago Cape Town was. It felt like I had left just a few days earlier, but when I checked the calendar I was amazed to see that since leaving South Africa I had been at sea for four weeks and had already sailed 7,000 miles.

I was so proud of my boat. She had taken everything the Southern Ocean could throw at her and each time she had simply shaken her deck free of water and plunged straight on. To me, she was more than just an Open 50; she was a good friend, someone I could read very well.

After a few more calls back home, Dad and I agreed it would be a good idea to put in to Hobart. I was really hoping to continue without stopping, but as I was so close and as I had a few fairly serious repairs that needed doing it was best to do them now. I could probably have managed without stopping but I think it was best to stop and sort them out before I started off on the longest landless stretch of my journey, across the Pacific Ocean.

Ever since the knockdown, I hadn't been able to use my generator to charge my batteries. Luckily I could still charge them using the engine and solar panels, so this wasn't too bad, but it was best to have all these sources operational, just in case. One of the other problems was that the bonding had come away from the rudder bearing/sleeve that had been repaired in Cape Town. Fixing it was simply a matter of sticking it back together. The third and final job was to repair the broken clutch on the ballast pump. I was able to fill the ballast without a pump but it was so much better to have it as it made filling the tanks so much easier.

Dad and I reckoned that these repairs shouldn't take longer than forty-eight hours. But then we'd reckoned the whole trip would take just four months.

As it turned out, my decision to stop in Hobart proved to be a life-changing experience.

36

There and Back Again

The wind fell away as I approached Tasmania, forcing me to put back my arrival time. I didn't mind at all, as it was just so beautiful. The sun was setting over the mountains and the thin, high clouds that sat above them were tinged with gold while lower, thicker clouds glowed a deep pink. The light was just incredible; it had a whole other quality like nothing I'd ever seen before. As I entered Storm Bay on the south side of the island, I could see lush valleys full of green trees. The water was lit up pink, gold and blue.

'What a welcome,' I thought as I sailed up the Derwent River.

I had 8 knots of breeze on a close reach when I saw the lights of Hobart, a large bright cluster. As I looked at them, I noticed that the lights seemed to be moving; in fact Hobart seemed to be heading straight towards me! It was then that I realized that the mass of lights belonged to an enormous cruise ship, which quickly motored past.

Once the floating city had powered by, the Derwent fell quiet as the night drew in. I stayed on deck the whole time, enjoying the most peaceful and relaxing sailing I'd had so far. I could just make out the shore on either side and, in the distance, the real lights of Hobart. I felt a surge of pride and exhilaration. I'd sailed the Southern Ocean; I'd won my long-dreamed-of battle to face all it could throw at me. I was triumphant, thrilled. Blasting across those seas was something I would never, ever forget.

A small boat from the Royal Yacht Club of Tasmania came out to meet me when I was about halfway up the river. Dad was on board, waving like mad. Practically the first thing I heard was: 'Hello there! Got any spare fuel?' They'd come out without filling their fuel tanks and were running on empty. I happily gave them one of my jerry cans of diesel. They thoroughly deserved it for coming out so late to meet me.

Once we were within port limits, Dad jumped on board (to achieve the solo part of my record the rules said I couldn't allow anyone on board unless I was inside port limits). I finally got that longed-for hug and we chatted non-stop all the way up the rest of the river. Dad had arrived four days earlier, with a little help from Richard Branson, who'd heard about my adventure after he got back from his failed attempt to break the record for the fastest crossing of the Atlantic in a single-hulled vessel. His team had helped Dad out with the flight and even got him into first class!

As usual, Dad had taken care of the onshore logistics, everything from getting me a visa to finding us a hotel, from talking to customs to contacting all the people who would help with the repairs. In fact it was often difficult for me to get a word in: Dad's phone was always ringing because he had so much to arrange.

We arrived at the marina a couple of hours later. I took down the sails and, with the help of a rib, we dodged our way through the moorings and berthed easily. Customs, who had been on standby all night waiting for me, boarded the boat and did all the paperwork pretty quickly, although they were a little concerned about my vacuum-packed dried beef, which had apparently been treated rather differently from the way their regulations require. In the end we agreed that instead of going to all the trouble of removing it, it would be made 'temporarily inaccessible' during my stay, and they 'sealed' the packs with their very own special yellow tape.

Also waiting for me, even though it was after one a.m., was Don McIntyre, a real adventurer, an Antarctic explorer and one of

Australia's most experienced sailors, having competed in the 1990 BOC Challenge Single-Handed Around the World Yacht Race, coming second in Class. In 2007 he'd become the first person to fly a gyro-copter round Australia. I liked his style! He'd emailed Dad when he heard I was coming to Hobart and asked if there was anything he could do to help.

Don greeted me with a powerful handshake and a hearty 'Hiya, mate, welcome to Tazzie!' We hit it off straight away.

As soon as we'd said our hellos and had a good chat with Don, Dad and I rushed off to the hotel, salivating at the thought of a good steak. But by then it was half one and of course the kitchen didn't run on Mike time, so I had to settle for a few slices of pizza from a takeaway shop, which turned out to be the best BBQ pizza I'd ever had.

I grinned. I'd just sailed over 7,000 miles from South Africa and here I was wolfing down BBQ pizza from a late-night fast-food restaurant! 'My glamorous life as a round-the-world sailor continues,' I thought to myself.

After four hours' sleep at the hotel I was wide awake and set for the day. I jumped in the shower and savoured the novelty of 'hot rain'. I marvelled at my body, which was covered in bruises of all shapes, sizes and colours. It was amazing. I simply hadn't realized just how much I'd been knocked about.

Dad had done it again. When we arrived at the marina the following morning, a mechanic for the engine and ballast pump, an electrician for the chargers and an engineer – plus Don and a few extra helping hands for the rudder – were all ready and raring to go. I climbed into the water in my Musto dry-suit where I bobbed about and guided the rudder out to prevent any stress on the lower bearing. We'd filled the ballast tanks on one side so the boat tilted enough for me to get underneath. I hadn't dropped the rudder in the water before and was interested to see that it was really very buoyant. I actually had to force it right down into the water (with the help of an anchor chain) to free it. It then just popped up to the surface where it was quickly pulled out by Don and his mates onshore.

The steel sleeve at the top of the shaft was repaired and bonded back on in the evening by a fantastic and brilliant guy called Maurice Crawford, a very experienced carbon engineer. I was so grateful for his speedy and precise work.

By the end of the day, the charging system was back up and running, the engine and ballast pump was fixed and the rudder had been bonded.

'Now that's what I call a very, very productive day, for sure!'

The fact that the following day was a Sunday didn't dissuade anyone from coming to help us, and Don and I got the rudder back in. I also took the chance to do some washing and turned my hotel room into a launderette. Every available space was taken up with drying clothes.

One of my laptops, which had worked perfectly all the way across the Southern Ocean, had gone haywire as soon as I arrived in Hobart and refused to work any more. That meant more time and money, as we had to find a tough sea-going laptop and then install and configure all the necessary software.

Money was becoming a real issue for us. Dad was still arguing with the boat charterers. We'd only chartered the boat for seven months and we were just coming into the seventh. They wanted a lot more money, money we simply didn't have. We felt that they'd given us a boat that wasn't exactly 100 per cent shipshape – the autopilot had malfunctioned right at the start and the bearings should have been better maintained. These were the problems that had led to the very lengthy delays that kept pushing my schedule further and further back. The charterers disagreed, and the discussions were starting to get pretty heated.

Dad and I took a couple of hours off to take a trip up Mount Wellington, the 5,000ft peak that rises above Hobart. We arrived at the top on the first day of winter and the ground was covered in ice and snow. We slid our way from the car park down to the viewing point where, once the cloud broke, we had a spectacular view over the city. I could clearly see the Derwent River; I hoped I'd be sailing out of it very soon. A few minutes later we were frozen and tried to make our way back to the hire car, but this proved pretty impossible as the ice seemed determined to foil our attempts to get back uphill. Eventually, freezing and with dripping noses, we made it to the car and clambered in gratefully.

Now that I was in Australia I was able to have a long chat with Beckie. She was distraught when I told her about the knockdown. It was awful. I wasn't there to hug or comfort her, I was just this crackly voice on the end of a distant telephone – not exactly the ideal boyfriend. Thanks to faulty equipment I'd been away for far longer than planned. I should have been nearly home by now, about to hold her in my arms, but here I was, still half a world away.

These delays were hard on both of us, and although we would still speak on the phone regularly, our relationship would change from being boyfriend/girlfriend to friends.

I wanted to get home more than ever now.

Dad had to head back to UK about five days after I arrived; he was chasing work and had picked up a couple of jobs. Of course I was sorry to see him go but the repairs had gone magically and I was ready to head off as well.

Don and his wife Margie came to see me off as I sailed out of Storm Bay with 10 knots of wind, which made for pretty graceful sailing, although once I was a bit further out the wind increased to 25 knots.

I was still grinning from ear to ear 15 miles later when I ducked my head into the aft compartment to have a check on the rudder bearing.

'Oh no!'

It was full of water, something you don't ever want to see. I grabbed a bucket and bailed out as fast as I could. I crouched down and studied the bearing. I couldn't believe it! Water was pouring over the lower bearing and into the boat.

I was furious. I knew I had to turn round but I could barely stomach the thought. After a couple of minutes I calmed down, phoned the marina, spun the boat round and headed straight back. I'd had a lucky escape, I told myself. I was about to head across the Southern Ocean again, south of New Zealand on my way to Cape Horn. If this problem had happened when I was hundreds of miles from land during a good old blow, I would have been in real trouble.

It was with some relief, then, that I sailed back up the Derwent River, a beautiful place and made for perfect sailing; there was something about the light there that charmed me. It was dark by the time I was back at the marina and Don and Margie were there, waiting to commiserate.

'Tough luck, mate,' Don said. 'Let's have a look.'

We removed the top cap over the bearing.

'It isn't aligned correctly,' Don said. 'Stay with us tonight and we'll sort it in the morning.'

This voyage was proving to be a real test of my emotional strength. The stress caused by the malfunctions was the hardest thing of all. It was these that kept me away for longer than I needed to be from my friends and family, from Beckie.

It was also getting quite late in the year to try to round Cape Horn. It was nearing midwinter in the southern hemisphere and the Horn's low 56-degree latitude meant I would face an increased risk of encountering some very nasty weather. A storm with 100mph winds had just hit the Cape.

My other option was to sail via the Panama Canal, which was arguably the safer option. Having said that, going via Panama would mean sailing through some very tricky weather and negotiating the very busy sea traffic near the canal would be extremely tough using sail only, especially in an area famous for its light winds.

It was agonizing, having to wait while a specially machined bearing travelled halfway across the world to get to me. Don told me not to worry, that he'd overcome a fair few setbacks in his time, and he inspired me to do the same with his attitude. He was right, of course, and although it was a struggle to cope with the fact that I should have been home by now, I had to be patient and get on with the job in hand.

I stayed with Don and Margie while I was waiting for the bearing. They were a fabulous couple, a real double act; they did absolutely everything together. They were so much fun and turned every day into an adventure. Bizarrely, they had a pet rabbit that was totally crazy and had the run of their house.

During my stay with these adventurers, I had a look round Don's aircraft hangar, which was in his huge backyard. It was full of all sorts of weird and wonderful toys, including rally cars, boats, a micro-light and a hut that Don and Margie had lived in for a year in Antarctica. It was incredible.

I was poking around when I noticed a particularly attractive-looking boat. I asked Don about her at dinner.

'She's a beauty, isn't she?' he replied with some pride.

She was a replica of a traditional eighteenth-century open whale hunting boat, 25 feet long with a beam of just over 6 feet. Don was planning to take her on the adventure of a lifetime, a journey he'd spent more than twenty years dreaming about: a replication of the extraordinary odyssey Captain Bligh and his crew completed following the infamous mutiny led by Fletcher Christian on HMS *Bounty* on 28 April 1789. Along with Ernest Shackleton's 800-mile Antarctic voyage in the *James Caird*, Bligh's 4,000-mile, forty-seven-day journey is regarded as the greatest open boat journey in history. Don wanted to replicate it as precisely as possible, with little food, no charts or toilet paper, and only the limited navigation implements that were available to Bligh, including an eighteenth-century octant and sextant and two pocket watches.

'We'll start the adventure on the same day at the same time and in the same place 221 years after the original mutiny journey, in April 2010,' he told me.

Don's plan was to sail to Tofua where he would catch fish, gather a supply of fruit and coconuts, and top up his small supply of 28 gallons of water with rainwater. He would then head westwards through the Fiji and the Vanuatu Island groups, bound for the Queensland coast, to land, like Bligh, on Restoration Island. Then he planned to sail north inside the Great Barrier Reef to Thursday Island, and then through the Torres Strait to Kupang and Timor. If successful, this would be the first time anyone had sailed the same course in the same way Bligh had.

'We'll have no torches, no iPods, no books, nothing like that,' Don told me, 'and we'll set off with the same weight of food and water that Bligh had.'

Don's planned menu was quite shocking:

Breakfast: ships biscuits 110g, 1 litre water
Lunch: nuts 50g, fruit 50g
Dinner: ships biscuits 100g, beef 85g, 1 litre water

So much has been written about Bligh and his journey but debates about the experience continue today, and there are still many unanswered questions. Don thought that by following in Bligh's wake exactly he would gain the finest insight yet into this astonishing open boat journey, in the process raising a small fortune for research into motor neurone disease. There was something very special, he told me, about putting yourself into situations that once inspired you as a child, or had left you in awe of the experience of others. I agreed.

He said he was still looking for three crew members to join him. Don didn't suggest that I should join up but a seed had definitely been planted in my mind! At the time I still had over half my round-the-world journey to complete, so I decided to think about it once I'd successfully completed that.

The next day I found myself on a small plane flying to Mooloolab near Brisbane. 'As we've got to wait a week for the bearing,' Don had asked me, 'why don't we go and see some good mates of mine?' The 'mates' in question were Jessica Watson and her family. Could there be any more sailing coincidences? First Zac, then Saito, now sixteen-year-old Jessica who was also hoping to become the world's youngest non-stop circumnavigator. Her trip was still in the planning stages and Don was helping her realize her dream by kitting out his boat for her.

I thought the Watsons were an amazing family. I was right behind Jessica's project, which was a totally different kind of round-the-world trip to mine. She was going to sail in a smaller, slower boat and I told her that was going to be mentally tough on her, but I was really, really impressed by her attitude. I had every confidence that she was going to get out there and live her dream, just like me.

As I was halfway through my trip, I was able to give Jessica and her family some useful advice on getting to the start line. At that stage they knew very little about the preparations involved, how to generate media interest and attract sponsors, and I was delighted to be able to pass on what I'd learned from my own experiences.

We also took Jessica's boat out for a sail. After sailing an Open 50 for so long, her 34-foot boat felt like a toy with its tiny winches, strings (ropes) and handkerchiefs (sails). Don and I had a great day's sail with her, though, and I was really impressed by her positive 'go-for-it' attitude.

On the fourth day we had to catch the plane back to Tasmania, so I wished Jessica good luck one more time and my thoughts returned to my own adventure.

I could hardly sit still the day the bearing was due to arrive; I was overjoyed when it appeared very early in the morning – fantastic! Don and I raced down to the boat, dropped the rudder and gave it a good test.

'Seems fine to me, mate. Looks like you're ready for the off.'

'Yes!'

It was now May, and time was getting short. I still had a massive distance to cover and it was with no little relief that

I left Hobart in the sunshine and with a good breeze that filled the sails. God, I'd missed sailing the girl so very much.

Then the alarms started. The autopilot! It was throwing out alarms for no wind, despite there being a good breeze. I called home, and Dad spoke to the AP company. I had to return: the pilot processor was broken. Dad ordered a new one but we wouldn't have it for at least twenty-four hours.

I had to force myself to get up, drop the sails and spin the boat back round. Of all the rotten luck! I'd been in and out of Storm Bay twice! I was pretty miffed, but at least I knew that this problem could be fixed. I did wonder whether I was going to discover any more problems the next time I tried to leave, but hey, I decided to let the frustration go. You can only worry so much, and setbacks are part of the adventure. Even so, as much as I liked Hobart, I really, really couldn't stomach any more delays.

37

Zoom, Zoom, Zoom!

Once the processor had arrived and been successfully fitted, Don and Margie filled the boat with fresh food for the third time, including a pair of roast chickens which I was looking forward to munching very much indeed.

I was completely indebted to Don and Margie. What a pair of stars they'd proved to be. I really hoped I'd sail with Don on one of his adventures one day.

For now, though, all I wanted to do was clear the Derwent River and start racking up some serious mileage. This proved to be quite tricky, as both the river and Storm Bay were almost windless. Eventually a 5-knot breeze helped me along, and as I started to clear the bay, the wind picked up to 25 knots. The sea was getting really choppy now, waves coming at the boat from my least favourite angle – on the nose – and I made the decision to reef.

I had soon passed the magnificent Cape Raoul, a set of wild, jagged and sheer 300-metre-high cliffs at the southeastern tip of Tasmania, and when I finally bore away downwind, boy, did we move! It was as if the accelerator had been pressed flat on the floor as the boat took off at 14 to 15 knots in 30 knots of breeze. I grinned, pleased to see the girl doing what she did best.

I put in another reef. Up until then the sea had been giving me a pretty rough ride, but it finally started to flatten as I pulled further away from land. The boat raced through the night at 13 knots until the wind dropped away a little in the morning, by which time I was feeling pretty seasick. I'd been looking forward to those chickens so much and now my sea legs had deserted me. Still, a couple of days and they should return.

Before leaving, I'd had a long phone conversation with Mike Broughton. 'Best to go north over New Zealand,' he'd advised me, 'as the weather window for going under doesn't look at all good. There's a very nasty low-pressure system sat just waiting to eat you up.' Once I'd passed New Zealand's North Island I'd be able to make my way leisurely back down to the 40-degree line of latitude, in readiness to round Cape Horn. For now, I looked forward to experiencing some warmer weather as I sailed further north.

By the next morning I'd made great progress and the boat was really romping across the Tasman Sea, occasionally surfing at 20-plus knots. It had become really gusty but the boat just accelerated out of each gust as it came through. It was a terrific feeling – proper sailing! Just the kind the girl had been built for.

My already high spirits soared when my appetite returned. I quickly polished off the first of my fresh chickens. I was just picking the bones that evening when the radar sounded an alert. There were ten boats on the radar. I looked to the horizon and sure enough I could see a couple of lights in the distance.

They turned out to be fishing boats. I hadn't expected to see any out here in the middle of the Tasman. 'No sleep for me then,' I thought. I was going to have to keep watch all night to make sure I didn't sail too close.

The following morning, yawning constantly, I checked the log. I was delighted to see that I'd travelled 300 miles in twenty-four hours (this was a point-to-point measurement and didn't take into account all the twists and turns I'd made, so I had in fact sailed even further). I took great delight in measuring the distance on my chart.

Now that the fishing boats were finally out of radar range, I wondered whether I'd be able to get away with a quick snooze. The problem was, we were still rocketing along at 20 knots in what was proving to be a very wet and wild ride. Tonnes of spray rained down on the coach roof.

Suddenly a strong 38-knot gust picked us up. Any thoughts of sleep were instantly forgotten as the boat shot down a wave at well over 20 knots. The bow started to dig into the back of the next wave, losing a bit of speed, and next thing I knew tonnes of water rushed up the deck towards the cockpit and filled it up. I flung myself up on to my beanbag, lifting my boots in the air to keep them dry. Suddenly I was surrounded by rushing, foaming water, and then, as quickly as it had arrived, it drained away, leaving the cockpit empty once more. The boat resumed her surfing as if nothing had happened.

Once my heart had slowed down, I cooked myself a large serving of porridge. 'Not bad,' I thought. 'A few more raisins needed, perhaps.'

I managed a short nap after breakfast but it wasn't easy settling back into the routine yet again, especially in such exciting conditions. I was sailing incredibly fast but everything was under complete control. The boat seemed to be really happy in these conditions: when 40-knot gusts hit she just leapt up playfully and charged right ahead. My crossing of the Tasman turned out to be one of the fastest on record for my boat-type; at this stage I was maintaining a 300 miles plus per twenty-four hours average.

On my next boat inspection I spotted a new old problem. I put my ear to the starboard rudder and could just hear a slight grinding sound. I could now tell whenever there was an odd sound on the boat; I knew her so well and could feel even the slightest difference. Sometimes I'd pause, just stop dead, during a phone conversation with Dad because I could tell something wasn't quite right. Then I'd quickly say 'I'll call you back!' before running off to investigate.

The top bearing had about 2mm of play. I called Dad and he arranged for two new custom parts to be sent from France over to him in the UK and he would then fly with them all the way to New

Zealand. It was the quickest way. The previous time it had taken a week for us to get something from Europe to the southern hemisphere. I really couldn't afford to wait that long this time.

I loved the boat more than anything but I cursed my rotten luck. I'd had the best sailing of my life on this stretch and I really, really wanted it to continue. It was so frustrating to have to stop again, but I had to live with the fact. The one thing I'd learned so far on this trip was that you never had everything under control and sometimes, especially when you're pushing the boundaries, you needed the patience of a saint.

I popped up on deck in the early evening, just as darkness was falling, to have a quick look for any ships. There was a bright white glimmer on the horizon, just below the clouds. I squinted at it for a second and then went to have a look at the radar.

As I reached for the power button on the radar screen, I glanced out the window and suddenly the dumb realization hit me: that was no ship, it was the moon! My first moonrise. I'd never seen one like this before. Its silver light quickly broke the horizon, steadily becoming rounder and brighter. I laughed at my silly mistake, grabbed a chunk of chocolate and a drink and went outside to watch the show.

I looked up. The sky was clear above me, lit by countless stars. As the moon rose, the deck was clearly lit by its silvery light. The feel of the boat moving effortlessly over the water at a graceful 9 knots made the moment even more special. At some point in the night I opened my eyes between naps and could just make out the lights of New Zealand in the distance.

By daybreak I could clearly see land. I prepared to round Cape Reinga, the northwestern tip of New Zealand's North Island. It's a really remote spot, over 100km north of the nearest town. It's known by the Maoris as the point where the spirits of the dead enter the underworld. I could understand how they'd got that idea: it's a desolate but spectacular piece of scenery. The Tasman Sea and the Pacific Ocean meet at Cape Reinga. From the automated lighthouse it's possible to see the two waters clash, creating some pretty turbulent conditions just off the coast.

I avoided this area and gracefully coasted round the island at a leisurely 5 knots. The sun was out and I made the most of it, spending time out on deck doing a spot of reading, just enjoying the day.

I was curled up on the beanbag when I heard an alien noise, a rushing, something I hadn't heard before on this trip. It sounded like an engine. I sat up and looked over the side of the boat, half expecting to see a speedboat of some kind.

And then I saw it. A low-flying twin-prop, heading straight for me.

What was the pilot up to? He eased back on the throttle and performed a perfect U-turn above the boat.

Then my VHF buzzed: 'Come in, this is customs aircraft.'

Nice of them to say hello.

Seeing the plane made me think of Dad, because the aircraft had known where to find me thanks to him. He'd always call ahead and alert customs and the coastguard about what I was up to, where I was headed, what safety equipment I had on board, my telephone number, and so on. He was in the air right at that moment, zooming across the planet to meet me. Although I hated the thought of stopping – I was worried that we'd find something else wrong with the boat once it was moored in the marina – I couldn't wait to see him.

I had one more night before I arrived in Auckland, and as darkness fell I once again spotted the glow of the moon on the horizon. 'Right,' I said, 'time to put my feet up and watch the show.' I treated myself to a hot chocolate and then sat outside on my beanbag in the cockpit, watching the water gleaming in the moonlight.

I grinned as I thought once again just how lucky I was to be there.

Sailing into Auckland Harbour the following morning was impressive to say the least. I passed the spectacular Little Barrier Island, an extinct 4-mile-wide volcano 50 miles to the north of Auckland. The uninhabited island looked like Jurassic Park, entirely green and full of deep ravines.

The spinnaker was up, the sun was out, the boat was sailing a happy 10 knots and I had a wide grin on my face as I sailed into the Hauraki Gulf.

I had arrived almost a day ahead of Dad so he wasn't on hand when I called New Zealand Customs on the VHF. Within a few minutes it was clear to me that they did not understand sailing. I was in squally conditions with 20-knot winds and I asked them if it was OK for a rib to come out and help me in.

They said no.

I asked if someone could come on board to help me berth, as I was on my own.

They said no.

'Then how do you plan to help me in?' I asked.

They wanted me to sail into the harbour on my own. This was impossible as this was a busy shipping port. They then said they'd give me a tug.

'That's a crazy idea,' I said. 'This boat isn't designed to be berthed by a tug; a tug will bring the rig down.'

They called a tug anyway, but the captain sided with me.

By now I was seriously annoyed and couldn't understand why they were being so difficult. My engine wasn't working that well and wasn't really powerful enough anyway; it certainly wouldn't provide me with enough manoeuvrability once I was in the marina. Besides which, they wanted me to head for some horrendous concrete berthing spots surrounded by big steel poles with very little in the way of padding, which was fine for tugs but a total nightmare for me.

'You are creating a dangerous situation here,' I told them. 'Do you seriously want me to go ahead?'

It was then that I spotted the coastguard heading towards me. As soon as I saw them I thought, 'Aha! They look official.' I called customs once more to ask if the coastguard could help me in. They were reluctant but eventually agreed, although they said no one, not even a coastguard officer, was allowed on the boat. But at least they could tie up alongside and manoeuvre me in.

Thank goodness for that!

The coastguard had been listening in on the VHF and had heard everything. They couldn't quite believe it either. They'd also brought a TV crew with them and I did an interview as we cruised in.

We had relatives in New Zealand, and my Great-Aunty Betty and Great-Uncle Graham very kindly put Dad and me up. The following day, as I waited for Dad to arrive, I met up with Derek Hatfield, a Canadian sailor who had sailed his Open 60 to New Zealand after having to pull out of the Vendée Globe. We had something in common in that he'd been knocked down by a rogue wave. He'd been sailing all night long in the wild seas of the Southern Ocean with 40 knots gusting to 55 knots. 'I was exhausted and lying in my bunk when *crash*, the boat went over and I ended up on the ceiling with all sorts of things whizzing past me. The boat came upright immediately, leaving carnage inside.' When he stuck his head out on deck, he saw that two of his spreaders were dangling limp on the shrouds. He knew then that his race was over.

Sailing really is about as extreme a sport as it's possible to get. I thanked my lucky stars that I'd come through exactly the same experience comparatively unscathed. I was so lucky not to have lost my mast.

Then Dad arrived with the spare parts, and after the obligatory rib-crushing hugs we got straight to work. I was in one of the world's premier sailing cities and we had a couple of guys, Alan and Tim, who were Open 50 and Open 60 specialists, so we were in good hands. The boat was lifted out of the water and the bearings were soon cut down to size.

Lots of people came down to say hello and wish me well, and by the end of the day I'd agreed to give a talk about my adventures at a local all-girl secondary school and to show a local group of Sea Scouts round the boat in the evening. When they arrived they were all pretty awed with her, which made me feel extremely proud.

Back at the dock, it took us a good ninety minutes to get everything reattached, the rudder bearings and the steering rods too. Alan and Tim eventually had to head off home but I stayed on a bit later to do a bit more tidying up – the kind that only I could do. By the time I was done she looked immaculate, just the way I liked her.

While we were in New Zealand, Dad and I had time to take a day trip to Rotorua. We drove down in a cousin's ute, a huge truck. Dad had been once before, when he'd backpacked round the world with Mum twenty years earlier. 'There aren't many places I want to go back to,' Dad had said, 'but this is definitely one of them.' Rotorua is famous for its geothermal activity – geysers, bubbling mud-pools and hot thermal springs. For some reason, the mud-pools fascinated Dad. Although I thought they were interesting, I was quite keen to escape their 'rotten eggs' aroma.

It was now the end of May and I couldn't wait to get moving again. Once again, it was terribly painful to say farewell to Dad, who flew back to the UK the day before I left. It was made a little easier by the fact that my stay in New Zealand had been a short one and I knew now that every mile I sailed was a homeward-bound mile.

Of course, I was now about to embark on a huge journey across the world's largest ocean with no land to stop at for thousands of miles if anything else broke on the boat. I couldn't help but feel apprehensive as the rib escorted me out of the harbour under the ever-watchful eyes of the customs officers.

I was still in the harbour setting the sails when the engine started to vibrate like mad. I switched it off, and decided to do without it. It was very weak anyway and I didn't need it, or rather couldn't use it, to get the record, so I kept going.

A helicopter hired by the TV company that was making the film for Channel 4 came to join me as I sailed out into the sea. It performed a series of low sweeps. Soon I was sailing past another beautiful volcanic island, Rangitoto, with its broad, low-lying and perfectly symmetrical cone. I then cruised back past Great Barrier Island and was out into the Pacific, free again.

I picked up the satellite phone and called Dad to let him know that everything was fine. Calls on the second half of the voyage were now being sponsored by Clearpoint Weather which was a big help to the trip's finances and made a huge difference to my life at sea. We would often talk about the future and reminisced over the past.

My mood lifted. I was full of optimism once more as I turned back to the task at hand and thought about warmer weather and the long, smooth swells of the Pacific.

PART FOUR

THE PACIFIC

Days at Sea: 42
Distance Covered: 7,675 nautical miles

Total Days at Sea: 129
Total Distance Covered: 24,375 nautical miles

38

Pacific Storm

My first night out from Auckland was particularly tough and I really struggled with sleep, having to stay alert for ships. There were loads of squalls around too, which didn't help. I couldn't leave the radar on watchman mode as it would instantly react to a squall cloud.

I gradually made my way further out into traffic-free open water and started to feel more relaxed. Once daylight arrived I was able to nap my way through to around ten a.m. I gobbled up my fresh roast chicken for lunch so then I was back on to the freeze-dried stuff again. Yum!

The wind had dropped off by the following morning, leading to some rather frustrating sailing conditions. The swell was knocking what little wind there was out of the sails. Every now and again a little breeze would come along and fill them with 10 knots of wind for ten precious minutes before dying away again.

I took advantage of the calm conditions and spent a good chunk of the afternoon out on the beanbag enjoying the warm sunshine and just taking everything in, watching the world go by, as I loved to do.

Then I was given a good example of the stormy conditions I could expect at this time of year around the Cape. Mike Broughton emailed to warn me that 'A pretty nasty low-pressure system with a secondary low is heading your way.' It had 70 knots of wind, so it looked as though a good old ding-dong was in store. I wasn't going to escape its clutches completely, but with Mike's help I thought I would at least avoid the very worst. Even so, despite a pretty dramatic course change to the northeast, I was still going to see some 40-knot winds in a couple of days' time – which was fine by me. I eagerly awaited the surfing conditions they would bring.

That night I approached Macauley Island, the slanted tip of a million-year-old underwater volcano. I wondered whether I was going to have to tack, but in the end I passed by with a few miles to spare and had a good view of the uninhabited lopsided island as the last of the light faded.

I was completely shattered. Pulling in and out of New Zealand had been pretty stressful and quite rushed. I was finding it difficult to recover after suddenly putting the brakes on in Auckland before once again leaping off into my 24/7 go, go, go routine. So I climbed back into my bunk and napped, and napped, and napped . . .

A few hours later I felt really refreshed, so much so that I decided to have a look at Raoul Island. I'd been looking at the chart when I realized it was kind of on the way to my next waypoint. It looked interesting; I liked its anvil shape. It was one of the biggest of the remote islands in the area, 1,000 miles from New Zealand, but un-inhabited, apart from a handful of scientists. People had lived there – first Polynesians, then Europeans in the mid-nineteenth century – but the island was still a very active volcano and erupted quite a bit, last doing so in 2006, killing one scientist. Earthquakes happened on a daily basis. Raoul is so active because it sits right on the Kermadec Ridge, the boundary of the Pacific and Indo-Australian plates.

I headed a little bit more to the north and the island appeared on the horizon at around midday. It was amazing to see this giant, barren lump of rock loom out of the sea before me. It's a good 5 miles wide so it definitely stuck out. I only came within 5 miles of the shore as there was no way I was going to risk hitting any rocks. I also wanted to make sure I avoided the island's wind shadow.

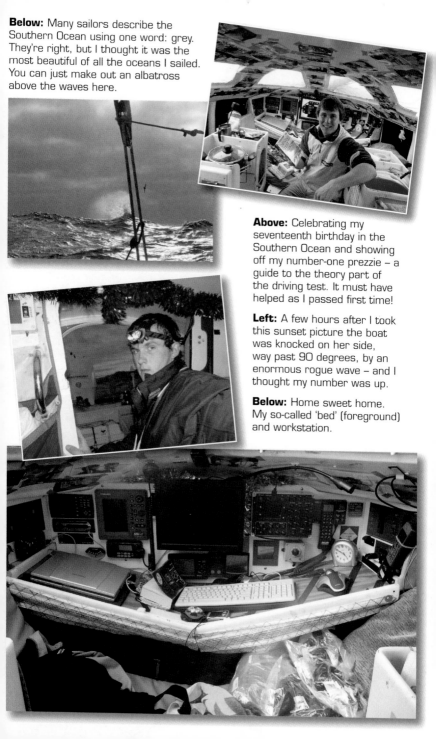

Below: Many sailors describe the Southern Ocean using one word: grey. They're right, but I thought it was the most beautiful of all the oceans I sailed. You can just make out an albatross above the waves here.

Above: Celebrating my seventeenth birthday in the Southern Ocean and showing off my number-one prezzie – a guide to the theory part of the driving test. It must have helped as I passed first time!

Left: A few hours after I took this sunset picture the boat was knocked on her side, way past 90 degrees, by an enormous rogue wave – and I thought my number was up.

Below: Home sweet home. My so-called 'bed' (foreground) and workstation.

Left: The waves of the Southern Ocean: These pics (taken the day after my knockdown) simply don't do justice to the size, power and speed of these incredible beasts, the biggest of which was 50 feet. Surfing them at speeds of up to 26 knots was a truly unforgettable experience!

Bottom: Water on board. A 38-knot gust powered the boat into the back of a wave that filled the cockpit to the brim. I managed to grab a pic just as the water was draining away.

Below: Food bags in the forepeak: I'd start a new one each week. They had to be eaten in numerical order so I'd get the right amount of food to match whichever part of the world I was sailing through and the different energy demands each part presented.

Middle: Nearing Hobart: I'd done it! After forty days, 8,500 miles and a near-death experience, I'd sailed the Southern Ocean.

Bottom: This sunset was one of the most amazing ones I saw.

Above: Aussie adventurer Don McIntyre:
I stayed with Don and Margie in Hobart.
They volunteered their help and were
amazing; we got on so well that I'm even
joining Don on his next adventure. Here,
Don and I are getting to grips with my
steering.

Left: Don and I hopped on a plane
to Mooloolab to see another teen
solo-circumnavigator, sixteen-year-old
Jessica Watson, who was planning to
set off in a few months' time.

Left: Leaving
Hobart: I couldn't
wait to get back out
on the ocean!

Approaching New Zealand: After zooming across the Tasman Sea in spectacular conditions I just wanted to keep going, but more problems with the steering meant I had no choice but to stop.

Rocketing along in the South Pacific.

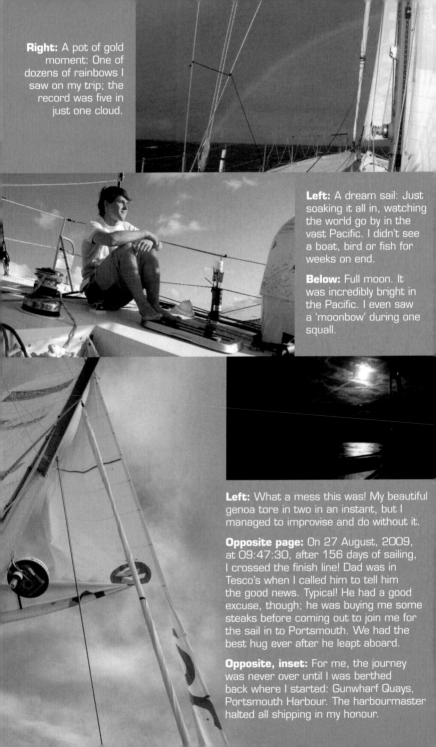

Right: A pot of gold moment: One of dozens of rainbows I saw on my trip; the record was five in just one cloud.

Left: A dream sail: Just soaking it all in, watching the world go by in the vast Pacific. I didn't see a boat, bird or fish for weeks on end.

Below: Full moon. It was incredibly bright in the Pacific. I even saw a 'moonbow' during one squall.

Left: What a mess this was! My beautiful genoa tore in two in an instant, but I managed to improvise and do without it.

Opposite page: On 27 August, 2009, at 09:47:30, after 156 days of sailing, I crossed the finish line! Dad was in Tesco's when I called him to tell him the good news. Typical! He had a good excuse, though; he was buying me some steaks before coming out to join me for the sail in to Portsmouth. We had the best hug ever after he leapt aboard.

Opposite, inset: For me, the journey was never over until I was berthed back where I started: Gunwharf Quays, Portsmouth Harbour. The harbourmaster halted all shipping in my honour.

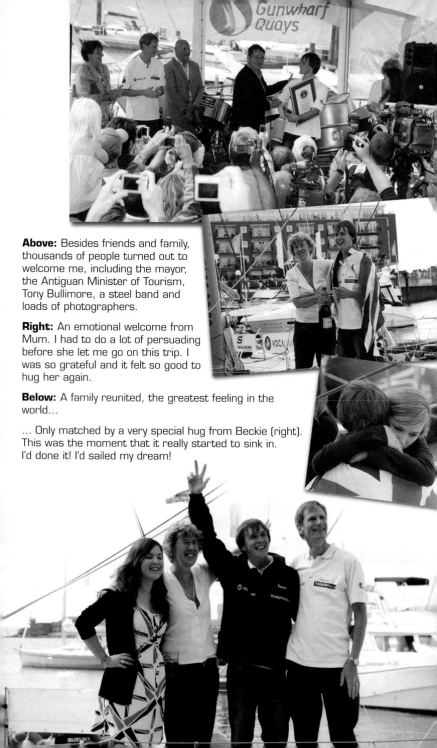

Above: Besides friends and family, thousands of people turned out to welcome me, including the mayor, the Antiguan Minister of Tourism, Tony Bullimore, a steel band and loads of photographers.

Right: An emotional welcome from Mum. I had to do a lot of persuading before she let me go on this trip. I was so grateful and it felt so good to hug her again.

Below: A family reunited, the greatest feeling in the world…

… Only matched by a very special hug from Beckie (right). This was the moment that it really started to sink in. I'd done it! I'd sailed my dream!

I thought of Dad and imagined what he'd say if he was here with me. Probably something like 'Yep, that's another lump of rock all right.'

I grinned.

Once I was past Raoul, I was over the Kermadec Trench, one of the world's deepest oceanic trenches. The water here is an unimaginable 10km deep. It was certainly the deepest water I'd ever sailed over and it amazes me to think that no human has ever ventured down that far to find out what creatures might live at that depth. Also below me were hundreds of active underwater volcanoes, enormous mountain peaks of the Kermadec Ridge, some of which were only 120 metres below sea level.

'I hope they're feeling nice and calm,' I thought. 'I wouldn't want to come all this way only to get blown out of the water by some random eruption.'

I carried on northeastwards to about 26 degrees south. I had winds of up to 28 knots to help me on my way, making for some fantastic sailing. Mike Broughton had warned me to expect gusts at over 50 knots so I braced myself for a very wet and wild ride. I was grateful to be avoiding the 70 knots that were blasting the ocean just a few degrees further south. That would have been no fun at all, just a straightforward battle for survival. I was so relieved that I'd managed to get a good bit of rest: I had a long night ahead of me and I was going to have to make a few sail changes to adapt to the increasing wind strength.

I decided to get changed and started to put on my oilies, but then stopped.

'Hang on a minute,' I thought. 'Fifty-knot winds?'

I stuck my head outside the cabin for one last look at the conditions as the light faded. I was pretty sure I could see some very, very dark-looking clouds on the horizon.

'Sod it, I'll bung on the dry-suit.'

This turned out to be a very wise decision.

Fifty-foot waves and 50-knot winds! The swell was huge, the

biggest so far, and I was hand-steering to try to keep the boat under some kind of control in what were incredible sailing conditions. The monstrous waves that reared all around me made the girl feel very tiny indeed. I had no choice but to keep the power on and sail with the wind so that I didn't get caught under any breaking waves. I was back on the never-ending log flume. Dad had been messaging again, having seen my ridiculous 20-plus-knots average, but I didn't have time to answer – my hand needed to be at the helm.

Every now and again the moon shone through the clouds and lit up the wild waves, and little old me surfing down them. The noise was phenomenal. The wind whipped around me and thudded into the sails, the sea raged and boiled, breakers roared, and the boat groaned, rattled and clattered as it plunged onwards.

As the surf of each wave began, the boat edged forward at 14 knots or so and began her descent. As the waves were both long and steep – typical for the Pacific – the bow dropped away and I felt the boat rapidly accelerate. The wave picked the boat up on to an incredible plane now, with only the back third of the boat in the water, and still the speed increased – 15, 16, 17 knots. It was dark and I wondered what was going to happen when we hit the bottom of the wave travelling so fast. We sailed faster and faster – 19, 21, 24 knots! I saw the bottom of the wave approaching and braced myself, hanging on with my aching hands, waiting for the deceleration. I could feel myself lifting up off the deck with the sheer force of speed as the boat dived down fearlessly, without slowing.

'OK, now *this* is nerve-racking!'

By now I was used to the idea that speed was my friend, the faster the better, but this was phenomenal. When the boat caught one 50-foot monster perfectly and roared ahead at an amazing 28 knots, Dad, who was anxiously watching the tracker at home, was so impressed he took a photograph of the screen.

I was having the time of my life. I was scared but I was certain the boat would see me safely through. I don't think I could have survived the night without my amazing dry-suit, which kept me warm and dry in these ridiculous conditions.

At some point during the storm I zipped over the dateline and the time difference between Mikeworld and home started to decrease at last.

The front passed through with dawn. The clouds raced across what was a cold, dark sky. The boat shot on tirelessly. I was exhausted but delighted. Once again I'd been pushed to the limit, right to the edge of what was humanly possible, and I'd sailed through it.

The front continued to ease and I waited another hour before doing a heavy air tack to bring me back to an easterly heading. I waited for the right wave and spun the boat round into the wind and through it, using the momentum I already had from reaching. As I turned the wind changed from one side to the other and we started to head east. Turning like this was much safer than gybing in these heavy conditions and was much better for the boat.

The wind was now blowing 30 knots so I had a good tidy up of the boat before heading below to get some much-needed zeds.

Later, the wind became pretty unstable and gusty with anything between 6 and 29 knots. This made it tricky to pick the right sails. I eventually settled on a full main and solent. This left me a little overpowered in the strong gusts but I was at least able to bear the boat away downwind.

It was now the start of June and I really wanted to keep things moving – as did the boat: she flew, surfing without question down huge waves, ever eastwards. It was sometimes hard for me to believe just how fast I was actually going.

It had been a week since leaving New Zealand, and I definitely needed a good wash.

'OK, here goes nothing.'

I lifted the bucket of seawater over my head and held my breath as I emptied its freezing contents. I shivered as I dried off and got my clothes back on before heading off to hunt for the giant chocolate bar I knew would be in the new food bag – very welcome indeed.

Thanks to a high-pressure ridge making its way across the Tasman Sea I was well and truly beating into the wind, trying to pull as far over to the east as I could. I had the forward and middle ballast tanks filled up so the boat was ploughing heavily through the waves at an impressive 9.5 knots.

Mike Broughton emailed to warn me about a tropical disturbance heading my way. 'It's heading south towards your position and may become a secondary low system but you should be able to route yourself around it by turning north.' Mike had been amazing this whole trip. He'd never put a foot wrong. My odyssey would have been far, far more difficult without his expert knowledge.

As darkness fell, I took advantage of the easier conditions and had a 'chilled' evening, lying down doing a bit of reading, munching my way through the remnants of the giant bar of chocolate. As I lay on the beanbag in the cuddy I looked back and watched the spray hitting the coach roof. I'd become so used to my washing-machine life now, it was normal to look out of my 'bedroom window' and see heavy spray constantly thudding down. I really was having the time of my life. I felt, much like the boat, that I could go on sailing for ever.

I felt a little differently the following day when I was forced to sail upwind in 26 knots of breeze with a lumpy sea. 'Urgh!' I thought as the boat landed with yet another massive slap and we pummelled head-on into the next wave and *slap* she went again. Sailing in these conditions was really unpleasant in this boat thanks to her flat hull. Eventually I decided I couldn't let her suffer any more and eased off the wind by a few more degrees, which gave me a little more speed as well.

The forecast suggested that the wind would continue to back round to the north over the next twenty-four hours, allowing me to open the sails and start heading fully eastwards. This was thanks to that tropical low, and it looked like I was going to clip its edge, giving me winds of 45 knots, so some more exciting conditions were on the way.

As I was sailing into the wind there was next to no ventilation and it got quite stuffy in the cabin. There were no air vents to bring some welcome relief. My little fan was whirring away but it really wasn't helping very much.

'Sod it! I'm going out for some fresh air.'

I put on a CD and sat outside on the edge of the cockpit, taking everything in. It was raining, dark, cold and pretty miserable but I didn't give a damn; it was my home and I loved it. There was nothing like the feeling of the boat moving purposefully across the sea, taking me towards my precious goal, back home to my family and friends. The feeling I got from seeing the water continuously rush past my beautiful boat's hull simply couldn't be beaten. I also loved to watch the dark squalls racing towards me, feeling the wind increase; they brought about a great sense of anticipation.

As one particularly heavy squall rumbled in my direction, I came to a decision.

'Right, time for a freshwater shower.'

I lined up my buckets under the mainsail, stripped off and had a great wash. As I did so I looked up at the sails and thought about how brilliant they'd been. I'd not suffered any serious damage so far.

The ever-changing wind conditions, however, were making me tear my hair out.

'Make up your mind!'

It had been up and down between 15 and 38 knots all morning, forcing me head-on into the walls of steep waves once more. I cracked off the sheets a little and scooted off northeast and this brought some welcome relief, but then the conditions changed again.

'Oh for goodness' sake!'

I was up and down the boat the whole day. As soon as I had

everything set just right, the conditions would change completely. One minute I was over-canvassed, the next I was heeling the wrong way because I had too much ballast in my tanks for a small sail set.

To add to my irritation, one of the windows just above the chart table had started to leak – right where I had my laptop. I had to lay towels over everything so it didn't get totally soaked. I wouldn't be able to reseal the window until it got a bit drier and a lot less rainy.

Finally, by nine p.m. the wind levelled off and I took myself outside with a snack to watch the full moon for a little while. It looked magnificent, so bright, like a giant spotlight. All I could do was think, 'Wow.'

A squall had been shadowing me for a while and it finally clipped me as it passed by, filling the air with a light drizzle. Thanks to the bright moonlight I could see the rain was much heavier about half a mile away. As I gazed across the horizon, just by the squall I saw something that looked like . . . like . . .

Was I seeing things? A full-coloured rainbow at night? Then the moon flashed out from behind the clouds, and my goodness, there it was, a . . . well, I suppose you'd have to call it a moonbow. I'd never even known it was possible. I watched, amazed, until the rain passed and the moonbow slowly faded to nothing. Yet another magical moment on this incredible journey.

Shaking my head in wonder at what I'd just seen, I climbed below and tried to get some sleep. The wind had eased and it remained light and variable, so I thought it'd be safe. I set the pilot to steer off the apparent wind angle so the boat could adjust herself if there were any wind changes while I slept. As soon as I lay down, I was gone.

39

An Unexpected Swim

I opened my eyes. Something was wrong. Something seemed to be pressing down on me; then I was rolling halfway across the cabin in the darkness.

'What on earth?'

We were on our side! We were pinned right over!

My muscles groaned as I sprang up and looked out of the window. The bottom set of mast spreaders were about a foot off the water. I really didn't want them to drop any lower. I thought of Derek Hatfield and the snapped spreader that had ended his dreams. I had to keep mine alive!

The wind had dropped while I was asleep, so much so that the pilot couldn't cope and had decided to take me straight into the wind. This wouldn't have been so bad, but then a sudden squall swooped in with 25 knots of wind. The combination of that, the ballast on the wrong side and the gennaker and main pinned up against the rig put the boat right over on her side.

I quickly threw on my harness and made my way out into the cock-eyed cockpit where I eased off the sheet of the gennaker. This proved trickier than normal as the weird angle of the boat meant the winch was now above my head. I slowly came a bit more upright into a slightly more sane position. After this I bunged on my running backstay and eased out the main until, finally, we were righted. The sails were still flapping so I immediately furled in the gennaker and shot out my solent, which caught the wind and turned me back in the right direction. 'Phew, what a wake-up call!' I thought as she took off downwind.

This is an example of just how dangerous sleeping for even the shortest time can be.

I took a quick look round the boat. There was some water inside but not too much, and a few things had bounced around the cabin, but all looked to be OK.

The deck, on the other hand, was a real mess. In my rush to get the gennaker away as quickly as possible I had bodged it a bit and it was now threatening to half unfurl itself at the top of the sail. If it unfurled in these strong winds it would tear. And this was my favourite downwind sail.

'Stuff it,' I thought, 'I need a quick solution.'

I decided to lower it, even though it was partly unfurled, then shove it down into the sail locker.

'Not the neatest of solutions,' I thought as I went back for the sheets and furling line and stuffed them below, 'but at least she's safe down there.'

Once this was done I sat down with a relieved sigh. I would wait for a calmer day to sort it out.

It was time to eat, but I was at the end of my food bag. I'd eaten all the best stuff first and had left my least favoured options until the end. I checked the galley glumly but I knew exactly what was there: no snacks, just a lonely chicken in unidentifiable red sauce. Bugger.

It was amazing how food could change my mood. I actually felt a little down at this point, but once I'd boiled the kettle and had started to eat I felt quite a bit better and began to think about the delights that would be in my new food bag tomorrow.

I soon had to get back to work as that squall proved to be the start of a chain. I put in a reef and finished tidying the deck. My wonderful boat started trucking along eastwards, just as the horizon gradually lightened, turning the clouds deep blue. I yawned. I'd had little more than two hours' sleep overnight.

Then the wind steadily backed round to the south and really started to pick up speed, climbing to a brisk 30 knots. 'That's odd,' I thought, 'I'm sure I was supposed to be getting gentle 10-knot winds from the north.' Still, I wasn't complaining as these unexpected winds really helped me make brilliant progress through the day.

The next morning I woke up with great excitement – my one hundredth day at sea! I was now almost two thirds of the way round the world. Hurrah!

My smile froze.

'What on earth?'

I was travelling backwards! The bow was pointing the right way but with the wind so light and on the nose she was sailing backwards at 0.7 knots.

I went and finished off what had become a three-point-turn. I started to make headway at around 1.5 knots, which wasn't terribly spectacular but much better than going in reverse.

The wind slowly filled in, and after a few squalls rushed by, presenting me with a series of wonderful rainbows, it moved round to the south. Now that's what I'd been waiting for! I cracked off the sheets and the boat sped away at 9 knots.

The weather remained really unpredictable and very localized, nothing like the predictions had suggested. I spent a lot of time trying to read the sky – after all, what was going on up there affected me directly down here – but it wasn't much help.

That evening there was another amazing cloudless sunset. The whole sky turned orange, then pink, then red – another one of nature's amazing displays. I'd now seen a hundred sea sunsets and every single one of them had been different. Some, like this one, had been joyful explosions of colour, others had been cold, grey and full of foreboding. I found all of them beautiful in their own way; each had stirred strong emotions in me. Whenever I could, I'd sit and watch them and think how lucky I was to be there, how much I was enjoying myself.

Every sunset signified the passing of yet another successful day at sea, that I'd overcome everything that had been thrown at me, which gave me the confidence to face whatever challenges would come next. After all, I had nowhere to run, no one to turn to. That was the thing about Mikeworld: it had a population of one; I was completely self-reliant. Some people might see this responsibility as a heavy burden, but it was something I treasured. I thought it gave me the ultimate freedom.

I was now sailing through a large area of the South Pacific that was full of small uncharted reefs, so I had to be careful. Although I was expecting them to lie much deeper than my 4-metre keel, they were always changing and growing so there was always the chance that some would be unexpectedly shallow. The main reason I wanted to avoid sailing over them was that they would lead to some unpleasant sea conditions with possible breaking waves.

These reefs would take two days to cross, and I had to base my route on the wind direction, which was still proving to be most unreliable. I'd had everything from northwesterlies to south-easterlies, ranging from 0 to 25 knots.

A big part of me would have loved to stop and explore this tropical area. Although I hadn't seen any yet, it was full of magical little islands that were barely more than reefs, just small crescents of sand with a dash of vegetation. It was also home to Mangareva, a once lush island that had been turned into desert by over-enthusiastic logging by its inhabitants – a small warning to humans as a whole.

'Perhaps in a cruising boat one day,' I mused.

The front that had been messing me around finally decided to move eastwards, giving me some steadier northwest conditions, which allowed me to make around 9 knots ENE. A couple of 30-knot gusts got my pulse racing – the boat accelerated out of them with the greatest of ease; she always seemed to handle everything with a good solid stride – but they quickly ran out of breath.

By morning I was cruising along slowly, pleased to see I had just three reefs left to clear. Once I was free of them I'd be able to relax a little and get some rest. If the boat was doing about 11 to 12 knots and a wind shift came through while I was sleeping, I could hit one of these reefs in no time at all. I was going to come pretty close to two of them, so I had an interesting time ahead of me.

After my hundredth sunset, the days had started to blur. It was really hard to tell them apart. With my jobs on the boat up to date I took the chance to unpack and raise the gennaker I'd packed away so quickly. It was great to see her flying once more.

After making sure I was totally happy with everything above decks I made my way inside for a good chat with Mum and Dad. It was their silver wedding anniversary and they'd just had a party at home with friends and family. I love them so much. They are such an incredible pair, a genuine match made in heaven. I can only hope for happiness like theirs in my own life. I felt these emotions keenly in the moments after I'd put down the phone. Sailing round the world on my own was all very well, but it sometimes made for a lonely existence.

I cooked up some breakfast – porridge with sultanas – and put my feet up for a little while, chilling out with bowl in hand, drink on the side and book in front of me. Soon I was almost totally becalmed, crawling along at 1 or 2 knots. It felt as though life had slowed right down.

When the wind altered course slightly, I decided to gybe to try to squeeze another tenth of a knot from my sails. As I did so, I saw that the fluffy white clouds that had been sitting still for hours were starting to move away – a sign of increasing winds. Sure enough, it suddenly picked up to a beautiful 8 knots.

I was just on my way back to the gennaker when the rope, which I'd only partially fastened, slipped from the deck and dropped over the bow. I dashed forward but it was too late. It passed under the boat and wrapped itself around one of my stern rudders.

'Oh crap!'

The steering suddenly became very sticky, and the pilot started to struggle.

I spent a frantic fifteen minutes trying to hook the line off where it was caught under the rudder but it just wouldn't budge, so I had to cut the rope at the clew of the sail and furl away the sail using the other rope to keep the tension on.

I couldn't have a flagging sail – that leads to tears or damage to the rig.

I cut the line and it fell into the water, floated under the boat, and got wrapped around my other rudder! Luck really wasn't going my way. It should have just floated due aft and hung behind the boat, making it easier to untangle the other end of the rope, but no, it had decided to somehow drift off 20 feet to the left before wrapping itself around my port rudder. My rudders were now literally tied up in knots.

I leaned over the aft and looked down at the rudders. They had started to make some weird noises. They were clearly straining against the rope, and damage was a real possibility. I tried using my deck brush to push the line down off the rudder but it was jammed on pretty tightly. I then managed to persuade the boat to sail backwards. I dashed back to see if it had loosened them at all. No good. I set up some lines to try to pull the rope from the bow, but it wouldn't budge. Next, I grabbed my anchor chain, fastened it to the tangled mess and dropped it to see if its weight would pull the rope off the rudder, but no, it was here to stay.

I pulled in my anchor chain and collapsed on deck, exhausted. All of my efforts had probably made it worse: all the yanking, pulling and pushing had tightened and jammed the mess in further. I tried to move the rudders but they weren't having it. I was pretty much at the mercy of wind and sea now.

There was only one option: jump in.

I had to go over the side with a sharp knife, swim underneath and cut the rope entangled around my rudders. And if I was going to do it, then it had to be now. The conditions were just right. For the moment the wind was light and I was sailing very slowly upwind in calm seas. Also, I only had an hour or so of daylight left. I couldn't afford to leave it overnight, nor could I risk going overboard in the dark.

For the first time since the knockdown, I was terrified.

Leaving the boat was my worst nightmare. Of course I'd tie myself on to the boat, but if the rope got caught and broke . . . well, the thought of watching my boat sail on without me gave me quite a chill. Then there was the possibility that a wave or a change in wind direction would throw the 5-tonne boat unexpectedly at my head, knocking me out or killing me instantly.

I pushed these thoughts aside. It was now or never, and never didn't bear thinking about. I simply didn't have a choice. That would teach me not to moan when things got quiet. You forget how lucky you are.

I stripped down to my shorts and found two knives. I kept one in my hand and, in case I dropped it, fastened the other to my leg. I put on my harness, tied the other end to the backstay bolt, checked both bolt and rope several times, took a deep breath and slipped over the side into the cold water.

I hated the feeling of seawater on my eyes but I forced them open. No wonder I hadn't been able to free the rope: it was jammed in much worse than I'd imagined, having managed to slot itself into the tiny gap between the skeg (the fin-shaped extension on the underside of the boat which was supposed to stop this sort of thing from happening) and rudder. I could see that the rope was firmly pinched and held in place.

I grabbed a good lungful of air before sticking my head below again. The water was clear and free of wildlife. I tried not to think about what might be swimming about below me and focused on my urgent task.

I'm a strong swimmer so I had no problem keeping myself in a good position by the rudders. I'd had to switch off the pilot while I

MIKE PERHAM

was in the water, so I moved the rudders myself to keep me in a very slow upwind position, doing around 1.5 knots. Of course I could only make slight adjustments to the rudders thanks to the rope I was trying to cut away. I was really worried that the boat would get shoved back by a large wave and would pitch into my head, knocking me cold.

I spent about thirty seconds at a time trying both to cut the rope away and get it out of its pinched position. My arms were soon pretty tired and were being chafed quite horribly by the rudders. They were red and raw in no time, and I was soon covered in sticky antifoul as well.

After twenty minutes I was exhausted but still hadn't finished. Every time I pushed my head above water to take another breath I was conscious it was getting dark. I pushed the cold, fatigue and fear out of my mind and redoubled my efforts.

Finally, after forty minutes, the lines were free.

As the sun set, I dragged myself out of the ocean and back on to the boat. I climbed into the cabin, switched on the AP and checked my course. As it all came to life, I collapsed. I was shaking with fatigue and adrenalin. My arms were sore and covered in bruises and were in agony after all the hanging on and cutting I'd done. The antifoul paint stung my skin. My hands were covered in cuts from where the skeg and the knife had caught me as I sawed away.

I cried with relief. That had been about as tough as it could get, and I'd done it. I'd made it. I looked at the sunset as I shivered. Another major challenge had been overcome. I wondered how many more I'd have to face before I got home.

It took a few minutes for me to stop shaking and calm down, then I vigorously soaped all the muck off. Afterwards I put on some warm clothes and cooked up some chicken curry, even though I still didn't feel particularly hungry. As soon as the first mouthful passed my lips I was suddenly ravenous, and after wolfing it down I followed it with a superhuman portion of Toblerone.

I climbed out on deck with my chocolate and star-gazed,

listening to the water rush by below; I preferred it to music now, it was the soundtrack to my life. Suddenly, a huge shooting star flashed across the sky. About half a dozen more followed in quick succession. A while later I set my alarms and tried to get some sleep.

40

That's Torn It

I awoke and bolted upright. I slept like a dog, one ear always open; the slightest change woke me up. I looked at my clock: six a.m. The boat wasn't behaving as she should.

'She's tacking!'

I dived for the helm but I was too late. With the sails pinned right up against the rig and all three ballast tanks full on the wrong side, down she went.

I fought my way into the obscenely angled cockpit and began my now well-practised routine of easing off the sheets and adjusting the backstays until we came up. I bore her away off the wind and we started plodding along SW, on the wrong tack and not even sailing close to the wind. I tidied up a bit, made a few adjustments with the ballast, then tacked her back over on to starboard, just as the wind increased to 26 knots and we shot off across the waves.

The increased wind speed meant that the time had come to furl away the genoa and replace it with the solent, especially as the forecast was for it to blow a little harder later on that day. I had got about four turns round the furler when I noticed a 2-inch hole a couple of feet from the foot of the sail.

'Where the hell did that come from?'

Was it something to do with the unplanned tack?

I immediately bore away to get the genoa as sheltered as possible behind the main. Then, with a loud *rrr-rrr-rrrriiiip*, the whole genoa tore in two in an instant.

I stared at it, dumbfounded. 'Bummer.'

This was, of course, a huge understatement. I was shocked to the core. The most beautiful of all my sails was in tatters. I watched aghast as it flapped against the main.

My next thought was that there was a danger the genoa could rip completely off the head at any second which would cause the sail to drop in the water, and I didn't want to run the risk of getting it wrapped around my keel or rudders. I certainly didn't want to have to get back in the water again. It was beyond repair, completely in tatters. I cut one of the sheets off with a safety knife I always had strapped up against the mast and made the other sheet ready to be released quickly. If it fell in the water I'd have to dump it.

However, after a few moments and no change it looked as if it was going to stay attached at the top – and this presented its own array of problems. Now it was a matter of containing it and sorting it out in such a way that it would be safe. Easier said than done! At one point it became caught around the spreaders and I dread to think what would have happened if it had separated from the head of the sail and dragged in the water still attached to the spreaders. It could well have brought the rig down.

In the end I managed to wrap the sail around the forestay using my spare spinnaker halyard to hold it in tight. It wasn't exactly the prettiest of solutions but at least it wasn't flapping everywhere and causing a danger to the rig.

I collapsed on to my beanbag and reflected on this disaster. The tiny hole must have developed when I was pinned down against the water. At the time I thought it was incredible that such a small thing had totally written off the whole sail. It felt pretty darn bad and I was quite upset, but looking back, I saw it was just another hurdle I'd overcome.

We later found out that the reason for the tear was the sun's UV rays, which had made the sails brittle. They had all come with a protective covering that kept the sun off for four months but this had now worn away. When the sailmakers heard about this they told Dad they were surprised they hadn't torn sooner. We'd done the right thing having them made stronger than normal.

Once I'd tidied up a bit more I got out the solent, came up to wind and started to head eastwards. I'd lost 25 miles to the west during the excitement, but hey, that's life. I raised the solent and emptied out a little ballast, and soon I was doing the same speed I would have done with the genoa. 'Excellent!' I thought, pretty pleased with my efforts, and I ploughed onwards over the ocean.

The winds held all day and within twenty-four hours I pulled off a 200-mile run, which I was pretty happy about. I crossed off the mileage on the chart and ticked the day's box with a flourish.

Then exhaustion hit me again. Two hours' sleep out of twenty-four just ain't enough. I dragged out my beanbag, laid it out in the cockpit, got some mellow music going and gazed up at the stars.

By now I was so far north across the Pacific, thanks to the 70-knot low-pressure storm I'd been avoiding, it kind of made what was a tough decision a little easier. I was heading for Panama instead of Cape Horn. There was no denying that winter was in full swing in the Southern Ocean and with the reduced daylight hours and much fiercer storms that were already raging, well, you'd have to be mad to try it then. Some people thought I was mad to be doing this at all, but I wasn't that mad! The only problem was, I needed to get my skates on otherwise I'd end up surrounded by hurricanes once I made it through the canal and into the Caribbean Sea.

I was gutted. I wanted to sail round Cape Horn, the Cape of Capes. I had dreamed of rounding it before I left, then sailing up the Atlantic side of South America before moving on to the home stretch. But it wasn't to be. Actually, what I'd dreamed about most was facing and conquering the Southern Ocean – its huge swells, its raging power, the unrelenting winds, the greyness and the isolation – and I was proud to be able to say that I'd experienced all that it tried to throw at me and I'd well and truly ticked that box.

I looked towards the South. Despite its greyness and its loneliness, I thought it was the most beautiful place on earth. Had I fallen in love with the South? Yes, I think I had. I knew I'd be back one day. There's unfinished business . . .

But now it was time to head northeast, to Panama, and the many unexpected challenges that would bring.

41

The Panamanian Way

The next day was a very special one indeed.

'HAPPY FATHER'S DAY, DAD!'

'Thank you, Mike!'

'None of this would have been possible without your love and support, that's for sure,' I told him as we chatted. He'd worked so hard to get me here; Dad was the engine that had powered my dream into reality. My calls to him were just the best ever. I knew I could always be entirely straight with him.

'Sorry I haven't sent a card,' I added, 'but I'm not sure where the local newsagent's is, or the nearest post box.'

'You could use airmail.'

'Or a carrier pigeon.'

'A paper plane . . .'

'I know! A message in a bottle!'

In the end I wrote 'Happy Father's Day' on my arm, took a picture and sent it by email.

I'd just cleared an area of high pressure, and the new winds made for much more comfortable sailing. Unfortunately, the stronger winds that had been forecast failed to materialize, but still the boat ploughed on, beating into a few metres of sea, with the forward ballast nicely pumped up which held the boat fast and stopped her bouncing and slamming over every single wave. I loved how I was able to alter her trim and stability. I had so many options. I could set her up nicely to punch through waves if we were sailing upwind, or if we were sailing downwind I could set her up so that she surfed down the fronts of waves with her bow in the air.

I had about fifty books on board, some of which had been given to me by friends and family. Some of these covered some serious, heavy subjects and were pretty awful. I much prefer adventure-style stories by Clive Cussler, who has written some great sea-based action epics.

That afternoon I was once again out on the beanbag in the cockpit, enjoying *The Sacred Stone*, when the boat suddenly punched her way through a wave in such a way that a few gallons of water came cascading over the coach roof straight into the cockpit, soaking both me and the book! Deciding to finish what this wave had started, I put the book down to dry, stripped off and had a very spur-of-the-moment shower. I grabbed my trusty bottle of saltwater shampoo, showered off using a couple of buckets of seawater, then finished off with a litre of fresh water to get the salt off my body. I dried off by once again sitting on the beanbag in the cockpit in the beautiful sunshine.

That evening's sunset was especially spectacular. The fireworks only really started about five minutes after the sun passed the horizon. The whole sky turned orange and pink. And I mean the whole sky. There was hardly any blue anywhere. Both the ocean and the boat turned light pink. It felt like I was sailing across some alien planet. It didn't last for long, but it was stunning to see. The boat was gracefully heading along upwind at 9 knots in a good 16-knot breeze at the time, so it was a pretty special moment.

I was closing rapidly on the equator now, just two days away. I couldn't wait to get this major box ticked. But the heat, the heat! The sea gleamed and glittered with a headache-inducing intensity. The bright white sails filled the boat with reflected sunlight. When I crossed the black painted section of my foredeck in my bare feet I gasped at how hot it was, like walking over a frying pan.

It's all too easy to forget that heat can be just as dangerous as the cold. When everything was permanently damp in the Southern Ocean, the skin on my hands became spongy and was always coming off in pieces. With the heat, my hands had started to become dry and extremely flaky. I spent more and more time outside, as it was just getting so hot on board. I had to take great care that I didn't get heatstroke. I didn't want my sore back to return. Fortunately, at midday, my large mainsail put the whole back end of the boat in the shade. I was incredibly grateful when a scattering of clouds moved in, giving me a little more shade, but they eventually shrank away and evaporated into thin air under the sun's fierce midday glare.

I'd begun a routine of having a shower on the foredeck every morning and every evening, but without rain to wash the boat, a good layer of salt had again built up. Soon it was impossible to touch anything that wasn't totally covered with the stuff. I would have loved it if a rain cloud had passed by, but there were none on the horizon.

I checked my water maker. I was drinking between 4 and 5 litres a day. This kept me going just nicely and I wanted to make sure I wasn't going to have any problems. I was the proud owner of a pretty powerful Sunshine Maritime Katadyn Desalinator. I'd usually run it for thirty minutes each day, during which time it produced 10 litres of drinking water. I didn't always need it all but I liked to run it every day so there was no chance of it clogging up. In case of emergency, I had a spare survivor hand-operated water maker in my grab bag (my 'abandon ship' bag) as well as 60 litres of emergency water kept in jerry cans lashed up underneath the cockpit.

I was out on deck performing my checks when a wave leapt over the side and jumped straight into my boots.

'Aw no! Dammit!'

As I squelched around the boat, I was reminded of the times when Dad and I would hunt down the biggest puddles we could find and then jump in them. In no time we'd be having great fun kicking water over each other. We'd always end up squelching our way home.

Normally I'd be pretty cheesed off if I got my boots wet while sailing – they'd got soaked not long after leaving Cape Town and hadn't dried out until I put them on a radiator in Hobart; luckily I had two spare pairs – but not now. They dried out quickly, along with all my other damp gear, once I put them in the sun.

That done, I relaxed on the beanbag as the sun finally set – another spectacular show. It was perfectly clear on the horizon, a glowing red ball that sank quickly and was gone. Soon the brilliant stars were twinkling away. I loved the time between sunset and the moment when the moon appeared over the horizon, as the stars and shooting stars were at their brightest then. I'd stop whatever I was doing and become conscious of the boat's smooth movement through the longer gentle swells of the Pacific. There was no slamming, just a feeling of a grand, majestic power as the boat ploughed steadily onwards, eating up mile after mile.

With the solent, I wasn't quite as powered up as I would have been with my lost genoa, but by emptying a little ballast it was possible to keep the boat speed high while keeping her on an even keel. I was delighted that losing the genoa had only slowed me down a fraction.

That night passed by very sedately, although I was shaken awake the following morning by a huge squall with a slow but ever-changing wind, forcing me to helm for an hour or so. The boat did a few crazy pirouettes as the wind shifted from one direction to the other, blowing between 1 and 5 knots.

I'd now been sailing for three weeks since Auckland and I was pleased to see that I was closing in on the Galapagos Islands, although they were still two and a half weeks away. My plan was to head north of the Galapagos before turning towards Panama Bay. I knew from my research that sailing there could be very tricky with very little wind at times and loads and loads of seriously busy shipping lanes. I really hoped I'd be blessed with a nice fresh breeze that would see me in safely.

In many ways sailing through Panama was going to be more challenging than trying to round Cape Horn. In a way, all that was required to get round the Horn was to weather the storms and keep sailing far enough out from the coast so you didn't hit any rocks. By coming to Panama I was going to face a whole heap of technical challenges thanks to the unpredictable weather and the masses of ships all battling to get through the canal, not to mention the sleep deprivation. There was no way I was going to get any rest whatsoever during the last forty-eight hours in. My biggest fear was being left with next to no wind in one of the busiest shipping areas in the world.

For now, though, the next big box to be ticked remained crossing the equator, and I was definitely going to make sure I didn't sleep through it this time!

It was the beginning of a new week, so I opened a new food bag, but this latest one smelled pretty weird. I rummaged around inside and discovered a tiny slit in the bottom through which seawater had managed to get in. This wasn't so bad as the food was in vacuum-sealed bags, but it was annoying as all the packets smelled intensely of diesel. I washed them with soap and water but they retained this peculiarly strong smell.

I always saw something different every day, even out on the open ocean where one day could be much like another. Very often the 'something new' came in the form of clouds. That particular evening, a really strange set of clouds appeared in the distance and travelled towards me. One had a base that was close to sea level but its peak was hundreds of feet above me. It looked very other-worldly, and as the sun set it took on a pink hue and reminded me of those pictures you see of giant gas clouds in space that are light-years away.

Another cloud passed right by my stern, its low base rising gradually off the surface of the ocean, raining steadily as it did so. The moisture twisted in the updraft as the cloud climbed upwards and I thought it might form a waterspout, but it seemed to decide against it and passed by peacefully.

Another cloud passed by with five separate rainbows. 'Now that's just showing off!' I thought.

I constantly read the sky. I knew that some clouds would have no wind on their far side while others were flying along, ready to punch me right on the nose. I did my best to avoid these if I could, but more often than not I wasn't able to do much to get out of the way – the weather tended to move much faster than I did!

I crossed the equator earlier than expected, before dawn, just like the last time, except for one very important difference: I was awake! It felt great to be back in the northern hemisphere; the knowledge that I was on 'home turf' again was a real boost. I toasted Neptune with a bottle of champagne – some for him, some for my wonderful boat, and a sip for me. I also presented Neptune with my day's ration of chocolate: a whole packet of chocolate digestives, an Aero and a Mars bar. Now I had just one champagne bottle left, and I was saving that for a *very* special occasion.

Mike Broughton had come up with a cunning plan for me to skirt just south of the Doldrums and use the southeasterlies that head into them to propel me eastwards. I hadn't thought of this tactical option before. I'd imagined I would be tacking along down at 10 degrees south or so before coming up for the final few miles into Panama, which sits right at the edge of the Doldrums.

The temperature inside the cabin was getting crazy, so I decided to move my bed outdoors to the cockpit. I crawled into the forepeak and grabbed my spare beanbag. I just about had a spare everything – everything but the kitchen sink. I'd made sure I brought an extra beanbag because losing it would have been a real blow. I practically lived on the thing! I wedged my second beanbag alongside the first, and *voilà*, I had a bed in the cockpit, and a pretty darn comfortable one at that. I laid a towel on top, grabbed a cushion, and got myself a nice bit of R and R with a book in hand in the shade of the mainsail. Lovely.

After a calm night the wind picked up a bit – but so did the current. It was very interesting to see the difference between the boat speed from the logs at the back of the boat and the speed over ground coming through from the GPS, which was also linked into the pilot. The boat speed was registered at 10.5 knots while ground speed was only reading 8.3 knots, so I was sailing with a lovely 2.2 knots of equatorial current on my nose. 'But hey, that's OK,' I thought. The current may have been slowing me down for now, but once I was on the other side of Panama and through the Caribbean I knew I'd be able to hook up with the Gulf Stream and make the most of that to shoot me back home.

Home! It still seemed so far away. I had quite a way to go before I could think about the Gulf Stream. 'Let's cross Panama off the list first,' I thought, and focused on just that.

These slow conditions were pretty trying but I knew I'd get there in the end. All it required was patience and the desire to squeeze every last tenth of a knot out of my boat in whatever conditions I had.

Cruising boats that made this trip from New Zealand or Australia used their engines during light conditions to make good progress, but I wasn't about to use mine to push me even one nautical mile around the planet (my engine had stopped working when I left New Zealand anyway). I did use the engine for berthing in marinas, just because it was safer, but I always made sure that when I left I sailed back across my track to meet all the requirements of sailing round the world. After all, it was manpower and wind power alone; using my engine just wasn't on. No one can say they've 'sailed' the world unless they genuinely haven't used an engine to do it.

I glanced at the horizon and noticed something small in the distance, right on the edge of my vision. I grabbed my binoculars, and yes, sure enough, there it was, the mast of a fishing boat. So there *was* other life out here then! It had sometimes felt as if I were the only object on the Pacific. I hadn't seen a single boat since leaving Auckland. I hadn't even had a boat pop up on my AIS, and that picked up ships over 100 miles away in gentle conditions like this. I couldn't remember the last time I'd seen a bird, fish or dolphin either. I always kept an eye out for any sea life and was really surprised by the lack of it in the Pacific. In the Atlantic I saw dolphins pretty much every other day, and birds were always following me. I really looked forward to getting on the other side of Panama; I knew I'd find plenty of dolphins and sea turtles in the Caribbean.

Weirdly, the fishing boat was doing pretty much the same speed and heading in the same direction as me, and it stayed 3 miles off my port bow for the whole afternoon. As evening approached it put on a little more speed and started heading east, around 2.5 knots faster than me. I watched as it left my radar screen and wondered whether the crew had become annoyed with this tall orange mast hanging around behind them. My boat certainly stood out!

42

Going Yo-Yo

Well, this was a first. After breakfast I sat on the chart table seat and thought, 'Oh, gee, what to do now?'

I'd never found myself thinking that before. There just weren't any jobs for me to do. No sails to change, nothing. There was simply nothing for me to do for the first time since leaving Portsmouth all that time ago, back in November.

This didn't last for long, however. I soon found myself greatly amused by a packet of four yo-yos I uncovered during some rummaging and tidying. The yo-yos did their job and travelled down to earth as the string played out behind them. The only trouble was getting them to travel back up the string again. That part didn't seem to work so well.

'Sod it, I'm calling home.'

I rang Mum and Dad and it was great, as usual, to hear all their news. They'd just been to a friends' twenty-fifth wedding anniversary BBQ in a thunderstorm (typical English summer). They'd returned home to find themselves in the midst of a power cut and were sitting in candlelight.

I loved hearing little bits of information from home – after all, I could hardly switch on the TV to get the day's news, or pick up a paper from the local newsagent's. It was mainly just snippets of what had been happening here and there that I liked to hear about most. It was great to be kept in the loop as it's very easy to feel a long way out of it when you're in the middle of nowhere. Mum would send me news snippets from the BBC so I was able to keep up with some of the goings-on in our crazy world.

After finding the yo-yos, I stumbled across a packet of ten party balloons. I blew up around half a dozen of them and had a great time whacking them around the cabin – being careful not to let any get outside and fly away – before popping them one by one. Soon the floor was littered with dead balloons. 'But hey, who cares?' I thought. 'Any excuse for a party!'

This was followed by a 'Hawaiian Day'. For some reason, Fiona had packed a grass skirt into one of my bags; in fact she'd given me loads of weird and wonderful odds and ends to keep me amused. When I saw the grass skirt, I thought 'Why the hell not?' and did a little dance for the cameras.

Some solo sailors find the extended isolation difficult to manage, particularly when the conditions are quiet. This is quite understandable as humans aren't used to living alone. At home we depend on one another for our day-to-day existence and can't survive without one another's help. Think about how little you are on your own, especially during the day. Few people are alone for longer than a few hours at a time, above all teenagers. I'm extremely sociable and love having lots of friends, going out and sharing experiences with them. I need their company, love, companionship and sympathy.

Although I sometimes felt lonely, I never felt the urge to talk to myself to keep myself company, to distract my mind, to occupy thoughts. I loved the incredible feeling of freedom my adventure gave me. I loved the majesty of the ocean, the fact that it was unchangeable. Man had tamed the land but not the sea, which looked the same now as it had done when Captain Cook sailed to Australia, and when Joshua Slocum, Sir Francis Chichester and Sir Robin Knox-Johnston sailed the world.

Of course, the knowledge that I could speak to whoever I wanted via the satellite phone (even though we'd been struggling to pay the bills for most of the trip) was a massive help, as was the fact that I had Mike Broughton on my side. I couldn't imagine having to sail round the world without his forecasts, perhaps sailing into a dead calm and being stuck for weeks. Certainly my happiness was very much related to my boat's forward progress. As long as we were moving in the right direction I knew I'd get home sooner or later, and that was the main thing.

In the meantime I was loving the journey, every wave, every cloud, every sunset, every storm and every moonbow. I had witnessed and faced everything on my own, from my first blow to a raging Southern Ocean storm, from going over the side to a torn sail. I had sailed over enormous waves, waves most sailors never get to experience in their lifetimes. And I had done all this on my own, with no one to offer me words of advice or encouragement until after the event, when I called home and told Dad about whatever I'd faced that day. I had been put to the test and I'd not only overcome each experience, I'd loved each and every moment. So it was extremely hard to stay gloomy aboard my boat, no matter what happened. Every day I had a grin on my face at some point.

Crossing the Atlantic when I was fourteen had taught me a great deal, but I had already experienced so much more on this trip. I was exactly the same Mike as the one who left Portsmouth back in November, but since then I'd been pushed beyond what I thought was possible and as a result I was definitely growing in confidence.

I estimated that I still had about a week of sailing before arriving in Panama, depending on how the weather behaved itself. Studying my route, it looked like I was going to have an interesting time of it, especially during the last couple of days. Panama sits bang on the Doldrums and the bay can be notoriously fickle, with no wind at all at one moment and with lots of squalls of up to 40 knots the next.

Dad had been busy arranging everything in Panama for my arrival and transit so I was hoping for a quick passage through. I had no repairs that needed doing, I just wanted to get the torn genoa untied and stored below, as I had to admit it wasn't the most cosmetically beautiful touch. I'm a tidy teenager and the little bits of sailcloth flapping about here and there really didn't look that good to me!

The following day I was treated to some gorgeous sailing by way of a very small tropical low that was forming in the Doldrums. I had wonderful 20-knot reaching conditions and the boat powered happily along at a fantastic 12 to 13 knots all day. There was no swell to speak of and with only a 2-metre chop the boat was in sailing heaven. She felt so very solid as she powered forward, passing smoothly over the waves without slowing a fraction. Once she was powered up with ballast she didn't get moved about at all, thanks also to her wide base. It's a very different feel to a standard sailing boat, which always rolls from side to side. The joys of sailing a 50ft surfboard!

I was even spared the burning sun as clouds rolled in and I was able to enjoy moving around the boat in just my shorts. It wasn't perfect, though: the humidity was still there and it still felt so very hot, with little easing of the temperature at night. Even a 20-knot breeze failed to bring much relief.

After another fantastic day's run, the wind began to drop off slightly as the sun neared the horizon and the boat slowed to 9 knots. I was still delighted with my progress through the Doldrums. I was only 650 miles away from Panama as the crow flew, but I guessed that I would end up sailing around 750 miles to get there. As ever, sailing in a straight line wasn't the quickest way to get to my destination. I was still heading east but I needed to stay south for as long as possible before peeling off north, almost straight up to Panama. This way I'd stay in the good winds for longer and would be able to make the most of the current.

I'd just finished looking at the charts and came out on deck when I saw, just 10 feet away, a large fishing buoy with a flagpole attached.

'Yikes!'

This was a typical marker for something like a lobster pot, which should have been tethered just a short distance offshore. It had obviously escaped and drifted all the way out here.

The moment I saw it I immediately thought that one of its trailing lines would wrap around my keel, which was nothing less than a perfect hook. I watched anxiously as we sailed straight past at 11 knots. The buoy stayed just where it was, thank goodness, and I watched it bob away into the distance and out of sight.

The sheer amount of random gear I'd seen floating out on the ocean was crazy. The ocean really is full of junk in places. Apart from several more mooring buoys, I also spotted countless random plastic bottles and small bits of rubbish just floating about – all over the world, but nowhere worse than in the run-up to Panama.

I was having a dream run, with no pressure on the boat or myself. I was experiencing the kind of glorious conditions sailors dream of, being able to lounge about and take a back seat while the boat sailed itself, in this case cruising at 9 knots with 17 knots of wind on the beam, even though there was a 2-knot current against her.

That evening I adopted an incredibly comfortable position on my beanbag in the cockpit and read my book until it got too dark. As I put my book down, I squirmed down into the beanbag even more – a total couch potato type of slouch – and gazed up at the night sky and the moon directly above. I could see everything from galaxies to shooting stars with crystal clarity. That night there were quite a few wisps of low cloud about. As they passed by the moon they were lit up beautifully, only to be completely blacked out into nothing the moment they left the area of brightness.

The new day brought with it another new food bag. Now that I was two thirds of the way round the world I'd really mastered preparing rehydrated food. The packets had a line to indicate the level to which you were supposed to pour the water, but in my experience this was rarely placed correctly. It had taken me much careful experimenting to get it right, because too much water and you ended up with a gloopy soup, too little and you ended up eating clumps of dry powder. And it was different for every meal: some required more water than others.

And some of the meals were much better than others. There was a spicy mince and rice affair that just did not work at all and I couldn't bring myself to eat those until I'd reached the end of the food bag and there was no alternative. Different parts of this particular meal rehydrated at different speeds; some ingredients just didn't want to rehydrate at all. So, for example, in between the soft mince and rice I'd sometimes bite down on a rock-hard pea. There was also a mild beef curry which was just dreadful; I struggled to get that down even when I was starving. But for the most part the food was excellent. It wasn't exactly home cooking but I really did enjoy it – which was pretty important as I needed to consume at least 4,000 calories per day.

I'd been on a starboard tack for so long that it felt quite odd switching to port once I tacked from the east to the north for the run into Panama. A few hours after doing this, at three a.m., I was lying on my beanbag catching some zeds when I saw a flash of light in the sky. This was followed by a good rumble just a few seconds later.

Uh-oh.

I got up and saw, as the grey clouds were lit by another bolt of lightning, that a rain-filled squall was heading straight for me. This was the first of a seemingly never-ending sequence. Every twenty minutes the wind rose to 26 knots before dropping down to a tiny 4 knots, sending me scurrying all over the boat. She needed lots of attention in these conditions.

I hated it when the wind fell off, causing the mainsail to lose its shape. It whacked back and forth in the swell until the wind filled it in again. It's a horrible sound and it made me cringe thinking of the chafe on the sail. If the wind had stayed light then I'd've adjusted a few things and made the sail much more taut to reduce the chafe. Unfortunately, because these light periods lasted for only a few minutes there was nothing I could do. By the time I'd have trimmed the sail, the wind would have leapt to 26 knots again and I'd need to open it up once more. I just had to grimace and bear it.

I managed to perform quite a few pirouettes as well, as the wind swung round 360 degrees on a few occasions.

The thunder, lightning and rain stayed with me until the following evening, when everything finally started to die away. Although I was shattered I was really excited by the time I'd passed through all the squalls because a check on the charts revealed I only had 360 miles to go to Panama. I started dreaming of fresh steaks and hot showers.

By the next day, steaks and hot showers seemed further away. 'Patience, patience, Mike,' I told myself.

This part of the world was making for some very frustrating sailing. I'd spun slowly round a couple more times as the wind once again turned through 360 degrees twice in short succession, before drifting through the night. This was followed by another very slow day. I whooped for joy when the boat hit a dizzying but short-lived 4 knots.

It was extremely tricky with the wind directly behind and me gybing on the wind shifts. The sails really struggled to stay filled. The small swell just knocked all the air out of them. I trimmed the main so that my gennaker stayed much fuller and took over as the real pulling force.

Besides all the tricky sailing, it didn't help that the temperatures were creeping higher and higher. The cabin was up to a pretty unbearable 42 degrees, while the outside air temperature was 39 degrees. Boiling the kettle for lunch wasn't fun at all, as it turned the insufferably stuffy cabin into a sauna. I had nowhere to run to cool off and I could only take so many saltwater showers.

I dreamed of those wonderful trade winds all the way over on the other side of Panama. But at least I was closing in, mile by mile. It was only about a day and a half until I'd have to begin my stay-awake marathon for the final run into the harbour, when I'd really be in the thick of some serious traffic. I wasn't looking forward to this bit at all, especially if there was no wind (and therefore no manoeuvrability). 'But hey,' I told myself, 'I'll take it as it comes.'

I plotted a course for the eastern side of the bay, as this area had a counter current that would hopefully be of help to my part-sail, part-drift into Panama. 'Here we go,' I thought. 'It won't be long before I'll be doing a bit of "*Hola*, can you see me here?"'

As we passed a very rainy and windless cloud I noticed a bird sitting on a bit of wood about 20 metres away from me. I had almost no wind so couldn't really sail, the bird had no wind so couldn't fly. 'Peas in a pod, really, aren't we?' We both sat there wondering when the wind would pick up a bit.

Other birds on bits of wood soon joined me, and we just watched one another as I drifted past. I heard a buzzing sound and saw a couple of dragonflies skimming the water as they shot by.

I grabbed my video camera to shoot some footage of all the plastic in the water. There was so much it was truly appalling. As a race, we should be ashamed of ourselves. More and more rubbish came into view the closer I got to Panama.

I crawled towards the harbour, peaking at 3 knots of boat speed as I crossed the main shipping lane. The traffic wasn't too bad at this stage although one ship came within 300 metres of me, altering course slightly to give me a nice wide berth.

A few hours later I was at the northeast end of the bay and had seven ships within a mile of me. I wasn't terribly pleased at all with this situation, especially as the nearly full moon vanished behind one of the wildest thunderstorms I'd seen so far on this trip. Soon the shipping was MAD; their bright deck lights were everywhere I looked. Every now and again forked lightning lit up the sky, and although it looked truly awesome it only added to the tension.

I didn't even think about motor gives way to sail. As far as I was concerned, might was right, and I did everything I could to stay as much out of their way as possible, pulling tacks whenever I could to get myself off collision courses with very large ships that were only about a quarter of a mile away.

By the time I was just 30 miles from the harbour I was truly exhausted, but still had no problems remaining on high alert through what was proving to be a very busy and sleepless night. 'Give me Cape Horn any day of the week,' I joked to myself as I darted across the boat to put in yet another tack.

Finally, at nine a.m., shattered beyond words, I coasted into Panama Harbour to be greeted by a very talkative gaggle of journalists packed aboard a small yacht. I struggled to answer a few questions as we headed into Flamenco Marina.

Berthing was always a little nerve-racking, especially when there were many eyes watching, and I had no engine. So, with many amazing yachts moored all over the place, I really took extra care on my way in. If you take your eye off the ball for just a few seconds it's very easy for events to quickly spiral out of control. I was only able to relax once my beautiful boat had been securely moored. I just couldn't wait to get my head down.

43

A Dream Surf

I opened my eyes and sat up. This was weird. It was quiet, I wasn't moving, and I was on an enormous bed in a huge bedroom. I got up and looked out of the window. A huge swimming pool sparkled in the bright sunlight. Luxurious gardens stretched ahead of me for a short distance to the tip of the headland. I could see ships passing in and out of Panama Bay, the water glittering in the morning sun.

Dad had been unable to meet me this time, thanks to a lack of cash, but he'd made a few calls and hooked me up with Monte, the wealthy owner of the Panamanian Sailing School. Monte was a big guy, larger than life, a real man's man, with the habit of saying one outrageous thing after another, usually in reference to a beautiful lady. I couldn't quite believe what I was hearing! But his heart was in the right place. He was generous, too, and he'd provided me with the use of his huge luxury apartment on the Panamanian headland.

I stepped over the pile of clothes I'd left on the floor and went into the kitchen to get myself something to drink. I was met by not one but two maids, both of whom refused to let me go anywhere near the kitchen and who tended to my every need. I actually found this a bit unsettling. When I returned to my bedroom a little while later it was as if I'd never been there. The bed was immaculate and my clothes had been folded into a neat little pile.

'Crikey,' I thought, 'whatever next?'

Monte had offered me the use of his two chauffeurs to take me anywhere I needed to go. Sure enough, a chauffeur was waiting for me, but he wasn't driving anything so mundane as a limousine, oh no. Sitting in Monte's private car park was a low-slung gold Maserati. It may seem odd, but this too made me feel slightly uncomfortable. I had never experienced this kind of lifestyle, but I was very, very, grateful.

We drove back down to the marina. I had been planning to head through the canal within twenty-four hours of arriving in Panama but I discovered, during a thorough boat check, that the double jaw toggle at the head of the solent had sheared on one side. That was very serious. If it had broken completely then the sail would have fallen, causing all sorts of problems. I was extremely relieved not to have lost the sail on my way into Panama. Replacing it was a big job and meant I had to de-tension and re-tension the rig. It also meant staying on for a couple more days until a brand-new one could be flown in.

A couple of guys from the Panama Sailing School met me at the marina and helped me take off the genoa. It was in complete tatters, quite a sight, and when we packed it up it was too big to get through my forehatch; it took some serious pushing, shoving and squeezing by the three of us to jam it down there.

People were always dropping by to have a look at the boat and to find out what I was up to, and I was always delighted to speak to them, happy to share my experiences with as many people as possible. This was definitely a good opportunity to get people excited about sailing.

One morning two guys turned up with a gift for me: a Spot Satellite Personal Tracker. This was completely unexpected, just the sort of generosity I'd met with throughout my trip. A Spot is a small pocket-size tracking device that you can use as and when you please. You just press the OK button and it will track your position and tell other people you're fine, or you can use it in an emergency and the rescue services will be immediately alerted to your exact position. The Spot tracker was now my third emergency beacon as I already had two EPIRBs (Emergency Position Indicating Radio Beacons) and a PLB (Personal Locator Beacon) kindly gifted to me by the manufacturers McMurdo.

After the boat was tidied and the genoa had been stuffed below, I still had some time to kill before the toggle arrived so I was able to take up the British ambassador's invitation to join him for a cup of tea. It was great to meet another Brit out there and all the pictures of London hanging on the embassy walls really brought back a lot of memories. It almost felt like I was home – temporarily at least!

When I got back to my apartment I saw the mail on the kitchen top and a huge grin appeared on my face: there was a letter telling me the new part had arrived. Yes! I got my gear and was down at the boat half an hour later.

Once that had been fitted, I spoke to the mechanics who had been working throughout the week on my main engine. It had a serious problem in that it jumped around all over the place whenever I tried to engage the propeller. It had of course been like this for ages but I hadn't been that bothered about fixing it until now, as I never used my engine in gear anyway. It worked just fine in neutral, so it was great for pumping ballast or charging batteries.

Monte arranged for a marine diver to go down and check the propeller (as well as the hull, keel and rudder), as that was the most likely cause, but he said it was all fine down there. A few days later the mechanics were unable to find anything wrong. I'd eventually find out that the propeller *was* broken. The marine diver had some-how managed to miss it (if he'd even bothered to look at all).

Sometimes I felt I'd had a tad more than my fair share of technical problems on this trip. This was one of those moments. It didn't help that I was also on a very tight budget and every delay like this cost thousands of pounds. But I'm a firm believer that things happen for a reason, that someone up there has a plan for us all. So, although I was gutted about my mechanical setbacks, I reminded myself once again what an incredible journey I'd had so far. It might not have gone to plan with my various stops and I hadn't rounded Cape Horn, but it had been all the better for it. I'd met some incredible people (meeting Don and Margie in Hobart would turn out to be totally life-changing) and I'd pushed myself to the limit when sailing into Panama.

I'd set off all those months ago knowing that sailing round the world would be really hard, but it was proving much more difficult than I'd ever imagined. And I still had so much to experience on the other side of the canal, negotiating the Caribbean Sea, Cuba, the Florida Straits and then the Atlantic to home!

With no time or money left to waste, and not realizing that the propeller was broken, I left the engine as it was. It wasn't as if I was planning to use the propeller anyway: I was going to complete this journey by sail power alone.

Unfortunately, my patience was tested yet again when the Canal Authority struggled to find me a slot – something to do with the type of boat, they said. I had another forty-eight hours to wait.

I kicked my heels until Carlos, one of the captains from the sailing school, told me he had the perfect thing to take my mind off the wait. 'Come on!' he said, climbing into his 4×4 Land Cruiser, 'you'll never forget this as long as you live!' He's an avid surfer, and he wanted to take me to a top-secret local spot.

We headed up the highway to Colon where we suddenly went off-road. I lost all sense of direction as we bounced around through a tropical forest and up and down several crazily steep inclines, Carlos grinning the whole way. After three quarters of an hour of bouncing around in our car seats like jack-in-the-boxes and lots of opening of random gates in the middle of nowhere, we parked up on the side of a track.

'Come on,' Carlos said, 'the ocean's just over the next hill.'

We grabbed our boards and ran to the hill. When we reached the top, I stopped and looked down.

It was breathtaking.

Below us, surrounded by cliffs, was the perfect surfing beach. It was deserted, not another soul in sight. The waves were long, smooth curlers that rolled gracefully in from a long way out before breaking on a shallow reef.

You have to be careful surfing on a reef break – if you fall badly it's easy to get smacked against the reef below – but we had a ball. Carlos really knew how to handle a surfboard. I'd surfed a few times before, but nothing like this. It was so perfect, heavenly even.

After a while I had a rest, sat on my board, watched the waves and thought, 'Wow, yet another amazing experience.' If you'd told me back in November that eight months later I'd be surfing on a deserted beach in Panama, I don't think I'd have believed it!

Meanwhile, Zac Sunderland had just arrived home after his thirteen-month trip. Very few people can even begin to realize how much Zac and his family had put into his project and I was so happy for him. I always knew that some people would try to pit us against each other to make a good story and it always bugged me when that happened. Was it Zac versus Mike? No. I'll tell you what it was. Two teenagers went out there, lived their dream and had the adventure of a lifetime!

PART FIVE

THE ATLANTIC

Days at Sea: 28
Distance Covered: 5,460 nautical miles

Total Days at Sea: 157
Total Distance Covered: 29,835 nautical miles

44

Collision Course

I was up at four a.m. and ready to go at six but, typically for Panama, everyone else was on *mañana* time and we left the dock at around 7.30. I was desperate to get away again but both the paperwork and timing had to be just perfect. I had to sign papers that absolved the port authority of any responsibility if my boat was damaged, even if it was their fault. As I left, the port captain, who would supervise my passage, noticed my lines were only 12mm in diameter instead of the required 25mm. Fortunately, after I explained just how strong the Dynema was, he relaxed a little, my boat was lashed to a motorboat which would escort me through, and at last we were off.

My pulse raced at the magnificent sight of a million gallons of water being let through the mighty gates of the Panama Canal, and my confidence lifted with the rising water as I passed through these first two enormous locks in my tiny boat. I even took some time to pose for pics in front of a packed tourist boat that was also passing through the canal. The next two locks went just as smoothly and we made good speed across Gatun Lake, the body of water that feeds the two sets of locks on either side of Panama.

After sitting out in the rain for a couple of hours we eventually reached the Gatun Locks. We went through the first two really smoothly, and as we entered the final lock I was in really high spirits.

And that's when things went badly wrong.

There was only one port hand waiting for us on the lock wall. He made the mistake of securing the bow-line before the stern-line, and before anyone knew it my stern was swept out by an extremely strong burst of current and the girl spun out into the lock. I shouted for the motorboat that was escorting me through to go full reverse to pull on the rope to try to get the stern back round, but even 400 horsepower couldn't save me. We continued to spin, and in next to no time the back end of the boat was heading directly for the menacing bow of a tug.

There was nothing to do but watch as the tug crushed half the stanchions with a horrible crunch. I wasn't so concerned about that though, I was more worried about the rig. With some quick thinking I got the backstay away extremely fast so that it didn't get caught. If it had it would have brought the rig down.

With some help we were able to push ourselves off the tug, and the port hand helped me winch my way back to the wall. Four stanchions were bent while another two had been completely ripped out. I was gutted, but hey, that's sailing, right? I managed to stay positive and deal with the problem, and with the help of a few calls from good old Monte, the stanchions were repaired in double-quick time, in less than twenty-four hours.

Usually I hated goodbyes, but this time, as I exited the eastern end of the Panama Canal, I was in high spirits, thinking about the hellos waiting for me on the other side of the Atlantic. Mind you, those thoughts were soon forgotten as I needed every ounce of my attention to dodge the traffic.

I raised my mainsail as soon as I cleared the breakwater. It was boiling hot and it took a good twenty minutes to do, and to make matters worse I started to feel really queasy. I took a couple of sea-sickness tablets and tacked the boat NE to head through the anchorage, where ships waited to head into the canal.

To add to the fun and games, as I tried to reef, one of the lazy jacks snapped and became entangled in one of the cars that slid up and down the main mast. The car was jammed and this meant I couldn't lower the mainsail. A mast climb was needed to sort this out before the winds became too strong. The fact that I was in heavy traffic in 28-knot winds made this quite a risky operation, but if I left things as they were it would be like driving a Formula 1 car round Monaco with dodgy brakes.

I got everything ready – my protective padding and the new line for the lazy jack. As with any mast climb, I phoned Dad to tell him I was going up and not to expect to hear from me in the next hour or so. Mum was there and she again spent the whole time waiting for me to call back cleaning the house. It was her way of dealing with the anxiety.

I bore the boat away off the wind a little to try to ease some of the slamming but she was still being pounded as I climbed. I was soon being battered like a ball in a game of ping-pong. Getting around the first spreader was really tough, especially as I had too much canvas up because I was unable to drop the main. I was really being bucked around, and anything that happened to the boat was magnified tenfold while I was halfway up the mast. The wind was increasing all the while, the boat shook like mad, and my shoulders ached so much from the effort of holding on. I wanted to stop, but I needed that sail down!

Halfway up, 30 feet above the deck, I wrapped my legs around the mast, unpicked the snapped line and began to thread in the new one, making sure it wasn't at all tangled. I didn't want to have to come back up to correct a mistake.

As I did so, I was suddenly overtaken by seasickness.

Not now!

Lightheadedness followed. Using all my concentration, I continued to thread the new line.

'Time to go, Mike,' I told myself once I'd finished.

I started to head down, gritting my teeth, bracing myself every time I felt the boat lift, losing count of the number of times I was whacked against the mast. It felt like an eternity. When my foot touched the deck, I unclipped myself and collapsed, totally shattered. I hadn't had any sleep for twenty-four hours, nor had I eaten – I was feeling so dreadfully ill in the lumpy swell.

Not a great start to my last leg.

'Sod it,' I thought, 'I'm heading home now!'

Sure enough, despite the exhaustion, that grin of mine returned. I was into the final leg of my trip. Just 5,000 miles to go!

45

Mercury Rising

Still, I knew I needed to rest and eat soon otherwise I'd be too weak to sail. The first few days out of any port were always the hardest as I tried to settle into a rhythm. My stomach settled the next day but I'd still had precious little time to rest, thanks to the traffic and the rising temperatures.

I cleared the choppy shallows off Nicaragua and pointed the bow towards Cuba, and boy, did the mercury start to climb. Soon I was in the hottest conditions of the trip. I'd faced problems with heat before, off the coast of Africa and in the South Pacific, but this was something else. It was too hot to go inside the cabin. There were no windows and vents to throw open to circulate the air, it was simply an oven, and it stayed at 40 degrees Celsius day and night. I put my Katadyn desalinator to work and poured fresh water over myself as often as I could.

Worst of all, my skin rash returned with a vengeance and I had to dismiss any notion of sleep.

'This last leg is turning into the toughest of the trip,' I told Dad blearily.

I slowly passed by the Cayman Islands in a gentle wind, crouched on the deck, hiding from the sun in the shade of the main. I couldn't wait to round the western tip of Cuba, where I'd have to face yet more shipping lanes and cope with lack of sleep once again.

I was still encountering plenty of traffic so I was already on high alert when Dad called with some amusing news. There'd been some chatter on the blogs about pirates of the Caribbean – and I don't mean the movie of the same name. Bloggers were commenting on the very remote possibility that pirates were hijacking boats off the Cuban coast. In response, Dad – more to appease the bloggers than anything else – decided to switch off the internet display that showed where I was, so pirates wouldn't be able to find me.

As far as I was concerned, pirates were the least of my worries. It was still so, so hot. I sat there melting (along with my entire chocolate supply) in the 40-degree heat; even the boat seemed sluggish as she nibbled away at the miles. I love the heat, but not when the deck gets so hot that it burns my feet! To make matters worse, my water maker started to make some pretty weird-tasting fluid. There was no hint of salt in it, it was just weird. I did the logical thing and changed the filter, and wow, what a difference! It tasted brilliant. I was always impressed with just how pure the water was and how much the desalinator was able to produce – I was using around 6 litres a day to shower with.

The winds stayed low. 'If only I could have another five knots,' I pleaded, 'that would just make it a bit easier to ship-dodge.'

The traffic really picked up in the evening with three ships passing within a few miles. I was pleased to see that a full moon was due in the next few days, which would make everything so much easier on deck. I wouldn't have to use my head-torch to get around, and having a bright light strapped to my head made it much harder for me to spot ships.

I passed by a broken-down tanker as darkness fell; black smoke belched out of its enormous funnel every now and again. They obviously had engine trouble. I wouldn't want to be stuck in a busy shipping lane in a ship with no engine.

My seasickness was starting to fade, but the heat remained. The night brought a distant thundery squall, but not cooler weather. I watched as forked lightning lit up the water. As I approached the western tip of Cuba, some mighty squalls blew in – although again it stayed hot and dry – and the air crackled with electricity. I saw a thick bolt of lightning hit the sea less than a mile away from me.

Not for the first time, I looked up at my tall mast. Always slightly worrying when I was the tallest thing around!

Whenever I saw lightning I made sure to put my VHF radio, satellite phone and GPS in my special Faraday boxes – two of Gran's biscuit tins!

Thanks to a ship-only traffic-separation scheme around Cuba, I had to sail on the inshore track, which meant I was only a few miles from the coast. I was practically past the island, just by the north-western tip, when the wind died away. I was without wind and without an engine, drifting towards some reefs at 2 knots. I reckoned I had about ninety minutes before the boat hit the reefs and my trip was over. This was ridiculously bad luck; I'd had plenty of wind going in and more wind was forecast. This part of the island didn't even have a wind shadow as the land was so low.

What on earth was going on?

I called Dad to let him know and to say that I was really worried. He called some friends, and they all prayed for me.

And then, I saw a squall forming on the horizon. I watched it, willing it towards me, and sure enough it moved in my direction at great speed. Saved! We took off again, away from the land. I called Dad with the fantastic news. A close shave, but I'd pulled through once again – with a little help!

As I sailed further out into the open, away from the busiest shipping lanes, I started to feel a little more relaxed. I continued north to get into the best wind and current before I tacked east-wards, towards home. Mike Broughton's latest email brought wonderful news: an ESE wind was set to blow at 15 knots.

The girl looked so impressive. Her sails were sheeted in tightly and their hems resembled knife-edges as she ploughed smoothly onwards. I was so proud of her, and as I sat on my beanbag, music playing, watching the sunset, I felt so privileged to be able to sail such a remarkable and beautiful boat.

The same afternoon I hooked into the Gulf Stream and picked up a 2-knot current, so although the log said the boat was doing 8 knots, the GPS told me she was doing 10 knots over the ground.

'Fantastic!'

As an added bonus, the temperature had started to drop at long last.

'Just a few more degrees and it'll be perfect!' I thought.

Once I'd passed Miami I closed in on the Florida Straits and that meant that once again I had to stay wide awake as the area was chock-full of passenger boats. I'd had almost no sleep, less than an hour out of the last twenty-four, but I was having little trouble staying awake thanks to all the traffic.

I checked the AIS to see one ship coming at me from behind. I was sailing at 10 to 11 knots while the ship was charging along at 22 – and I was slap bang in his way. It was a bit unnerving seeing this ship skirt by so close, but he did move aside to overtake, giving me about 300 metres of space, and I had plenty of room to scoot off downwind if I needed to.

This was followed by another ship travelling at the same speed, in the same direction, once again right behind me.

'Hmm. Have I plonked myself right in the East Cuba–Florida shipping lane?' I wondered.

My sleepless night caught up with me the following day. It was as if the conditions conspired to make it even harder to stay awake as the winds were light and the sea was so quiet. The girl ghosted along for 3 knots (ground speed 5 knots) for most of the day and I sat in the cockpit my head nodding, feeling pretty whacked.

Once I'd passed the Straits and the Bahamas, the shipping started to ease, but only slightly. I still needed to keep my eyes peeled as I hugged the Florida coast for a bit longer to make the most of the Gulf Stream.

That night the breeze picked up to a very pleasant 9 knots and soon the boat was making a good 7.5 knots through the water with the gennaker up. I'd started a new food bag and I munched and snacked away a little more than I should have done.

'Steady on, Mike,' I thought, 'that's got to last another six days!'

But I was starving and I couldn't help myself, so I boiled up a chicken curry and ate it on deck in a refreshing breeze while watching the spray off the bow fly into the moonlight. I don't think a curry has ever tasted so wonderful.

As ever, though, I could never afford to get really comfortable. I somehow managed to sail out of the Gulf Stream and straight into a counter current of 2 knots. The sea got really ugly in this wind-against-tide situation; the wind was all over the place for about four hours, making it hard work to get back into the Gulf Stream. On a number of occasions I found myself with a course over ground going south at half a knot as I sailed through the water at a knot and a half to the north! I eventually managed to hook back into the Gulf Stream, and the difference in sea state was quite amazing. The sea flattened and the boat took off, sailing along under the spinnaker at 9 knots.

'That's more like it!'

A tiny bird joined me as dawn rose. After a brief rest on the stern rail he took off and gave my boat a thorough inspection, flying into all the rope bags and all around the cockpit and perching on every edge imaginable, including inside the cabin. 'Make yourself at home, why don't you?' I thought, laughing as the bird tweeted merrily away. I shooed him out of the cabin and into the cockpit but he went straight back inside. After shooing him out again, I shut the cabin door for the first time since leaving Panama. Even this didn't dissuade the determined bird and he tried to peck his way in through the little porthole in the door. He flew around the deck landing once again, searching every nook and cranny, then, seeing that there was nothing to scavenge, finally departed, flying back to wherever home was.

As he flew off towards the horizon I spotted a huge ship in the distance. It was heading straight for me on a collision course. It was still a long way off so I decided to let it come much closer before I did anything.

I couldn't figure out what kind of ship it was at first. 'It's no cargo ship,' I thought as I looked through the binoculars. 'That looks like . . . oh boy.' I'd spotted the distinctive set of radar dishes and the giant gun barrels pointing out at every angle – a US warship! It came within half a mile of me and sailed on a parallel course, at the same speed. The US Navy had obviously decided that I was suspicious and had come to check me out. After about five minutes it turned away and headed back towards Florida, its curiosity satisfied.

The fun really began after sunset. The moon vanished behind black clouds and then the craziest electrical storm I've ever seen started up. The wind went berserk, zipping from zero knots to 20 knots, first on the nose, then on my back. By five a.m. I hadn't slept a wink in almost twenty-four hours and was so, so tired. Then there was a sudden blinding flash, a deafening *crack-ack-ack*! I jumped out of my skin. I checked the boat. To my immense relief, nothing had fried or melted. Perhaps having a carbon mast rather than the standard steel kind had saved me.

It had finally cooled down, and at long last I had the perfect shorts and T-shirt weather I'd been waiting for. Now I just couldn't wait to get into clearer water and away from the incredibly busy shipping lanes running up and down the American coast. I didn't have much further to go. I was going to carry on up the coast, making the most of the Gulf Stream, all the way to Cape Hatteras on the coast of North Carolina where I'd start to cross the Atlantic. It's a beautiful part of the world. The Cape is known for its many shallow sandbars, called the Diamond Shoals, which lie up to 14 miles offshore. The warm-water Gulf Stream collides with the cold-water Labrador Current just off Cape Hatteras, causing some very turbulent waters. Fortunately, I wasn't going to go anywhere near this area, known as the 'Graveyard of the Atlantic' because so many ships have been wrecked there.

As I kept to the coast I used my VHF to eavesdrop on all the banter going on between the many ships in the area. The US Navy was out in full force, warships inspecting loads of boats, sometimes sending armed crews to look them over. I watched as a couple of planes passed by overhead. A man had been lost overboard and all shipping had been advised to keep a very good lookout. I said a prayer for him, hoping he'd be found safe and well.

After the planes, my next visitor turned out to be a huge container ship that rocketed past at 22 knots just 300 metres away. I was only doing 4 knots so wasn't much competition for him. Sometimes, if they were doing about 12 knots and the conditions were right, I was able to match a ship's speed. I enjoyed the company and the sail versus engine aspect; I loved to be able to show just what a good boat and a bit of wind could do.

I made the turn east the following day and immediately noticed a big reduction in shipping. 'Finally, some rest,' I thought. I'd slept for just three hours in three days. I was exhausted, and I looked it – unshaven, deeply tanned and red-eyed, just like the typical solo sailor.

The boat was moving along at a good smooth pace so I decided to snap some pics from the bow looking back towards her wake. She suddenly shot down the front of a wave at quite a pace. 'Uh-oh!' I thought and tried to duck but it was too late. As we hit the trough, loads of spray flew up into the air, splashing down on me and ruining the camera. She obviously hadn't wanted her picture to be taken!

I still had a spare but I was running out of electrical equipment to ruin. So far I'd destroyed three video cameras, two still cameras, a number of chargers, two inverters, two battery chargers, one sat phone, one laptop, one autopilot, all manner of audio and video leads, two sets of headphones and two hands-free kits. I think it's safe to say that an Open 50 – which, let's be honest, is a very wet boat – is just not the place for electrical devices, which tend not to be splash-proof. It gets very damp and humid inside the cabin, too, and in most of the compartments. Put that together with being continually shaken for about 150 days and I think we can say the cause of death of all these instruments has been successfully established.

Talking of equipment, it was time to move my clocks forward again – another great sign that I was getting closer to home.

I had the gennaker up all day and the boat loved the conditions, surfing away at a steady 11 to 12 knots. It felt like I hadn't sailed this fast in a good little while. By the time evening arrived I was umming and ahhing whether to keep the gennaker up or take it down and replace it with a smaller foresail. By this time the boat was storming along merrily, right at the limit of wind speed for the strength of the sail. 'OK,' I thought, 'I'm going to play it safe. I don't want to lose this sail.' I took the gennaker in and bunged up the solent.

Just an hour later it turned out that I'd made exactly the right call: the wind picked up to 28–29 knots, sending me flying over the 3,000-miles-to-go mark. I was in the cabin when we were hit with a gust of 34 knots but the girl just took it in her stride and surfed out of it at 19 knots!

'What a boat!'

I was being blown home, the air had cooled, my back had healed, I was able to sleep – this was the life!

I took the opportunity to have a good tidy up of the forepeak and bailed out a little water that had collected from the wet sails I was always shoving in. I soon had it looking organized.

Everything was going so well.

Of course, you know it's never going to last.

46

Homeward Bound

That night the wind picked up to a steady 30 knots and the boat surfed along in a short and steep swell. At dawn a couple of really nasty squall clouds raced in, blasting me with 40 knots of wind, and the boat really took off. We shot along at a breathtaking pace.

Once I'd passed under the second cloud, the wind dropped right back down to 10 knots and turned from the southwest to the east without any warning – and the boat did a big U-turn and sailed right back in the opposite direction!

I couldn't quite believe what I was seeing; there were obviously some serious local effects here. I had too much sail area up for beating and no ballast, so I couldn't turn myself back to face the wind. I was stuck! It was infuriating. I decided to let the local cloud conditions pass by before doing anything to fix the situation. It felt really, really horrible sailing directly into the waves, which were really lumpy and ugly. I cringed as the boat slammed unpleasantly into their troughs.

Eventually, after what felt like a very long ten minutes going the wrong way, the wind suddenly spun round to the south and then southwest and off I went again, except with less wind. Once the conditions had stabilized and I could see it was going to stay fairly light, I hoisted the mainsail up to the top from the first reef point and bunged up the gennaker again.

After that bizarre incident I had a day's plain sailing. The wind held in the teens and I was able to tick off a good few miles under a hot sun while grabbing some fantastic and much-needed rest.

After a series of naps I realized I'd overdone the sunbathing a little; my tan now had a slight reddish hue. I cooled off with a sea-water shower, shivering as I dumped a bucket over my head. 'Damn that's cold!' I thought, and then grinned at this sign of my progress. I'd left the warm waters of the Caribbean Sea far behind me. Now I was well and truly into the North Atlantic on what would be my third crossing in just over two years. It was great to be back!

As ever, there was no time for complacency. A good handful of ships were still showing up on the AIS each day, so I certainly couldn't afford to let my guard down.

And then, just as darkness started to close in, the boat demanded my urgent attention. After gybing northeast to put myself in a slightly better position for the ever-changing current, I glanced up at the rig and spotted that one of the batten attachments to the cars on the mast track had sheared (battens keep the sail flat and rigid). The batten was now hanging loose and banging into the rig, which meant it could gradually needle its way into the mast, creating a hole and weakening the structure. It also made it very difficult to raise and lower the sail, as it would potentially catch on everything it passed, causing more damage, or getting so tangled that the sail would become stuck.

I was straight into action. I dropped the shortcake I'd been munching on the beanbag, which I quickly wedged back in the cuddy area, and dived inside to find the spares I needed to replace the attachment with the all-important Allen key. I had to get this done before dark.

After gybing, I unfurled the solent, so I could head into the wind. I then brought the girl on to a very close reach and after flaking out the main halyard I quickly dropped the main down (there were certainly no points for neatness!). She wasn't happy about this at all. She started to roll about a bit in the swell and her motion became pretty ugly without the mainsail driving her along.

I replaced the broken part which had sheared off the batten attachment, and as I quickly checked the other cars I spotted another one that was totally bent and looked like it was about to go as well, so I replaced that one too.

Having replaced the parts and got the battens rigged up to the cars again I set about the worst part of the job: getting the main up. It took half an hour of grinding and a lot of patience as the fourth reef kept getting stuck in the lazy jacks. It was with a great grin that I finally got the main all the way up.

I bore her off downwind and looked up with a smile to see the mainsail back to full health. I gybed back over to starboard and unfurled the gennaker. She accelerated nicely and we were soon sailing along beautifully at around 9 knots in 15 knots of breeze.

I was delighted with my evening's work, and I was rewarded with another of those moments. The sun had already set by the time I climbed on to my bright orange coach roof, chocolate bar in hand. The sky was full of mesmerizing soft misty pinks and oranges and the boat ghosted along quite happily at 8 knots or so. My favourite music now was the sound of the boat passing through the sea; she really was just so graceful. She'd quickly become my friend, a thing of beauty that never seemed to tire, who wanted nothing more but to keep sailing towards the sun for ever.

The night passed peacefully and I was able to have a good rest, and the following day I ticked the 2,500-miles-to-go box. I always set myself short-term targets. Having lots of boxes to tick mentally, each one a clear marker signifying I was that much closer to my goal, really kept me going.

That goal seemed very far away the next day as the wind dropped and I found myself in a 2-knot counter current.

I'd missed the sight of my friends the dolphins since breaking through into the Atlantic. I hadn't seen a single one. In fact I hadn't seen any sea life on this leg, nothing, not so much as a flying fish. I'd also missed the starry nights; with non-stop cloud cover I'd barely caught sight of the moon, let alone the stars. I hoped some wind would come and blow them away. Mike Broughton's forecast for the following day looked promising, with the wind set to build.

I grinned from ear to ear the next morning when the wind did increase, to a beautiful 14 knots. It really was music to my ears as I listened to the sails fill and the boat surge forward, maintaining a solid 9 knots. These steady conditions were very calming and re-assuring, and once again I was able to get some much-needed zeds.

That evening, as the sun disappeared, I dropped the gennaker as I came up to the wind a bit more – the apparent wind speed had risen a little too high for the strength of the sail. After going through my now much-practised routine of dropping it and bagging it up inside the forepeak, I let loose the solent and pumped in a little ballast. Off she shot, blast reaching at a steady 12 knots. Spray flew over her bow constantly but the boat stayed rock solid as she skipped over the sea.

I loved the feel of being nicely powered up; right then it felt as if there was a big bit of elastic between home and us, pulling us in. I climbed into the cabin and grinned every time I felt the deceleration as the boat ploughed through a wave, carving up a great plume of spray before jumping into the trough.

Although she was storming along over the water at 12 knots, I was only doing 9 knots over ground thanks to a not-so-nice counter current of 3 knots. I hoped I'd shake this off some time soon as I headed north towards colder air. Soon I'd be just 100 miles from the exact spot where the RMS *Titanic* sank in April 1912.

I opened a new food bag and was startled to see not one but four chicken-in-white-sauce meals. This was one of my favourites but I wasn't sure how I'd ended up with four! It turned out that when the bags were being packed someone had told Mum we were out of chicken in white sauce and she'd rushed off to the supermarket to get a load more – too much more it seemed! I loved the stuff but this was my second bag with four meals the same.

'Oh well,' I thought, 'it could have been worse. I could have ended up with extra meals of beef in unidentifiable red sauce curry, or spicy beef something with dry peas!'

Once dinner was done I stayed in the cabin, going over the chart. When I'd finished, I switched off all the cabin lights and went outside into the cockpit. I gazed upwards, and as my eyes got accustomed to the dark an infinite number of stars appeared above me, as if someone had just scattered them there by magic. The moon hadn't risen yet, so it was still incredibly dark. I was totally blown away by their beauty. I sat back and, as I'd often done, made myself look at the sky until I saw a shooting star – the law was that only then could I go back inside the cabin. This didn't usually take that long, but this time I waited a good twenty minutes before one zipped across the sky.

'About time!'

By then it was getting quite cold on deck. The cabin, however, was nice and warm as I'd just been running the generator.

The temperature continued to fall, and for the first night since the South Pacific I actually woke up not to the sound of my alarm but because I was cold. Shorts and a long-sleeved top were no longer enough for the North Atlantic. As I was still sleepy and feeling a little lazy I couldn't be bothered to dig out my sleeping bag, so I grabbed one of my thick fleeces and jacket and draped them over me as I slept. My legs still felt a little nippy but I slept much better from then on.

I'd dream of eating all manner of NON-freeze-dried meals. I longed for my all-time favourite breakfast of lightly toasted FRESH and THICK white bread with MELTED butter on, and some really good pâté SMOTHERED all over it. Whenever I thought about it I started to drool and my on-board stores started to look more and more unappealing, especially as I was now overdosing on chicken in white sauce.

I also looked forward to being in my own bed and getting a really, really good night's sleep. I looked forward to laughing with my friends, too. I looked forward to going back to college. More than anything I looked forward to seeing my family again, waking up with them again, sharing everyday life with them again.

And then there was Beckie. We'd started to talk every day on the satellite phone and I could sense the excitement in her voice as my return drew nearer and nearer. Would we get back together? I certainly hoped so.

I was so close now; I didn't want to do anything that might jeopardize the trip. So much had gone into getting me this far, and to crash out now . . . well, it was something I didn't even consider.

I had so many cherished memories, such as surfing down mountainous 50ft waves at breakneck speeds on my wonderful surfboard, terrified and ecstatic all at the same time, and seeing countless dolphins jumping effortlessly alongside the girl as she flew purposefully through the water. But as I looked back over my odyssey, the one memory that stood out above all others – at this time, at least – was pulling into Hobart after completing my crossing of the Southern Ocean. Just hours earlier I'd been in 40-knot winds trying to tame the boat in wild seas as she careered forward, faster and faster. As soon as I rounded the headland into Storm Bay the wind dropped off to a nice 15 knots, thanks to my being in the lee, and I witnessed the most beautiful sunset I'd ever seen in my life. Suddenly I was ghosting along at 4 knots on the calm River Derwent under a pink sky with gold-lined clouds with the Tasmanian Hills as a backdrop. There was barely a sound as we slipped through the water. I was exhausted but ecstatic at having just survived the Southern Ocean, and I felt so incredibly lucky to be there. The hills of Tasmania rose on either side the further upriver I sailed, and as the soft, extraordinary light faded, lights twinkled in the small houses dotted along the banks.

Needless to say, I'd had a grin on my face beyond all grins.

47

Trouble at the Top

Another sunset, another day closer. The sun was just about to touch the horizon when I saw a great puff of water burst into the air. A whale! Right next to me! I leaned over the side and stared wide-eyed but it didn't surface or blow out again. It must have just grabbed a lungful of air before returning to the deep.

I was standing by the mast the following afternoon when I heard a loud splash close to the boat, almost as if something large had fallen into the water. 'What on earth?' I thought, and turned to look over the side. There was white froth in the water under the gennaker. 'What was that?' I wondered. And then I grinned. It had been so long since I'd seen them I'd forgotten the noise of their splashes. My friends the dolphins! Suddenly a great line of them appeared next to me. I counted about fifty, all jumping and racing alongside.

'I've missed you guys! Where've you been?'

They broke up into three separate gangs. One group went left, one stayed off the bow and one played around about 50 metres away. They hung around only for a minute or so, just enough time for me to grab some pics with my spare camera.

A short while later I emerged from the cabin to see six jet-black pilot whales just cruising along next to me, having a good look at the boat. They were quite stocky, their square heads and large bodies quickly tapering into a tailfin. They swam alongside for a few minutes before dropping below the surface and into the deep.

I had a bit of a rough night thanks to some light winds but I didn't mind too much as I was inside the 2,000-miles-to-go mark. I knew I'd be sailing more than that, though, as I never ever sailed in a straight line. Just call me the zigzag man.

Once the winds came in, we started moving through the water at 2.5 knots. I was so grateful for any wind that held the sails in one position, enabling me to get some sleep. I was out in seconds. I could have slept for hours but I set my alarms as usual.

A little later I was awake, just sitting on the beanbag, when all of a sudden *whoosh*, two dolphins jumped up right next to the stern, only about a metre away.

'Wow!'

They looked really, really impressive. Spray flew everywhere and they hung for a moment at the top of their arc before crashing back into the water, smiling and gleaming in the sun. These two playful guys hung around for a couple of minutes before disappearing.

I made fantastic progress through the night and managed to stay in front of a high-pressure bubble, which was really good news. Meanwhile a low front was approaching, and that would keep me speeding along. Before long the sea started kicking up into a steep and lumpy swell. I was about to experience all the lovely wild weather that was being brought up by the massive lows making their way across the North Atlantic.

My thoughts once again turned to home and I gave the cabin a good clean. I wanted the girl looking her best for our homecoming at Gunwharf Quays. To my disgust, a tin of chicken had managed to split open in one of my drawers; sauce had got over all the food packets and had also dripped into the drawers below. Half an hour later, thanks to a J-cloth and a fair few baby wipes, everything was sparkling once more.

It got colder the further across the Atlantic I sailed and soon I was in my cold-weather fleeces. It felt weird to be back in shoes and socks; I'd been barefoot since Panama. And now I had to tog up in all my oilies once more. Every time I went on deck I was hit by loads of spray, so I spent a lot more time in the cabin rather than out in the cockpit on the beanbag.

I was so near and yet so far, just ten days from home. Dad was on the edge of his seat every time I called.

'Everything is going great,' I'd tell him.

He'd always reply, 'Just be careful, Mike, just be careful.'

Of course, this plain sailing wasn't going to last.

The boat was rocketing along at some speed in 25 knots of wind. I was having a wonderful time, standing in the cockpit on the back of my 50ft surfboard as we rode the waves home. My grin hardly left my face all day. I loved to feel her so powered up and rock solid as we blasted over wave after wave. I'd ticked the 1,500-miles-to-go mark and was very excited.

I'd just flicked off the cabin's light switch and plonked my head down on my pillow when I glanced at the autopilot and saw that its screen was blank with no power.

'Bummer!'

The boat had just come out of a big surf at 18 knots and I could feel her instantly gearing up for the next. She was starting to lean a good bit downwind. I immediately looked through the hatch at the position of the tiller and noticed that the pilot had left it off to one side. We were on our way into a full-on crash gybe.

I sprang up as quick as lightning, just wearing socks and thermals – no boots or foul-weather gear – and dived into the cockpit where I grabbed the helm and pulled it fully across, just managing to avoid what would have been a nasty, nasty crash gybe in heavy seas.

'Phew!'

But what had happened? The last thing I wanted was another malfunctioning autopilot. Then I realized. 'Idiot!' I thought to myself. 'You're the one that's malfunctioning!' When I'd leaned over in half-asleep mode to turn off the light switch on the switchboard, just as I did this the boat had bounced on a wave and my finger had dropped a couple of centimetres or so down to the next switch and turned off the autopilot.

Once she was under control again, I dropped down into the cabin, flicked the switch back on and set the pilot up again. It was all over in seconds, but it certainly woke me up out of the dreamy mode I'd been in. My dad was right to be on the edge of his seat. 'No more mistakes like that one, please!' I told myself.

More hair-raising incidents lay ahead, though, for now I was interested to see an email from Mike Broughton telling me about the 'Bad Boy Low' (as he called it), a deepening storm spiralling my way which would bring some very strong winds. Although there's always an element of danger in such extreme conditions, I was thrilled as they were blowing in the right direction, towards home. From Mike's report it looked like a real whopper but the wind strengths looked like they'd be manageable. I just hoped they wouldn't fall on the wrong side of 40 knots.

Mike also mentioned the rather more worrisome Hurricane Bill, the strongest hurricane of the new season so far, also moving very quickly at 38 knots towards my position from Newfoundland, where it was currently blowing at 70 knots.

Sure enough, just a few hours later, the boat leapt and started to turbo-surf. I was back on the log flume, covering 140 miles in twelve hours.

I celebrated this progress with a tad-too-refreshing bucket-over-the-head shower. I had rather mixed feelings about how wise this decision was the moment the freezing water hit my head.

Another sign of my progress was that I'd started to get a few calls from the media, wanting interviews and live radio link-ups. It was a little weird to think I was only just over a week away from the finish line after I'd been gone for so long. I couldn't wait to share my adventures with friends and family. My heart raced with anticipation at the thought of seeing the English coastline, and seeing Beckie again. I wondered again what that would be like.

I was just thinking about this while changing up from solent to gennaker when I ran into a large flock of birds that had been happily bobbing about in the water. Oops! They flew around the boat for ten minutes or so before settling down again.

Meanwhile the dolphins were back in force. Their appearances became more and more frequent; no more big groups, just a couple here and there, which was a real treat for me. I loved to sit on deck and watch them sprint through the water, easily outrunning the boat.

Dad continued to be just as impatient for me to get back home – probably more so. 'Take it easy, Mike,' he kept saying. 'No need to take any risks.'

Naturally, I agreed wholeheartedly, but then I called him to say, 'Dad, I'm going up to the top of the mast.'

'What? Again?'

Poor Mum and Dad! Dad was so far over the edge of his seat while he waited for me to call back he nearly fell off. Meanwhile, Mum scrubbed the house from top to bottom yet again.

Really, what is it with me and mast climbs? My fourth one of the trip while at sea, three of them in heavy seas. I didn't like it any more than they did, and I was in the middle of my Bad Boy Low with a nice strong blow of 25 knots, just to make it all the more interesting. The last thing I wanted to do was swing about 70 feet above the boat.

The problem occurred after I'd gybed round to head up NE, which went without a hitch – or so I thought. I looked up at the rig and noticed something really odd. Part of the running backstay, which supports and goes about two thirds of the way up the mast, was hanging a little limply and wasn't in tension like the other two (masthead and halfway point). This totally threw me. I couldn't understand why on earth this one was hanging limp while the others were bar-tight.

I grabbed the binoculars, lay back on the deck to get into a steady position, and scoured the rig. Nothing stood out. I checked everything on deck too, every forestay and fitting. Nope, nothing wrong there either.

I furled away the foresail to take a bit of pressure off the rig and reached the conclusion that the middle backstay was so loose because the top backstay had somehow caught and was pulling much more than necessary.

The wind had eased and I reluctantly wound on the mainsail as tight as I dared, which would give the rig some support, and I let off the backstays completely. This wasn't the safest thing to do. Just one powerful gust and the rig would want to fall forward. I took the mast-head backstay off the block and put the other two back on to give the rig some support while I tried to figure out what was wrong.

All of the backstays are made of PBO, very, very strong fibre which is just as strong as wire rigging. As I thought that the backstay was caught right at the top, I tried everything I could think of to try to loosen it a little more, but seeing no change through the binocs, and with strong conditions forecast for the next day, I knew I had no choice. I couldn't leave it like this, not with some serious storms closing in.

So I donned the harness and padding, and after checking and rechecking all my gear, I took a deep breath and began my ascent.

Climbing the mast as a solo sailor, as I've said, is a daunting experience. Obviously once both feet are off the deck you're not there to look after the boat and take care of any unexpected dramas, such as rescuing her from autopilot failures or potential collisions. Once I was at the top I was about thirty minutes from climbing back down to the deck so it wasn't as if I could nip down if anything looked like it was going a bit wrong.

Eventually I was right at the top, 70 feet above the deck, the first time I'd been there at sea. Every time the autopilot corrected or the boat bounced awkwardly over a wave it felt ten times worse up there, especially as I'm no fan of heights and as we had a good 25-knot breeze.

I immediately saw what the problem was. My theory was incorrect! There was no problem! Which was bad/good news. Because, what on earth was affecting the backstay?

I looked to the horizon and saw a set of extra dark clouds heading my way. A squall. Time to head deckwards. This time, what with the wind and waves throwing me against the mast, it was a good thirty-five minutes before my foot touched the deck. I checked every fitting along the way and was pleased to see nothing was amiss. I unclipped myself from the halyard using the two carabiners and practically collapsed. I spent a minute or so getting my breath back. I felt pretty elated that I'd made it all the way to the top and safely down again. Now that was some serious box-ticking done.

But the job wasn't finished by any means. I phoned Dad again. He was extremely relieved to hear that I was fine, apart from a lovely new collection of bruises from being bashed into the mast.

I put the backstay back on the block with the other two, checked all the lashings, wound it back on nicely, and what do you know, it was suddenly perfect! I don't know what I did during the course of taking it off and putting it back on to fix the problem but I was thrilled. Job done, I unfurled the gennaker and the boat started careering along once again. I sat down for a well-earned rest and a large ration of chocolate.

Hurricane Bill was still racing towards me and Mike Broughton reckoned it would catch up in four days' time, when I'd be somewhere in between the Fastnet Rock (the most southerly point of Ireland, the midpoint marker for one of the world's classic yachting races, the Fastnet) and Land's End. In his words, Bill was expected to provide me with 'some fun and games'.

Bill was the strongest hurricane so far that year, but he still couldn't compete with the nastiness of some of the systems I'd managed to dodge while I was in the Southern Ocean. I was confident that the girl and I would handle Bill. She filled me with confidence; thanks to her speed I could easily position myself in the best possible place to experience the best conditions. If I'd been in a slower normal boat, dodging the really bad weather would have been much harder, if not impossible.

48

One Last Ding-Dong

I was standing on deck, leaning on the coach roof, gazing out across the sea, when suddenly *whack*! The boat shook. The tiller started to judder. The autopilot beeped its warning alarm.

'What on earth?' I thought. 'Have I broken a rudder? Is something snagged? Is the shaft bent?'

Then came the gut-wrenching sound of tearing fibreglass.

I ran to the stern and, checking the stern compartment, I saw that the mount for the autopilot ram was partially torn away. I shook my head. I was really being tested to the limits in my final week but I remained as determined as ever to face any problem. It was incredible how one second everything was fine, the next everything was going wrong.

I turned off the pilot and steered manually. The tiller shook violently in my hand; something was caught on the rudder. I peered over the back but couldn't see anything amiss.

I had a spare ram to hold the rudder for the autopilot and had an idea how I might free the rudder of the mystery object. It was one of those 'it's a crazy idea but it might just work' scenarios.

This was something else my trip had taught me. There were plenty of events you could never train for, especially ones that required a fast, sometimes split-second decision. It was also essential to keep a calm head in a crisis, focus on the task in hand and believe in yourself enough to complete it successfully, even if it was something you'd never tried before, or even heard of anyone else trying.

I needed to slow down a bit for this job in case anything went wrong, so I furled away the solent and put a reef in the main for good measure. I then went below and crawled my way into the stern compartment, which is not as easy as it sounds – it's a tight squeeze. As the pilot was off I steered by instinct. As the tiller rods passed into the stern compartment I was able to push them in the right direction as and when the boat moved. Despite my best efforts, the boat was still doing a lot of weaving through the water.

I picked my moment and knocked out the pin for the ram and hoisted it over to the other side of the tiller. All the while I continued to steer by 'feel', pushing and pulling the steering rods forward and back. But I was down for a little too long and I couldn't feel the boat well enough. As I changed the ram, the boat started to gybe. The main whacked up against the running backstay, and because it was pinned there, we rounded up into a stiff 30-knot breeze, sending the boat into a powerful gybe which, even with all my strength, I couldn't possibly pull out of.

The first time this happened, somewhere in the Atlantic on my first leg, it was quite a shock. But now I knew exactly what I was doing. When the main is pinned and rounded up, I'd learned to leave the preventer on, rather than let the main swing to the other side fully, and this in effect created a sail. With the wind on the bow and the main pinned up, the boat started sailing backwards, just as I had hoped.

As we sailed backwards (peaking at 6 knots!), the rudder started shaking horribly. After about twenty seconds I suddenly felt the tiller go 'free' – it moved easily again. Whatever was caught on there had been swept off during my dramatic reverse manoeuvre.

YES!

Once I had enough speed I swung the tiller over and we turned, still travelling backwards, just as if we were backing in and out of a parking space – not that I'd been able to try that yet! The main caught the wind on the side and the boat set off sailing forward again, reaching nicely.

It wasn't over yet. Next, I had to reconfigure the pilot to work on the other side of the boat as all of its lefts and rights were mixed up. This was easier said than done, and as the pilot performed its 'test' we came a little too close for comfort to both broaching and gybing; but the pilot managed to find its feet after a few seconds and we plunged onwards.

'Phew!' I thought. 'Anything else?'

I turned back to check the mainsail as it had suffered quite a bit of abuse during that manoeuvre. Almost immediately I saw that the fun and games were still not over, not by a long shot.

When I'd accidentally gybed, the batten attachment had snapped clean right by the head of the sail and the batten had now slid out from the front of the sail by about 10 inches. Not good! I had to get the main down to fix it. As I wound the sail down, the batten caught on every part of the rig on the way. I grabbed the deck brush to help it over certain parts of the sail. I must have looked quite a sight, see-sawing in heavy winds and seas, trying to winch down the main, jabbing it every now and again with my brush.

After an exhausting hour, the main was down. It was a quick fifteen-minute job to replace the attachment, put the batten back in and tension it up, and then put it back on the mast track.

Then came the really hard bit: getting the main up the mast again. It was blowing 30 knots, and because the head of the sail was so flipping large it was forever catching on the lazy jacks. It took even longer – an hour and a half and lots of up-and-down and up-and-down – to finally get the main up to the first reef mark. I threw in the reef, got everything tensioned and set, and dived down into the cabin, cold, wet, pretty knackered and, more than anything, starving.

I may have been getting a little tired of the chicken in white sauce, but that night it went down a treat.

I'd barely had time to think about home for a while, and I continued to focus on trying to get through the storm without further incident. And then Hurricane Bill declared his arrival with a good old ding-dong, wild 45-knot winds and one 45-foot swell after another. The Bad Boy Low had delivered its payload the previous night, and I had found myself in a seriously rough 40-foot swell with 35 knots of wind. By dawn the boat was still flying down some tremendous swells, the largest of which were close to 50 feet. But she simply flew onwards just as fearlessly as she had done since day one. Even after nearly 30,000 miles she looked almost as fresh as the day we left. It pained me to put the brakes on and reef down the sails but I didn't want to be caught too near the continental shelf with Bill; it was much better to be in open deep water where the sea state made for better sailing. Even with just a handkerchief up the boat still flew along, as eager as I was to get home. Even a hurricane wouldn't stop me now.

More signs of how close my homecoming was started to appear. I was emailed a complete schedule of radio, TV and newspaper interviews, one straight after another. Dad called to tell me the BBC had broadcast a special weather forecast on TV just for me, to show how I was coping with the tail end of Hurricane Bill.

'How are you coping?' he asked.

'Just fine,' I replied. 'I'm ahead of schedule as well.'

I was so excited at the thought of seeing Dad and his cheesy grin and hearing his crazy laugh and terrible jokes. I couldn't wait for my hug.

Another sign I was nearing the finish line was the crazy amount of shipping. I took the helm and marvelled as the boat came alive in my hands and surfed down every single wave.

'Gosh,' I thought, 'I'm really going to miss sailing her. She's like family now!'

As I started to reflect on my global odyssey, so many feelings washed over me. Knowing I was near the end filled me with joy and sadness. I wanted to keep going, to have more adventures, but at the same time I couldn't wait to be back home with my family. Such thoughts circled through the night as I watched out for dozens of fishing boats. 'It's going to be strange to have to think about things that aren't related to the trip,' I thought. But more than anything I couldn't wait to cross the finish line off Lizard Point and then see my family again.

First I had to get there, and Bill was still having a good old blow. The wind was still increasing hour by hour. The cold front that would deliver a real kick up the backside was expected to pass through between midnight and four a.m.

Even though it was blowing a really good gale, I decided to try to get some rest as I knew I wasn't going to get any sleep once I was in the English Channel, thanks to all the crazy shipping. This didn't really work as the sea soon turned into a choppy mess filled with more than enough fishing boats to keep me busy through the night.

Still, by now I knew I could see it through. I knew I could keep going, that I could push myself through increasing levels of exhaustion. This was a lesson hard learnt throughout my trip; it was the price I had to pay for my freedom, to be the captain of my own destiny.

I was still the same Mike as the one who'd left, but some things had changed. I was more confident. I had sailed beyond the edge, beyond what most sailors would ever have to deal with, and I'd succeeded. I'd not only survived high winds and huge waves, I'd outrun storms and hurricanes, dodged ships, coped with countless on-board repairs and adaptations, climbed my mast too many times to think about, and overcome extreme exhaustion. One of the greatest tests of my strength and will, if not the greatest, was my struggles with the autopilot at the start of the trip and the problems with the bearings that forced me to stop. To have to return to port again and again was about as tough as it was possible to get.

Yes, there was one priceless thing I would take from this trip: the knowledge and experience of what is possible when you're at the very edge of your physical and emotional capabilities, when you're pushed to the absolute limit time and time again.

49

The Finish Line

Even though I was shattered when dawn broke the following morning, I was so tremendously excited because I was due to cross Lizard Point. HMS *Mersey* and a Royal Navy helicopter did me the honour of escorting me. A number of ribs full of TV crews closed in on me as I drew nearer to the finish line.

At 09.47:30 on 27 August 2009, after 157 days of sailing, I crossed the line as HMS *Mersey* blasted all her horns. A message was also relayed from the First Sea Lord, Admiral Sir Mark Stanhope, which was quite something: 'This is a remarkable and inspirational achievement in one so young, another impressive event in the rich maritime history of this island nation, and of the Perham Family.'

Dad had earned this praise. He'd made the impossible happen, thanks to his unshakeable faith in me and his amazing ability to talk people on board, so to speak. Both Mum and Dad had given so much to this trip. I'd put them through plenty of stress and the family finances were still pretty ropey.

After receiving the message, I lit two red flares and stood at the bow, grinning from ear to ear. It was a wonderful moment. As I'd imagined, the sense of accomplishment was out of this world. But, as far as I was concerned, my trip wasn't over until the girl was moored at Gunwharf Quays.

In the meantime, the media boats converged for interviews and we shouted back and forth until I was hoarse. The best feeling at that moment was the realization that I didn't have to be alone any more.

As soon as I got a chance I grabbed the phone and called Dad.

'I've done it!' I yelled.

'Well done, Mike,' he replied. 'I'm in Tesco at the checkout at the moment. I'll call you back in just a second.'

Typical!

Dad had been shopping for steaks and fresh white bread for me. He was in Falmouth and was going to join me for the sail through the Channel to Portsmouth.

Dad left the supermarket, went straight to Falmouth Harbour, leapt on a rib provided by the Falmouth Sailing School and zoomed out to meet me. I saw him zipping across the water and waved.

He leapt over the side, and in what we both later described as 'the best hug in the world' – a real rib-crusher – he squeezed the breath out of me.

'I love you, Mike. I'm so very proud of you.'

'I love you too, Dad.'

The last time I'd seen Dad was in New Zealand, half a world away. It felt unreal holding him and having the luxury of talking to him face to face once more. We talked non-stop, and I told him off when he turned the cabin into a total tip after only five minutes of being on board. He may have been my dad but I was the captain here and he respected that!

Family friend Phil and Adam, a cameraman who was going to film my sail into Portsmouth for the Channel 4 documentary, joined Dad on board. I couldn't believe how much stuff they'd brought with them. 'What on earth's all this?' I asked as they hauled one large cardboard box on board. I opened it and grinned. I couldn't quite believe what I was seeing. Lots and lots of steak!

Dad soon got to work in the galley. I drooled as the aroma filled the boat. We ate them in the teeth of Hurricane Bill's last gasp.

'Not bad at all!' I exclaimed.

Our spirits soared ever higher as we neared my homecoming at Gunwharf Quays, from where I'd departed all those months ago. It was so wonderful to be sailing this last part with Dad by my side. Mum, Fiona and Beckie were waiting for me there along with my friends and extended family. One of the restaurants had been turned into a media centre and I'd been warned to expect a very busy few hours after arrival, which was just fine with me! I couldn't wait to see Mum and Fiona again, now I was back from my 'gap year'. And Beckie. We'd been able to have a couple of quick chats after I passed the Lizard and she'd sounded as excited as I was.

The gale continued to bounce us around, and as we were ahead of schedule for our arrival on Saturday morning, we dropped into Lyme Bay for a bit of shelter and to kill some time. The wind dropped from 38 to 30 knots and we sailed up and down, telling jokes and eating more steak.

As night drew in, I made the call to turn the girl's bow out into the Channel once more. I'd hardly closed my eyes for forty-eight hours and was grateful to grab some shut-eye while Dad kept watch.

When my turn came the gale had fallen away; the night was clear and bright with stars. I watched for a shooting star and didn't have to wait long before I was rewarded with a real beauty that crossed the sky right above us. 'It can only be a good omen,' I thought.

We passed the Needles and the Isle of Wight at daybreak. I loved seeing these landmarks. Although Tasmania was pretty special, nothing could quite match seeing the familiar sights along the south coast of England!

Not long after dawn we were joined by another Royal Navy vessel, HMS *Puncher*, which escorted us towards Portsmouth. Just outside the harbour I spotted a very antique-looking airplane, which performed a few barrel rolls, loop-the-loops and low fly-pasts in my honour. That was most unexpected and totally crazy!

As we entered the harbour I was amazed to see that thousands of people were waiting for me; they lined the whole quay, several bodies deep. I could hear the shouting and clapping from half a mile away. I broke out two more red flares and was fit to burst with happiness. No one could take the smile off my face, that's for sure! I laughed all the way in as dozens of ships sounded their horns. What a welcome! It was amazing. The Queen's Harbour Master had suspended all shipping while I made my way in, so that meant all the passenger ferries were forced to wait for me to pass. I was joined by dozens of yachts that came by to shout and wave their congratulations.

I'd mentioned to Dad before I'd set off that it would be great to be welcomed by a steel band, and I was amazed to hear that he had found one to come and play me in!

Mum, who was hopping with excitement and impatience, and Fiona were first on board once I'd berthed. It was the first time I'd seen Mum in eight months and it was quite a moment being able to hug her again and tell her I loved her – in person!

The press waited until we'd finished our hug and then started shouting questions. The photographers were desperately trying to get me to look at them, but I was busy looking for Beckie. I finally caught sight of her on the jetty. Neither of us had any idea what was going to happen.

Then Dad handed me my last bottle of champagne and draped the flag around my shoulders. The press yelled at me to spray the champagne, which I gladly did, being careful not to get it all over their cameras.

That done, I spotted Beckie again, caught her eye and waved her on board. She was crying as she wrapped her arms tightly around me and said, 'I'm so proud of you.' For a few moments, everyone and everything else went out of my mind. It was as if the two of us were entirely alone. I was back with Beckie.

As we came out of that moment, it finally felt like my journey was complete. I'd done it! I was home. At last, we were a family together again.

And that, I can most definitely say without question, was the greatest feeling in the world.

Total Days at Sea: 157
Total Distance Covered: 29,835 nautical miles
Average Speed: 7.92 knots
Average Daily Distance: 190 nautical miles

Epilogue

Within a couple of days things were getting back to, er, normal . . . well, what passes for normal in the Perham household anyway. I'd woken up in *my* bed, in *my* bedroom. I couldn't quite believe it. No more rocking about, no clonking, creaking or whooshing.

The house was already in a proper mess. My dirty clothes were scattered about everywhere and the kitchen was piled up with stuff to go in the dishwasher after a night of celebrations with friends, family and neighbours. The whole house was full of boat stuff and all my gear (thank you so much everyone who stuffed their cars full to help us get it all back to Potters Bar). It did look a bit like I'd taken over, and it certainly smelled like it. Everything had a 'boat aroma'.

Amid all the chaos sat a very special piece of paper. The proof, the reminder, as if I needed it, of what had been achieved: the certificate from Guinness World Records. I was officially, at seventeen years and 164 days, The Youngest Person To Sail Around The World Solo. It had been presented to me amid the whirl of press conferences and interviews while we were at Gunwharf Quays.

As things became a little more settled, I looked back over the past few days' events. Just after I'd arrived, while we were still on the quayside, a reporter asked me why I'd done it.

'For the adventure! Because I'm a dreamer!' I replied.

For as long as I could remember, since the day I clapped eyes on our first boat *Blue Jay*, I'd wanted to sail further and further. When the reporter asked me her question, I had to throw her back a quick answer, but that was it in a nutshell. I did it for the feeling I got once I'd lost sight of land, for the sense of adventure, the independence, the thrill of the boat moving through the wild water, for the feeling of accomplishment once my journey was complete.

One other popular question that day was 'Would you do it again?' Yes! I'd even like to try racing my way round. But not just yet.

The rest of the day seemed to pass in a daze, a blur of congratulations, cheers and photo calls with dignitaries including the Mayor of Portsmouth and the Antiguan High Commissioner, who happened to be in the UK at the time. I loved every moment, although it was a bit overwhelming after spending all that time alone in my boat suddenly to be surrounded by thousands of people. At the press conference in Tiger Tiger, so many people had crammed on to the first floor that the staff had to start turning people away. When I looked at a building across the way I could see more cameras pointed at me, and there were yet more looking up at me from below. The number of people who had turned up was truly amazing.

I started to relax once I was on my way back to Potters Bar. I drove with Beckie and two of my best friends, Ben and Mark. I'd been away so long that Mark had got his driving licence. We were all on such a high. I was cuddled up with Beckie on the back seat. 'It feels like you've hardly been away now!' she said, and I agreed. When we pulled into our road and I saw the Perham family home right at the end of our street, I was so happy. The neighbours had put together a fantastic display of bunting and a large 'Welcome Home Mike' sign. Minutes later my first party was well and truly under way!

Since then, the phone hadn't stopped ringing with messages of congratulations, and emails had come in from all over the world. An incredible sense of pride stayed with me the whole time.

I slotted straight back into college and picked up friendships like I'd never been away. Friends and teachers remarked on how I was just the same as when I'd left. My family said the same, although Dad told me that I now walked faster than I used to! It was wonderful to be able to reach out and touch Mum and Dad, to be able to talk to them properly again.

I'd had so many wonderful 'hellos', but there had been one very tough goodbye: the boat. I was going to miss her. I still do. By the time I reached journey's end I felt like I could have kept sailing with her for ever. I'll never forget her and how amazing she was, seeing me safely and speedily through so many wild and dangerous seas. We'd certainly been through a lot together, that's for sure!

Many people had doubted us, and that was understandable. I was pushing the boundaries after all, which is what breaking records is all about. I'd faced more than my fair share of malfunctions which turned the trip into a far greater challenge than even I was expecting, but I'd done it. Now I didn't have to daydream. When I shut my eyes I could see myself surfing down the mighty waves of the freezing Southern Ocean.

I'd sailed the dream.

Afterword

Sailing round the world has changed my life in more ways than I could have imagined. One evening, a few weeks after I'd berthed in Portsmouth, I was due to give a talk near Tower Bridge in London. I'd arrived half an hour early and so decided to walk across this magnificent structure. I took stock as I admired the view of the Thames, which was full of boats as usual. Just a few weeks ago I'd set off on my journey and I'd stood in exactly the same place; full of thoughts about all the adventures I was going to have. So much had happened since that day. I wondered what on earth would happen next.

As I approached Portsmouth at the end of my journey, I received over a hundred emails a day – it was simply impossible to reply to them all. How I wish they answered themselves! It's been like that ever since. Somehow, in between all the interviews, public engagements and writing this book, I found time to take my driving lessons and, I'm very happy to report, I passed my test first time.

Also not long after my return to Potters Bar, I signed up to join Don McIntyre on his *Bounty* Boat trip. Don was planning to attempt to recreate one of the world's greatest sailing journeys in April 2010, the 221st anniversary of the Mutiny on the *Bounty*, when Fletcher Christian cast William Bligh and eighteen of his men adrift in a 23ft open boat. This marked the beginning of one of the greatest open boat voyages in maritime history. During the following seven weeks, Bligh and his men sailed over 3,700 nautical miles in an overloaded boat, with little food or water and no charts, from Tonga to Kupang in Timor. Don, with a crew of three, was planning to relive Bligh's 'nightmare', by attempting to sail the same voyage under similar conditions, no charts, no toilet paper, not enough food or water, in an 18th century traditional open timber whale boat.

This was just the sort of adventure I wanted to be a part of. I flew out to Australia to begin training but things didn't go to plan. On the very first morning I fell ill with terrible stomach pains. I threw up and then fainted a couple of times before being taken to hospital where the docs diagnosed a nasty case of appendicitis. This, unfortunately, was the end of my adventure, as it took quite a while for me to fully recover. I was gutted to have to pull out of the adventure because wow, did it sound incredible!

Don got on with finding a replacement before setting off on his own dream that April. Meanwhile, life didn't slow down for me for one moment. One of my favourite jobs has been giving talks to schools and businesses about my adventure as part of the 'Live the Dream' schools programme. I've also become an Ambassador for the Prince's Trust. There isn't much that can beat the thrill I get from seeing everyone's faces light up as I describe what the Southern Ocean can be like in a blow. I've done these talks all over the world, from Hong Kong to Australia, and the reaction is always the same, whether I'm talking to primary school children or middle-aged businessmen. It's great being only eighteen and sometimes delivering a talk to an audience with an average age of forty-five.

Somehow I managed to keep up with all my college work and by Christmas I was really looking forward to a good break with my family. I wasn't disappointed and to top it all it was the first white Christmas in years, making it especially magical to be at home in the snow. There certainly were lots of memorable snowball fights.

One of my highlights of 2010 was flying out to Sydney to see Jessica Watson complete her round-the-world voyage. Jessica had been away from home for 210 days. She left Sydney Harbour on 18 October 2009, sailing on her dream to become the youngest person to sail solo, non-stop and unassisted around the world, and arrived home triumphant seven months later.

Jesse Martin (the previous youngest person to sail single-handed around the world unassisted) and I had been given the fun task of helming *Ella's Pink Lady* from the Sydney Heads all the way up the Opera House, which was a pretty exciting prospect. The flotilla around Jessica was totally huge, with reports of up to 1500 boats in the area, which is pretty mad. The buzz in the flotilla was amazing though and I couldn't take the grin off my face. It was fantastic to jump aboard and hand Jessica some fresh food because I knew how much I missed it and I knew she would have too!

We safely berthed at the Sydney Opera House. Jessica was greeted by thousands of cheering fans on the shore. The atmosphere was electric; it sent shivers up my spine. Jessica jumped off into the waiting arms of her parents and family and it was fantastic to see them all reunited again. Jesse Martin and I then finished berthing *Ella's Pink Lady* and then followed Jessica up the pink carpet into the area right in front of the stage reserved for her close family and friends. Her speech was pretty awesome and I was pretty darn proud of her. Another dream realized!

We later caught up with Jessica at a small but brilliant get-together at a hotel in Manly where all her close family and team were. Amazingly, Jesse Martin, David Dicks, Brian Caldwell (the first under twenty-one-year-old to sail the globe), and Jon Sanders (the first person to complete a double circumnavigation) were there too. Six people who had sailed solo around the world before in the same room, and four of us who had once been the 'youngest'. It was brilliant to meet these guys and we all had a great laugh together.

A couple of weeks later I sailed *Ella's Pink Lady* with Jess up the coast to her hometown of Mooloolaba. It was fantastic to be out at sea again and we talked incessantly about sailing and our adventures, comparing notes.

It was during this trip, in June 2010, that we heard that Abby Sunderland's EPIRBs had been activated and that her team were unable to reach her. Needless to say we were extremely concerned for her and her family. Abby is Zac Sunderland's sixteen-year-old sister and she had set off on her own world record attempt in her Open 40 boat, *Wild Eyes*, in February 2010. Now she was lost somewhere in the Indian Ocean. This was a chilling reminder of the dangers solo sailors face and a reminder of how fortunate I had been in my knockdown not to lose my mast. Fortunately it wasn't long before we heard that a plane had spotted Abby and she was fine, if shaken. *Wild Eyes* had been dismasted during a tremendous storm. Abby and her family still faced a further day's anxious wait until the nearest vessel, a fishing boat, was able to reach her. Fortunately, by the grace of God, Abby was reunited with her family and she still hopes to complete her dream of sailing around the world one day.

Also in June, Don successfully completed his incredible Bounty Boat trip. You'll be able to read all about that soon enough in his own book.

Next on my list of things to do – now that I was eighteen – was to sit my Yachtmaster exams and I'm very pleased to say I passed no problem.

Now I've just announced my next adventure, which is to become the youngest person to fly solo around the world. If I'm successful I'll become the first person to both sail and fly solo around the world.

Circumnavigating the globe in a small plane is the ultimate flying adventure. The planning and logistics required for such a trip are hugely challenging. Studying the weather systems en-route and dealing with eighteen worldwide bureaucracies and regulations look to me to be very daunting. I'll have to cope with massively different flying conditions on the three-month trip, which will be both mentally and physically gruelling. To get the record I have to start and finish at the same aerodrome, cross all the meridians of longitude and fly not less than 19,864nm (equal in length to the Tropic of Cancer).

So, just a few months after passing my driving test, I found myself in a small plane, ready for my first flying lesson. It's truly amazing to experience the freedom that flying gives. There is a lot to learn, but I'm loving every moment, and it's superbly exciting to say the least.

One of the recent flying lessons I had was covering stalls. In this lesson was an exercise to show me how the plane will effectively fix itself if balanced. I let the plane stall, and as the nose dropped away, I let it go into a partial dive to increase the airspeed over the wings and once this happened the airplane started to level herself out impressively, without any help from me. The feeling of losing a thousand feet in a few seconds was simply amazing. As we flew back towards the airfield I thought about how incredible this was. I'd gone from the sea to the air in such a short time.

A lot of people often ask me, what is it that drives me? What is it that makes me work that extra bit harder, time and time again to get to where I want to be? Sometimes I simply say it's because I want to achieve my dream, but honestly it goes a lot deeper than that. I don't just want to achieve my dream, I want to show others and especially young people, people my age, that if you want something bad enough then you truly can achieve it with enough sheer passion. If I can look back at a project and feel that I've achieved that, then wow, does it make all the additional hard work well worth it!

If only more people of my age realized they too could live their dreams. Nothing is impossible if you want it enough. I come from landlocked Potters Bar, yet I managed to sail around the world – so go for it, if I can do it then you can too!

Acknowledgements

In his congratulatory message to me as I crossed the finishing line, the First Sea Lord, Admiral Sir Mark Stanhope, was quite right to use the phrase 'the Perham Family'. And into our family I'd like to welcome all the people who believed in me and helped make my dream come true.

Without my mini-army of sponsors, especially TotallyMoney.com, VocaLink, Skechers, Kemp Sails, Mastervolt, Hill Dickinson and Underwriting Risk Services (to mention only a few), none of this would ever have happened. They believed in the adventure, and it's thanks to their passion that we reached the finish – because it wasn't just *me* who did this trip, it was *we*. My friends and family did everything they could to get me to the finish line, not to mention everyone who took the time to send me some wonderful messages. It all added up to a massive wave of support that helped carry me home.

So, to everyone who helped this project get underway and contributed to its success and my safe return: thank you so much!

Main Sponsors

VocaLink The first major contributor to get on board, VocaLink gave us a tremendous boost and showed us that businesses were prepared to support a sixteen-year-old on such a big adventure.

TotallyMoney.com Without TotallyMoney's generous last-minute cash injection we would never have made it past the drawing board.

Skechers USA These guys have been with me since the Atlantic trip so they've helped me live my dreams twice!

Mastervolt They kindly made a huge contribution to my crucial and expensive electrical equipment and it was thanks to them that I stayed fully powered up throughout my trip.

Kemp Sails I couldn't have sailed without them! They not only provided a full set of beautiful sails for the voyage, but went above and beyond the call of duty and helped with some custom design and strengthening.

Underwriting Risk Services Thanks so much for removing the insurance risk from our budget.

Supporting Sponsors

WinningWind.com
Hill Dickinson
Clearpoint Weather
Graham High Group
Furuno
National Boat Shows
Marlow Ropes
Blakes Paints
Viking Liferafts
Elite Performance
B&G
McMurdo
Tesco
Tek Tanks
Expedition Foods
Harken
MarineTrack
Plastimo
Ultima Computers
Spinlock
C-Map
Parkwood Health and Fitness
TenScope
Hollographics
Virgin Group
Tiger Tiger, Gunwharf Quays, Portsmouth
Red Ensign Training
The Marine Travel Company
Pick n Pay
Pigbags

RM Tool Company and RM Sealers
Draper Tools
Sunshine Maritime
Green Marine
Francis Taylor Building
Mikuni Heating
Gunwharf Quays
Falmouth School of Sailing

Several amazing marinas provided me with a warm welcome and did all they could to help: Clarence Marina, Portsmouth; Gunwharf Quays, Portsmouth; Falmouth Harbour Marina, Falmouth; Cascais Marina, Portugal; Muelle Deportivo Yacht Harbour, Las Palmas; Royal Cape Yacht Club, Cape Town; Royal Yacht Club of Tasmania; Hobson West Marina, Auckland; Flamenco Marina, Panama.

Key people who were a massive help when I was forced to stop due to equipment failure/damage: Afonso Zagalo, John Crouch, Manuel Mendes, Don and Margie McIntyre, Dr Monte Friesner, the Langridge Family.

Special thanks to the Royal Navy, the Queen's Harbour Master in Portsmouth, Phil Baughen, Mike Broughton, Dave Letham, Kizzi Nkwocha, Barry Pickthall and Kris Hollington. And to everyone who made personal donations or organized corporate hat-passing events. And to everyone who blogged on my site. You all provided a huge amount of encouragement to my family, more than you can ever know! And also to all those who prayed for my safety.

In fact, thank you to everyone I know and everyone I don't know. That should cover it.

Photo Acknowledgements

All photographs not credited below have been kindly supplied by the author.

Picture Section Two:

Page 7: Crossing the finishing line © Barry Pickthall/PPL.
Page 8: A hug from Beckie © Robin Jones/Digital South.

Index